GRANT & LEE

A Study in Personality and Generalship

GRANT & LEE

*A Study in Personality
and Generalship*

by

MAJOR GENERAL J. F. C. FULLER

℈

INDIANA UNIVERSITY PRESS
BLOOMINGTON

First Midland Book Edition 1982

Manufactured in the United States of America

Fuller, John Frederick Charles, 1878–
    Grant & Lee, a study in personality and generalship.
Bloomington, Indiana University Press, 1957.
    323 p. illus. 21 cm. (Civil War centennial series)
    Includes bibliography.
    1. U. S.—Hist.—Civil War. 2. Grant, Ulysses Simpson, Pres. U. S.,
1822–1885. 3. Lee, Robert Edward, 1807–1870. 4. U. S.—Hist.—Civil
War—Campaigns and battles.   ɪ. Title.
E468.F96 1957   973.7   57–10723 ‡

ISBN 0-253-13400-5
ISBN 0-253-20288-4 PBK

2 3 4 5 86

FOREWORD TO SECOND EDITION

WHEN some twenty-five years ago I set out to write this book, I decided, so far as it was possible, to base it on contemporary sources, because I felt that, as its subject was a very human one, the opinions of officers who had served under Grant and Lee, or of persons closely acquainted with them, would be of greater value than those of later-day commentators and historians. Although, since then, a number of personal memoirs of people in these categories have appeared, those which I have read, as well as the monumental works of Kenneth P. Williams on Grant, and of Douglas Southall Freeman on Lee, have not led me in any radical way to change my estimates of the two great protagonists of the Civil War.

But a more important question is: Is a study of generalship as displayed in a war of nearly a century ago of any practical value today? Has not the advent of nuclear warfare, of guided missiles, and all the many scientific military inventions which World War II gave birth to, so completely changed the character and nature of war that the generalship of a hundred years ago, of fifty years ago, of even twenty-five years ago, is now no more than of academic interest? I do not think so, and for the following reasons.

Should the next war be solely or mainly initiated with hydrogen bombs and guided missiles, then, all but certainly on the continent of Europe, the result will not be a speedy victory, but a chaos that will give rise to a guerrilla war which may well last for years. If, however, nuclear weapons are not used, but instead held in leash as a mutual deterrent, then the war will be waged on conventional lines. In both these types of war generalship, in the traditional meaning of the word, will be as important as ever; in the one case men like Forrest and Mosby will be at a premium, and in the other men like Grant and Lee. Therefore, as I hope my readers will appreciate, because generalship is so largely built on character and personality, and because human nature remains constant, or practically so, there is no war in history from which we cannot learn something about leadership and command. Weapons, however destructive they may be, do not cancel out the need for courage, endurance, resolution, cool-headedness, audacity, and all the other moral virtues which go to build up generalship, if only because, in the words of old Marshal Saxe: "The human heart is the starting point in all matters pertaining to war."

March 15, 1957   J. F. C. F.

PREFACE

THE object of this study is to examine the influence of personality upon generalship. It is not primarily a history of the American Civil War, nor is it a detailed account of the campaigns fought by Grant and *Lee*.* In place it is an analysis of two personalities, in which the outline of the war as set forth is no more than the background, and the campaigns and battles described are no more than illustrations of the influence of these personalities upon events.

I have adopted this course because in nearly all the histories I have read on this war the writers have concentrated almost entirely upon events, overlooking the fact that the supreme value of military history is to be sought in the personalities of the generals who shaped them. At base, seven-eighths of the history of war is psychological. Material conditions change, yet the heart of man changes but little, if at all, and as Marshal Saxe once said: "The human heart is the starting-point in all matters pertaining to war." Strategy is important; administration is important; tactics are important; yet what is of greater importance to the soldier is to discover what does and what does not constitute generalship, because the general is called upon to use these three branches of the military art as a workman uses his tools.

Until a few years ago I accepted the conventional point of view that Grant was a butcher and *Lee* one of the greatest generals this world has ever seen.

* The names of Confederate soldiers are throughout this book printed in italics.

7

I accepted this because I had been taught that this was so. Then, after the close of the World War, it occurred to me that a study of the American Civil War might have taught us, not only how better to have waged the European Civil War, but even how to have altogether avoided it. From school history I turned to the sources of history—the records, the memoirs, the letters, and soon discovered that much I had been taught as fact was little short of fiction.

Like most British officers, I had been fed upon Henderson's *Stonewall Jackson*; but historical research soon revealed to me that this justly popular book was almost as romantic as Xenophon's *Cyropaedia*. Interesting and instructive both these works are, but neither can be considered as wells of historic truth. Cyrus of the *Cyropaedia*, is Xenophon's ideal of a soldier, and so is *Jackson* of Henderson's only less famous book. What was my astonishment when I discovered that *Jackson*, though he possessed certain remarkable qualities, was possessed by so many equally remarkable idiosyncrasies as to leave one in doubt as to his sanity. Then I turned to Grant, and found him to be nothing like the Grant I had been led to picture; lastly to *Lee*, to discover that in several respects he was one of the most incapable Generals-in-Chief in history—so much for school education.

I did not arrive at these conclusions hastily, but after having read over two hundred books and articles on the Civil War and consulted as many more. That certain of my conclusions are erroneous is more than likely, for an American correspondent once informed me that he had collected a library of over twenty-three thousand volumes and items on the Civil War period; consequently, my reading, though considerable, has in no way been exhaustive.

I have kept this book as short as possible, and yet

8

I think I have included sufficient background to enable a reader not well acquainted with the history of this war to look at the whole of it as if through a diminishing glass. In some cases it may be considered that I might have said more, and in others less. For example: I have dismissed *Jackson's* vital Valley campaign in a few words, and have devoted a page or two to Buell's campaign in East Tennessee, which was only distantly related to Grant's operations at the time. I have done so because the details of *Jackson's* campaign are unnecessary in order to understand *Lee's* plans, whilst Grant's Chattanooga campaign is difficult to grasp unless its origins are outlined.

In this book I have given chapter and verse for practically every statement of importance relating to Grant and *Lee*, and I have made use of so large a number of references in comparison to the length of the book, that style, such as I may possess, has undoubtedly suffered. But as my object is not to write a romance, and as my opinions on Grant and *Lee* run counter to many of those held by former writers, I have considered it only just to marshal my evidence, and if the reader will trouble to glance through the references he will find that most of my witnesses were men and women personally acquainted with Grant and *Lee*. I have paid particular attention to the opinions of staff officers—men such as Porter, Badeau, *Long*, *Taylor* and *Marshall*, because these men are likely to have gained a better insight into the personalities of their chiefs than others. I have also placed considerable reliance on the opinions of foreign witnesses of the war, for their outside observations enable one to check inside estimates.

Finally, this book, though a short one, includes so many of the major operations of the Civil War that to the general reader it should, I think, provide a fairly clear sketch of what this war was like. To the military student it may be looked upon as an introduction, *based on facts*, to a more extended study which is to be found in no single book; for, curious to relate, though an individual can collect twenty-three thousand volumes and articles on this period, a full and unprejudiced military history of the American Civil War has still to be written.

J. F. C. F.

November 20, 1932.

CONTENTS

SKETCHES IN TEXT

MAPS

(at end of book)

GRANT & LEE

A Study in Personality and Generalship

ℰ

CHAPTER I

THE TWO CAUSES

The Two Orders

THE Wars of the Roses in England and the Civil War in America were both intestinal conflicts arising out of similar ideas.   In the first the clash was between feudalism and the new economic order; in the second, between an agricultural society and a new industrial one.   Both led to similar ends; the first to the founding of the English nation, and the second to the founding of the American.   Both were strangely interlinked; for it was men of the old military and not of the new economic mind—men, such as Sir Humphrey Gilbert and Sir Walter Raleigh—who founded the English colonies in America, and it was men of this type who settled in Virginia.

The ending of the Hundred Years' War with France, in 1453, by consolidating the attention of the English on home affairs at once led to the Wars of the Roses; so also did the ending of the Seven Years' War with France, in 1763, by removing the fear of French hegemony in America, consolidate the colonists on their own affairs, and led directly to the War of the Rebellion.   Though this rebellion liberated the colonists and enabled them to establish a nation in being, a greater revolution, namely, the industrial, was at this moment emerging from its cradle, and no sooner had independence been gained than the new-born nation was split into two hostile factions, or orders of society—the agricultural on the one side and the industrial on the other. These halves were ultimately fused into one whole by the Civil War of 1861-1865.

This may clearly be seen to-day, as clearly as the poet Stephen Vincent Benét saw it when he wrote that this war was:

> "The pastoral rebellion of the earth
> Against machines, against the Age of Steam,
> The Hamiltonian extremes against the Franklin mean";[1]

but, from 1789 onwards, it was not seen clearly, and not at all by Jefferson Davis who, as late as 1881, explained how though the substitution of the Constitution for the Articles of Confederation amended the form of government, "no new PEOPLE was created. . . . The people, in whom alone sovereignty inheres remained just as they had been before." Then he adds: "No doubt, the States—the people of the States—if they had been so disposed, might have merged themselves into one great consolidated State, retaining their geographical boundaries merely as matters of convenience. But such a merger must have been distinctly and formally stated, not left to deduction or implication."[2] From the purely legal point of view this is correct; consequently, when in 1861 the Southern States seceded they had the law on their side. But what Jefferson Davis did not see was that the industrial revolution was rapidly merging the individual States into "one great consolidated State," and that force of circumstances had in fact replaced law. "The monstrous conception of the creation of a new people, invested with the whole or a great part of the sovereignty which had previously belonged to the people of each State, has not a syllable to sustain it in the Constitution,"[3] is true in theory,

18

yet in fact it is not true; for, between 1789 and 1861, a new people was unconsciously created by changes in environment.

It was the unconsciousness of this fact which led to the war. The economically-minded North felt that prosperity depended upon the maintenance of the Union; the agriculturally-minded South felt otherwise; not that Southerners did not realise the value of the Union, but that they scorned to place prosperity above individual freedom. It was the South which had led in the rebellion for freedom, and to the aristocracy of the South freedom was beyond all price. Here on the one side is presented to us an economic ideal, on the other an ethical one. To the Southern gentleman the Yankees were a despised "race," inferior in courage and honour. General *Magruder* "spoke of the Puritans with intense disgust, and of the first importation of them as '*that pestiferous crew of the Mayflower*' "[4]; and when the war was declared, Mrs. Clay, a woman of high intelligence and wife of Senator Clay, of Alabama, laid the blame upon the shoulders of the Northern capitalists.[5]

For years the South had dominated the North, and though the Constitution of 1789 had made of the United States a nation, it was nationality of a limited order; for a fundamental principle of this Constitution was the right of each State to secede if it so willed, and form a separate government.

The first serious difficulty arose in 1794, when the Federal Government laid an excise on distilled spirit; this gave rise to the Whisky Insurrection in Pennsylvania, which Washington suppressed not only by using the militia of this State, but the militias of New Jersey, Virginia and Maryland. As Bryce says: "This was the first assertion by arms of the supreme authority of the Union, and produced an enormous effect upon opinion."[6]   The next arose out of the 1812 war with Great Britain; this, in 1820, led to the "Missouri Compromise," which was in reality a truce between antagonistic revenue systems. The trouble throughout was at bottom economic. The South was paying the largest share of the national expenses; in the third decade of the nineteenth century, out of a total revenue of $23,000,000, the Southern States furnished $16,500,000; and, depending upon agriculture, their policy of free trade clashed with the rising industrial interests of the North, which demanded protection. The tariff laws passed between the years 1824-1828 threw the main burden of taxation upon the Southern people, "who were consumers and not manufacturers, not only by the enhanced price of imports, but indirectly by the consequent depreciation in the value of exports, which were chiefly the products of Southern States."[7]   For instance, as one Southerner writes: "Only the other day I got a consignment of hardware from England, it had come through a Northern agency, and the charges over and above the freight and duties amounted to about 30 per cent on the invoice."[8]

The friction which arose from these contending economic interests led to a definite split in 1832, when South Carolina entered a protest against the tariffs in the form of an Ordinance of Nullification. Then, this same year, into the controversy was thrust the question of slavery which, like a fog, distorted and magnified the economic differences.

The first negroes were brought to America by the Dutch in 1619, and the first opposition to slavery originated among the Quakers. In 1772 Chief Justice Mansfield's historic judgment rendered slavery illegal in England. In 1790 two petitions to abolish slavery were presented to the first Congress convened under the Constitution, and might, within a decade or so, have secured their object, had not Eli Whitney's saw-gin, invented in 1793, given an enormous impetus to the production of cotton, and, as always, though in the end morality triumphs, economic necessity for the time being won through. In 1829 slavery was abolished in Mexico, and five years later in the British West Indies. In fact the morality of the day was against its continuance; for, on account of the increasing power of machinery, it was found not to pay. This morality, reduced to an emotional vapour under the white heat of political argument, poisoned all reason. Thus it happened that economic issues became blurred by hysterical emotionalism, and as Edward Lee Childe says: "Like the Trojan horse, it [slavery] offered a very convenient vehicle by means of which to introduce discord and confusion into the heart of the edifice of the Constitution."[9]

Though, in 1787, Madison had recognised that slavery divided the country into two economic interests,[10] it was in fact a dying institution. In 1776 it existed in all the thirteen States, and was first abandoned by Massachusetts. By 1861, when the Civil War broke out, it had also been abolished in Connecticut, New Hampshire, Rhode Island, New York, Pennsylvania and New Jersey, and was about to be abolished in Delaware and Maryland. It would have died a natural death had it not been used as a moral fulcrum upon which to move the political lever. As the States are equally represented in the Senate, between 1832 and 1860 the slave-holding interests were eager to extend the area of slavery "in order that by creating new Slave States they might maintain at least an equality in the Senate and thereby prevent any legislation hostile to slavery."[11]

The Abolitionist movement, which took form under

Garrison's leadership in 1831, soon gained strength. Before the Senate, in 1839, Henry Clay said: "Civil war, a dissolution of the Union . . . are nothing [with the Abolitionists]. . . . In all their leading prints and publications the alleged horrors of slavery are depicted in the most glowing and exaggerated colors, to excite the imaginations and stimulate the rage of the people in the free States against the people in the slave States."[12] In 1842-1843 a petition was presented to Congress by citizens of Massachusetts and Ohio, asking that steps should be taken toward "the peaceable dissolution of the Union." Already, in 1840, the slave question assumed such importance as to bring about the formation of a political party, securing 7,059 votes for its President and Vice-President. In 1844 these votes were increased to 62,300, and the Anti-Slavery Society rejected the Constitution as "a covenant with death and an agreement with hell." In 1848 the anti-slave party nominated for the Presidency Martin Van Buren, and for the Vice-Presidency Charles Francis Adams, these two receiving 300,000 votes. In 1856 this party became known as the Republican Party, and John C. Frémont was nominated and received 1,341,264 votes. So the contest swept onwards, until Thomas Carlyle in England cynically exclaimed: "Glod bless you and be a slave. . . . God damn you and be a freeman."

Behind all this turmoil what do we find? That in order to preserve its economic order the South was forced by the anti-slave attacks of the North to fall back on the Constitution for *legal* support. The State was sovereign, and the Union, as founded by the Constitution, was nothing more than an alliance between sovereigns. The original Confederacy was a loose-jointed league, and the Union was only a better articulated one. There had been constant threats of secession from 1786 onwards. In 1804 the New England Federalists threatened to establish a Northern Confederacy. The same happened in 1812, and again in 1814; and now the Abolitionists demanded it in the North; in fact, the idea of breaking away from the less progressive South was endemic in the Northern half of the community.

On December 20, 1860, South Carolina passed an ordinance dissolving the Union, and early in the following year the Southern Confederacy was established. "Technically, the seceding States had an arguable case; and if the point had been one to be decided on the construction of the Constitution as a court decides on the construction of a commercial contract, they were possibly entitled to judgment. Practically, the defenders of the Union stood on firmer ground, because circumstances had so changed since 1789 as to make the nation more completely one nation than it then was, and had so involved the fortunes of the majority which held to the Union with those of the minority seeking to depart that the majority might feel justified in forbidding their departure. Stripped of legal technicalities, the dispute resolved itself into the problem often proposed but capable of no general solution: When is a majority entitled to use force for the sake of retaining a minority in the same political body with itself? To this question, when it appears in a concrete shape, as to the similar question when an insurrection is justifiable, an answer can seldom be given beforehand. The result decides. When treason prospers none dare call it treason.

"The Constitution, which had rendered many services to the American people, did them an inevitable disservice when it fixed their minds on the legal aspect of the question. Law was meant to be the

23

servant of politics, and must not be suffered to become the master. A case had arisen which its formulæ were unfit to deal with, a case which was fit to be settled on large moral and historical grounds. It was not merely the superior physical force of the North that prevailed; it was the moral forces which rule the world, forces which had for long worked against slavery and were ordained to save North America from the curse of hostile nations established side by side."[13]

Legal rights are founded on physical force, political rights on moral force; by insisting on the former and not the latter the South challenged the North to combat.

The Two Peoples

Behind these two orders, the agricultural and static and the industrial and mobile, lived two peoples— the men of the field-lands and the men of the cities. The one an aristocracy, for no true peasantry existed, and slavery demanded mastership; the other an emerging democracy, crude, determined and self-seeking, a mixture of many nations and, consequently, a latently anarchic people. In the South the military, religious and artistic spirits preponderated; in the North, the commercial, matter-of-fact and practical. The South was eighteenth century, the North nineteenth century; the one looking backwards to Cavalier and King's man, the other forwards to the Roundheads and Cromwells of an all-conquering mechanical age.

In the South there were three classes of society— the slave-owners, the poor whites and the negroes; also, in the North were there three classes—the men who had made money, were making money, and those who had failed to do so. To the autocrats patriotism was founded on blood, to the plutocrats on gold. Power thus gazed upon power: the power of the past defiantly glowering into the eyes of the power of the future.

Life, interest and outlook, in both North and South, were strangely different; occupation and climate separated them into two peoples, almost into two nations. In the North the blizzard and the sea-wind had beaten Puritanism into men's bones, and to survive the rigours of the climate and the barrenness of the soil, of necessity the liberty of the individual was merged into the self-preservation of the mass; further still, the mixed nature of the population demanded amalgamation. In the South it was other-wise. In Virginia the greater part of the population was of English and Scottish stock, field-men, Cavaliers "wearing wide-brimmed felt sombreros, riding-boots, and gloves with beaver-skin backs." Men of legend and tradition, men of the romances of Sir Walter Scott. Men of a proud age and a gallant, an age of luxury and refinement; when women were worshipped as women, and the point of honour lurked in the point of every sword. When "cracked ice rattled refreshingly in the goblet; sprigs of fragrant mint peered above its broad brim; a mass of white sugar, too sweetly indolent to melt, rested on the mint; and, like rose-buds on a snow bank, luscious strawberries crowned the sugar."[14] Such was Virginia before the blast of war swept over her hills and down her dales—a mint-julep stirred with a sword-blade.

> "The girls were always beautiful. The men
> Wore varnished boots, raced horses and played cards
> And drank mint-juleps till the time came round
> For fighting duels with their second cousins
> Or tar-and-feathering some God-damn Yankee. . . .

The South . . . the honeysuckle . . . the hot sun . . .
The taste of ripe persimmons and sugar-cane. . . .
The cloyed and waxy sweetness of magnolias. . . .
White cotton, blowing like a fallen cloud,
And foxhounds belling the Virginia hills. . . ."[15]

Nothing in modern times has quite resembled the
social life of the South; it was feudalism, but of a
refined order, in which chivalry and above all the
spirit of gallantry endowed the ruling aristocracy
with an exalted pride in itself and its cause. Behind
the Southern soldier stood the Southern woman—
mother, wife, daughter, sister and sweetheart:

"The gentleman killed and the gentleman died,
But she was the South's incarnate pride
That mended the broken gentlemen
And sent them out to the war again,
That kept the house with the men away
And baked the bricks where there was no clay,
Made courage from terror and bread from bran
And propped the South on a swansdown fan
Through four long years of ruin and stress,
The pride—and the deadly bitterness."[16]

These words of the poet are no exaggeration, for
General *Lee* writes, in a letter to Mrs. Lee, how, in
November 1863, he met a soldier's wife who was on
a visit to her husband. "She was from Abbeville
district, S.C. She had not seen her husband for more
than two years and, as he had written to her for
clothes, she herself thought she would bring them on.
It was the first time she had travelled by railroad,
but she had got along very well by herself. She brought
an entire suit of her own manufacture for her husband.
She spun the yarn and made the clothes herself. She
clad her three children in the same way, and had on
a beautiful pair of gloves she had made for herself. . . .
Her greatest difficulty was to procure shoes. She sat
with me about ten minutes, and took her leave—

another mark of sense—and made no request for herself or husband."[17]

The heroism of the South must not blind us to the fact that behind it and within it lay much ignorance and selfishness—the backwash of autocracy. The contempt for the North was profound, so profound as to obscure the fact that in modern wars industries are as necessary as courage, and that the strength of the North lay not in her prowess but in her manufactures, her engineers and her mercantile marine. In the South these essentials were almost entirely lacking; the art of organizing and of creating was unknown, the saddle horse was the common means of locomotion, for roads were little better than tracks. Of his journey through Texas Colonel Fremantle writes: "Two of my companions served through the late severe campaign in New Mexico, but they considered forty-eight hours in a closely-packed stage a greater hardship than any of their military experiences."[18] It was a country and a people totally unprepared for war and, consequently, a country difficult to fight in, and a people difficult to subdue, for courage which scorns preparation is apt to defy defeat.

The Two Presidents

To turn from the two peoples to their political leaders, Abraham Lincoln and Jefferson Davis, it would be difficult to discover two men so different in appearance and character. Lincoln was the son of the soil, Davis the artificial product of the study. One had breathed into his soul the freedom of Nature, and like primitive man, could best express his inner feelings through parables. The other had breathed the air of the cloister, and his soul had grown stiff as the parchment it had fed upon. "Lincoln," as Edward Lee Childe describes him, was "a true Cherokee white, with straight hair, high cheekbone, unfathomable aspect, with a stony nature in the large hands, destined to manual labour, a nature withdrawing from intellectual work as much as possible. A mind of mediocrity, honourable and upright through the absence of passions; vulgar, but by no means wicked, loving allegory in the manner of common people; full of self-confidence, a believer in his own mission, a true representative of the most recent form of American democracy."[19] Davis, artificial, autocratic, and for ever standing upon the pedestal of his own conceit. A man of little humour, who could dictate but who would not argue or listen, who could read but who could not penetrate deeply. Logical, inflexible, inhuman, a man who scorned advice, for he could not tolerate either assistance or opposition. When *Lee* suggested that General *Whiting* should be sent south, Davis endorsed the recommendation: "Let General *Lee* order General *Whiting* to report here, and it may then be decided whether he will be sent south or not."[20] A man who, as Mrs. Davis relates of their first meeting, "has a way of taking for granted that everybody agrees with him"[21]; who was for ever suspicious of ability, and whose "cabinet was made up in great part of feeble and incapable men."[22] "He [Toombs]," says Mrs. Chesnut, "rides too high a horse for so despotic a person as Jefferson Davis."[23] Yet withal a man of invincible will and courage, as indomitable as the last proclamation he issued to his countrymen on April 5, 1865—to rely on God, and "meet the foe with fresh defiance and with unconquered and unconquerable hearts."[24]

In the hands of these two men was the destiny of

a divided people thrust. Davis, relying upon European intervention to scuttle the war, had no foreign policy outside establishing cotton as king. Early in the war the Hon. James Mason, Confederate Commissioner in Europe, had proclaimed that all cotton in Europe would be exhausted by February, 1862, "and that . . . intervention would be inevitable";[25] yet before the end of 1861 Europe was learning to do without it. Davis, however, could not believe that he was wrong; he staked the fortunes of his government and his people on this commodity, and lost. On the other hand Lincoln pinned his faith on what he believed to be the common right of humanity. In spite of division he saw one people, and in spite of climate and occupation—one nation. To him the Union was older than any State, for it was the Union that had created the States *as* States. He saw that whatever happened, the nation could not permanently remain divided. His supreme difficulty was to maintain the unity of the North so that he might enforce unity upon the South; whilst Jefferson Davis's ship of state was wrecked on the fundamental principle of his policy that each individual State had the right to control its own destiny, a policy which was not only antagonistic to his nature, but which was incapable of establishing united effort.

From the military point of view both men were incapable in the extreme. Davis thought he understood war, Lincoln acted as if no one could understand it. Davis himself says: "At the commencement of the year 1862 it was the purpose of the United States Government to assail us in every manner and at every point and with every engine of destruction which could be devised. The usual methods of civilized warfare consist in the destruction of an enemy's military power and the capture of his capital.

These, however, formed only a small portion of the purposes of *our* enemy."[26]   This shows his ignorance of the nature of modern warfare.   Lincoln, though he possessed military insight of a kind, such as when he suggested to Hooker "not to take any risk of being entangled upon the river, like an ox jumped half over a fence,"[27] relied on a military Junta, consisting of himself, the irascible Stanton and the egregious Halleck.   He leant upon councils of war and, in consequence, ruined the initiative of his generals. For instance, as the Comte de Paris informs us: "After ordering the preparations which McClellan had so long solicited, Mr. Lincoln relapsed into hesitancy, and insisted that the general-in-chief should submit his project to the examination of a council of war.   Twelve generals assembled on the 8th of March, not to receive the instructions of their chief, but to constitute a tribunal for passing judgment on his plans."[28]   Not until he discovered Grant did he cease to interfere, but Jefferson Davis was too self-centred to attain to such wisdom; from beginning to end he was *de facto* the Southern Commander-in-Chief, and though his admiration for *Lee* was unstinted and sincere, he treated him little better than a clerk.

The Two Problems

The secession of South Carolina and the other States did not in itself precipitate the war, for it was not until Fort Sumter was bombarded on April 12, 1861, that the emotionalism of the North swept through all argument, and though both sides were totally unprepared for the impending struggle, this insult to the national flag demanded immediate retribution.

What were the problems which now faced the contending parties? In themselves they were exceedingly simple: to re-establish the Union the North must conquer the South; and to maintain the Confederacy, and all that the Confederacy stood for, the South must resist invasion. On the one side the problem was offensive, on the other defensive. To conquer the North was out of the question, consequently the Southern problem resolved itself into inducing Europe to intervene and stop the war, and in tiring the North out and so compel the Union Government to abandon the contest. As it was uncertain what Europe would do, this second half of the problem was the more important; consequently, what was equally important was: how long could the Southern resources stand the strain?

The Northern problem of conquest meant not only defeating the enemy's armed forces and occupying his capital, but subduing the will of an entire people and occupying the whole of their country. This subjection could only be carried out by force of arms, for solely to rely upon blockade would not necessarily have led to this result. Blockade was important, but only as a strategic attack on the Confederate lines of supply with Europe. The main problem was tactical— the disarming of the enemy and the occupation of his country. The political object of the war was so clear, namely, union or disunion, that no other course could be adopted.

Jefferson Davis, as I have shown, totally misunderstood the nature of the war. He looked upon it as a war between two governments, when in fact it was a war between two peoples not quarrelling over some territorial or economic question, but a question so firmly established in the heart of every man and woman that it took upon itself a religious form. Both

31

sides were fighting for something dearer than life, consequently this civil war and most other civil wars find their nearest comparison in the wars of religion.

Lincoln dimly saw it thus: On April 19, 1861, he proclaimed a blockade of the Southern ports, but called for the enrolment of only 75,000 volunteers. Grant, then a clerk in his brother's leather store, considered it would be a ninety days' affair. *Lee* believed that it would prove a long war; but the only man who appears to have seen it in its true perspective was the Federal Commander-in-Chief, Lieut.-General Winfield Scott, who considered that "300,000 men under an able general might carry the business through in two or three years."[29] This seems a moderate enough estimate, seeing that the problem, simple though it was to realize, entailed the occupation of the entire South.

I will now turn to the theatre of the war, the area in which the two problems were to be resolved.

As the defensive, by force of policy and circumstances, was thrust upon the South, Jefferson Davis should have at once recognised that the strategic frontier of the Confederacy ran from the Potomac, by Washington, along the Alleghany Mountains to Chattanooga, thence along the Tennessee River to about Savannah, across to the Mississippi at Fulton, and from there to Little Rock on the Arkansas River. Had he done so, and had he realised that the States of Kentucky, Tennessee and Missouri could only be looked upon as advanced positions, or tactical outworks, to the main strategic line of defence, then his strategy would have taken on a concrete form. South of this strategic frontier ran two main lateral railroads, the first from Richmond via Chattanooga to Memphis, and the second from Richmond via Branchville and Atlanta to Vicksburg. Both were intersected by railroads running from the seaports of Wilmington, Charleston, Savannah, Pensacola, Mobile and New Orleans. The maintenance of these railways and the security of these seaports were vital to the Confederacy: the first in order to carry out troop movements from east to west and west to east, and the second to maintain communication with Europe. In place, what do we see? "With every month of the war the railroads of the Southern States become worse and worse, until a long journey by rail—say from Montgomery to Richmond—was as hazardous as picket duty on the Potomac,"[30] so says *Heros von Borcke*, who was chief-of-staff to General *J. E. B. Stuart*. And though it was of infinite importance to keep the Southern ports open, which could only be done by strengthening their land defences and adequately garrisoning them, in place "the Confederate Government wanted ships to cruise and to destroy the enemy's mercantile marine."[31] To attack Federal shipping was a direct violation of the defensive problem, because, though it might damage the supplies of the enemy, it could not enhance the supplies of the South. Strategically it was a wasteful diversion of force, particularly so as the Confederacy had few ships.

The question of supplies, which from the start to the finish of the war was a question of daily anxiety, was never adequately tackled, and eventually, more so than Federal pressure, lack of supplies wrecked the Confederate armies. Not only, by May, 1862, were the ports of Newbern, Beaufort, Savannah, Brunswick, Pensacola and New Orleans occupied by Federal troops, but no proper steps were taken to control, economize and amass supplies at strategic centres. Though totally unprepared for the war, throughout 1861 the apathy of the South was astounding.[32] As *Heros von Borcke* says: "Had the Confederate authorities, following Napoleon's example, established at the beginning of the war (when it might easily have been done) large depots of army-supplies at points not exposed, like Richmond, to raids of cavalry, I am convinced that it would have had a material influence on the final issue of the great conflict. The difficulties that were experienced during the last two years of the war in supporting the army, and the terrible privations to which men and animals were subjected in consequence of early maladministration and neglect, can be known only to those who were eye-witnesses of the misfortune and participants in the suffering."[33] It was not that supplies were unobtainable; they were plentiful. In May, 1862, Mrs. Clay says: "We had sugar in abundance, and pyramids of the richest butter, bowls of thick cream, and a marvellous plenitude of incomparable 'clabber';" and then again, in March the following year: "The contrast between the comfort in this pretty city [Macon] of lower Georgia, a city of beautiful homes and plentiful tables, and our poverty-stricken capital [Richmond] and meagre, starving camps, was terrible to picture. I wrote impulsively (and alas! impotently) in reply to my husband's letter:

" 'Why does not the President or some proper authority order on from here and other wealthy towns, and immediately at that, the thousands of provisions that fill the land? Monopolists and misers hold enough meat and grain in their clutches to feed our army and Lincoln's! Put down the screws and make them release it. Talk of disbanding an army at a time like this? No! empty the coffers and granaries and meat houses of every civilian in the land first!' "[34]

Why did not Jefferson Davis do so? "Right, weakness, invasion!" had detonated the South. "Was it not the God-implanted instinct which impels a man to defend his own hearth. . . . Within me is Right, before me is Duty, behind me is Home."[35] This enthusiasm, through which he could have accomplished almost anything whilst it burnt fiercely, left him cold. Cotton was king, Europe would intervene; then behind these dim possibilities stood the spectre of State Rights. What right had the Confederate Government to lay hands on the supplies of individual States? Had not the Conscription Act of April, 1862, caused trouble enough; was not it in fact an infringement of the Constitution? At first there had been fear of a slave rising:[36] this had died down; then there had been the consoling thought that the credit of the North would be unable to support the war:[37] this also became more and more unlikely. Nevertheless, State Rights stood daily, hourly, at every minute of day and night at Davis's elbow. Supplies could not be seized, taxes could not be enforced. Colonel *Marshall* says: "Everyone remarked how the people clamoured to be taxed to save the country when a timid Congress was hesitating to impose taxes. This indisposition to exert its power so often manifested by the Confederate Government, was a natural consequence of the theory upon which that Government was formed. Recognizing no power to coerce a State, holding that any State might nullify a law of Congress, and that the league rested entirely in the consent of the parties composing it, the Confederate Government endeavoured to shape its policy so as to conciliate the States and secure their acquiescence in its measures."[38]

The importance of State Rights as the controlling factor in Confederate strategy cannot be exaggerated. It was not only the cause of the war, but also the prime cause of the Confederate downfall. Though Jefferson Davis was hoisted by this constitutional

petard, after the war he never wearied of pointing
out that according to the "Declaration of Independence each State retained its sovereignty and freedom." He acknowledges that "the Government thus
constituted was found inadequate," and that "the
first idea of . . . reorganization arose from the
necessity of regulating the commercial intercourse of
the States with one another and with foreign countries,
and also of making some provision for payment of
the debt contracted during the war for independence."[39] Further, that the "prohibition" to exercise certain functions of sovereignty, such as making
treaties, declaring war, coining money, etc., was not
imposed upon the States "from without, or from
above, by any external or superior power, but is
self-imposed by their free consent"; consequently,
these prohibitory clauses "are not at all a denial of
the full sovereignty of the States, but are merely an
agreement among them to exercise certain powers of
sovereignty in concert, and not separately and
apart."[40]

Though Jefferson Davis acknowledged that the
General Government "had . . . the exclusive right
and power of determining on peace and war,"[41] and
that, as I have just shown, he realized that federalism
had originated through economic necessity, he could
not see that economic necessity was a far stronger
factor in 1861 than in 1789, or that State Rights were
of little value unless each State could back its rights
by military force. As the army was the common
property of all the States, there did exist a union by
force and compulsion as well as a union by agreement.
And when his coadjutor, Vice-President Stephens,
said that there was not such a thing as a citizen of the
United States, but the citizen of a State, quoting
Rawle in support of this contention, and that "the

object in quitting the Union was not to destroy, but to save the principles of the Constitution,"[42] what he, as well as Jefferson Davis, was doing was to foster and cherish the spirit of the first rebellion in place of eliminating it and so unifying the nation.

This pedagogic point of view and this scholastic reasoning were utterly antagonistic to unity within the Confederacy; whilst unity was the principle, though by no means a firmly established one, of its antagonist. No military dictator could be appointed, and "Instead of finishing the war, and then thinking how to establish a stable and definite government, the Confederate statesmen wished to do both at once."[43] Susceptibilities had to be considered, and though *Lee* and *Joseph E. Johnston* were of opinion that the more remote frontiers should be abandoned, and the scattered forces of the Confederacy concentrated, political reasons overruled their judgment. Further still, the general policy of defence, thrust upon the South by force of circumstances, magnified in the mind of each State the importance of local defence. As Colonel Henderson says: "Though all the States were willing to fight, each singly was unwilling to be left unprotected"[44]; consequently to abandon, for instance, Kentucky or Tennessee, or to refuse to support any frontier State in strength, would have led to acute political friction; yet this problem could have been solved as I will show a little later on.

From the first, the incurable jealousy of the States, especially of those not immediately affected by the war, established a dry rot within the Confederacy. Thus, each State not only furnished units to the Confederate Army, but raised local and irregular troops as well, and as service in the home areas was safer and more congenial than at the front, the establishment of these units was one of the outstanding causes of desertion. Also, as many of the irregular corps and guerilla forces were little better than bands of brigands leading a roisterer's life without a roisterer's expenses, the Federal Government was compelled to devastate vast tracks of the Confederacy in order to rid its armies of this pest.

These jealousies led to many serious absurdities. Thus Colonel *Marshall* tells us that when, largely through General *Lee's* efforts, conscription was enforced, in order to palliate the States, the Conscription Act "provided that the men of the existing commands retained in service should elect their field and company officers. . . . Thus by the provisions of this law the armies in the immediate presence of the enemy, like that of General *J. E. Johnston*, on the Peninsula, were authorized to change all their officers by a popular election." These elections "actually took place in the Yorktown trenches, and men had to come from the skirmish line to decide by their votes whether the officers who placed them there should continue to command them."[45]

From the political aspect of the problem I will now turn to the strategic. The first point to note is that the Alleghany Mountains cut the main theatre of war, which lay between the Mississippi and the Atlantic, into two sub-theatres—the Eastern and the Western, which may better be called the political and strategical theatres; for in the first the security of the two capital cities and their governments was the predominating factor, whilst the second was largely influenced by the great river lines of approach, namely, the Mississippi, Tennessee, Cumberland and Ohio. Throughout the first three years of the war politics so completely obscured strategy that both sides committed one blunder after another. Both Washington and Richmond were important railway centres, but neither the one nor the other was vital to either cause. It is possible, as Henderson points out,[46] that a Confederate occupation of Washington might have led to the Southern independence being recognized by Europe; yet such an occupation could have been a temporary one only. General *Gordon's* opinion on this question is worth recording. He gives us it in a conversation between two Confederate soldiers.

" 'I say, Mac, what do you suppose we are going to do with the city of Washington when we take it?'

" 'That question reminds me,' replied Mac, 'of old Simon's answer to Tony Towns when he asked Simon if he were not afraid he would lose his dog that was running after every train that came by. The old darkey replied that he was not thinking about losing his dog, but was just wonderin' what dat dorg was gwine to do wid dem kyars when he kotched 'em.' "[47]

Though from the west Washington was easy to strike at, to have established the Federal capital elsewhere was out of the question; for the initiative being with the North, to have done so would at once have been proclaimed a moral defeat. In the Confederacy no such question arose; the first capital selected was at Montgomery in Alabama, and it was moved to Richmond early in 1861, mainly because of Virginian influence, which demanded that it should be situated in Virginia, which was considered to be the vital area in the theatre of war.[48]

This was the initial strategical mistake made by Davis, for though Richmond was a good railroad centre, and was difficult to attack from the north, it possessed the disadvantage of being close to the sea coast. Further, the real strength of the Confederacy lay in the Mississippi region, and as the Federals would most certainly direct their operations against their enemy's political centre, the further it was away

from direct attack the better. In my own opinion the
capital should have been removed to Atlanta, the geographical centre of the Confederacy, an important
railroad junction not only connected to Charleston,
Savannah, Pensacola, Mobile and New Orleans, but
also with Memphis and Vicksburg on the Mississippi.
Had Atlanta been selected, then, whilst a covering
force, based on Richmond, was maintained in Virginia, its object being morally to threaten Washington,
the main forces, based on Chattanooga, could have
carried out a defensive-offensive campaign in Tennessee. Such a campaign, if pushed with vigour,
would not only have protected the great supply States
of Mississippi, Alabama and Georgia, but would have
kept open the vital crossings into Missouri, Arkansas
and Louisiana, as well as have stretched out a helping
hand to Kentucky. It may be said that had this
distribution been decided upon, Virginia would have
been occupied by the Federals, and thence they would
have pushed south through the Carolinas.

This is unlikely, even if Virginia had been over-
run, not only because the Confederate operations in
Tennessee would have drawn the bulk of the Federal
forces westwards, but because the topographical conditions in the East would have proved as difficult to
overcome as they did to the English in 1775-1783.
What did General Nathaniel Greene do in North
Carolina in 1781? He avoided pitched battles, and
relied on rapidity of manoeuvre to strike at weakness
and at his enemy's line of communications. Had the
Federals penetrated into North Carolina they would
have had to rely upon the Danville railroad; every
mile of advance would have laid this line of supply
open to more certain attack, consequently its protection would eventually have crippled their field
army. In actuality, to protect this central line of

supply, they would have been compelled to have advanced on an enormously extended front, their right on the Lynchburg-Knoxville railroad and their left on the Richmond-Weldon, consequently their progress would have been excessively slow. Had Jefferson Davis but remembered the words of Fredcrick the Great, "If I were mindful only of my own glory, I would choose always to make war in my own country, for there every man is a spy, and the enemy can make no movement of which I am not informed,"[49] he would have realized not only the value of a centrally placed capital, but the dangers a Federal advance from Washington into North Carolina would be subjected to. But State Rights once again interposed, and it is most unlikely that *Lee*, heart and soul a Virginian, would have looked with favour upon any weakening of the military forces in his native State.

The strategic strength of the Confederacy lay in its size and also in its lack of communications, for its conquest demanded its entire occupation, and how to effect this occupation was the outstanding military problem of the Federal Armies. For three years Lincoln, Stanton and Halleck were obsessed by conventional strategical considerations. They believed that the capture of Richmond would end the war; "how" and "why" does not seem to have entered their heads. Had McClellan occupied Richmond in 1862, the war would in fact have been indefinitely prolonged, for the Confederates would simply have established a capital elsewhere. Had they, however, restricted themselves to a limited offensive in the east; had they captured the sea ports, and particularly Wilmington, during the summer of 1862, as undoubtedly they could have done, then they would have been able to have launched a strong, well-organized offensive in the West. To attack from Washington was to strike at the roof of the Confederacy and drive the Confederate forces *into* the Confederate house. To attack in the west from Tennessee on the line Vicksburg and Chattanooga was to crash through an outer wall and sever its ground floor from its upper storey; in fact, to drive the Confederate forces out of the greater part of their house, and so gain entrance and occupation. The Washington and the Richmond Governments read strategy according to rule, they struck at strength and political power, when they should have struck at weakness and the national spirit, because weakness accentuated undermines strength, and loss of national spirit undermines political power.

Until General Grant assumed command, as we shall later on see, the grand-strategy of the North was beneath contempt. The immensity of the problem which lay before Lincoln and his generals was totally unappreciated. He called for 75,000 volunteers, yet look at his problem! This is how Colonel Henderson sees it:

"The city of Atlanta, which may be considered as the heart of the Confederacy, was sixty days' march from the Potomac, the same distance as Vienna from the English Channel, or Moscow from the Niemen. New Orleans, the commercial metropolis, was thirty-six days' march from the Ohio, the same distance as Berlin from the Moselle. Thus space was all in favour of the South; even should the enemy over-run her borders, her principal cities, few in number, were far removed from the hostile bases, and the important railway junctions were perfectly secure from sudden attack. And space, especially where means of communication are scanty, and the country affords few supplies, is the greatest of all obstacles. The hostile territory must be subjugated piecemeal, state by state, province by province, as was Asia by Alexander; and after each victory a new base of supply must be provisioned and secured, no matter at what cost of time, before a further advance can be attempted. Had Napoleon in the campaign against Russia remained for the winter at Smolensko, and firmly established himself in Poland, Moscow might have been captured and held during the ensuing summer. But the occupation of Moscow would not have ended the war. Russia in many respects, was not unlike the Confederacy. She had given no hostages to fortune in the shape of rich commercial towns; she possessed no historic fortresses; and so offered but few objectives to an invader. If defeated or retreating, her armies could always find refuge in distant fastnesses. The climate was severe; the internal trade inconsiderable; to bring the burden of war home to the mass of the population was difficult, and to hold the country by force impracticable. Such were the difficulties which the genius of Napoleon was powerless to overcome, and Napoleon invaded Russia with half a million of seasoned soldiers." [50]

The Two Tactics

This war was an epoch-making one, not only politically but tactically so; for besides uniting a nation, a nation which to-day is giving to the world the fullest expression of the Industrial Revolution, it initiated a new cycle in tactics.

The extraordinary thing about this initiation is that it sprouted from out of one tiny seed—the rifle bullet—which, like the Indian fakir's mango tree, during the four years of the war grew at such an astonishing speed, that on its conclusion the tree resulting could not be seen for the tactical wood; consequently the lessons of this war were lost to military thought, and are still far from being fully appreciated. The old tactical school learned nothing, the new died with the war; so it happened that the grim lessons of Malvern Hill, Shiloh, Fredericksburg, Chancellorsville, Gettysburg and the Wilderness had to be relearned in every succeeding war right up to the World War of 1914-1918, when they appeared in their most tremendous form; yet soldiers still hesitate to accept them.

Lord Wolseley, an able and an educated officer,

though for a brief period he saw the war as it was, totally misread its meaning. In 1887, he wrote: ". . . from first to last the co-operation of even one army corps of regular troops would have given complete victory to whichever side it fought on,"[51] and, in 1898, he repeated this statement, saying: "Had the United States been able, early in 1861, to put into the field, in addition to their volunteers, one Army Corps of regular troops the war would have ended in a few months."[52] To-day such a contention appears far-fetched, for the regular soldier of 1861 was not vastly different from the regular soldier of 1815 or of 1755. In 1755, on the Monongahela, Braddock's Red Coats were worthless against Beaujeu's Red Skins; and, in 1815, what happened to Pakenham at New Orleans when he met Andrew Jackson's rough riflemen of Kentucky, Tennessee and Louisiana?

"There followed a horrible scene: the 44th Foot were literally mowed down by a storm of bullets; other regiments took their place and shared their fate. In fifteen minutes the first attack had been swept away. But Pakenham was brave, and so were his soldiers. The British general formed a new column of attack, and with his staff behind him, his hat raised in the air, rode at the head of the Sutherland Highlanders back into the fearful zone of fire. Only one thing could happen. Once more the rifles blazed. Pakenham went down, killed outright, and every one of the British staff went to earth at the same moment. The Highlanders were decimated, but heroically struggled on, a few getting within a hundred yards of the entrenchments—but no further. Placed on four ranks, constantly firing and stepping back to reload in rotation, Coffee's buck-hunters had too easy a target, and when General Gibbs, succeeding Pakenham in command, brought up the Scots Fusiliers and the 43rd Light Infantry, dealt out the same fate to him as to his predecessor. General Lambert followed, and he, too, with magnificent but senseless British courage, attempted to continue the attack; but it was no longer possible; even Wellington's veterans could not face such an ordeal, and there was nothing left but retreat."[53]

44

What was the result of this engagement? Out of 9,000 British troops, of which 7,000 took part in the attacks, 3,300 were killed and wounded, and 500 taken prisoners; the American losses were 8 killed and 13 wounded, out of a total of 4,500 men! Why this extraordinary disproportion in casualties? First, the American losses were exceptionally light because the British troops were armed with the Brown Bess musket, and the British abnormally heavy because the Americans were armed with the long Tennessee flintlock rifle. Yet, had the British also been armed with this weapon—and this is the point to note—their casualties would have been nearly as great, because their tactics would still have been of the Brown Bess order. Their formations were rigid and their discipline unintelligent, and such was also the case in all foreign armies of 1861. Even in 1866, 1870, 1878, 1904 and 1914 history tells us that Brown Bess tactics died an exceedingly slow death, and even to-day are still very much alive in several European armies.

The supreme tactical fact was: that the rifle had rendered the defence the stronger form of war. "My men," said *Stonewall Jackson*, "sometimes fail to drive the enemy from his position, but to hold one, never!"[54] and though Henderson, an astute student of war, notes this remark with approval, he nevertheless considered that "against troops which can manoeuvre earthworks are useless,"[55] failing, so I think, to see that the art of entrenching is to make trenches manoeuvre also, as Sherman and *Lee* so successfully did in 1864-65. The truth is, that because of the rifle and its mates, the axe and the spade, the defence had become at least three times as strong as the attack. This point is noted by two independent witnesses. Colonel Lyman says: "Put a man in a hole, and a good battery on a hill behind him, and

45

he will beat off three times his number, even if he is not a very good soldier,"[56] and Frank Wilkeson writes: "Before we left North Anna I discovered that our infantry were tired of charging earthworks. The ordinary enlisted men assert that one good man behind an earthwork was equal to three good men outside of it."[57] The fact is that the whole practice of fighting had changed without it being realized. Here is a graphic description of a "1914" battle fought in 1863:

"I had taken part in two great battles, and heard the bullets whistle both days, and yet I had *scarcely seen a Rebel* save killed, wounded, or prisoners! I remember how even line officers, who were at the battle of Chancellorsville, said: 'Why, we never saw any Rebels where we were; only smoke and bushes, and lots of our men tumbling about'; and now I appreciate this most fully. The great art is to *conceal* men; for the moment they show, *bang, bang*, go a dozen cannon, the artillerists only too pleased to get a fair mark. Your typical 'great white plain,' with long lines advancing and manoeuvring, led on by generals in cocked hats and by bands of music, exist not for us. Here it *is*, as I said: 'Left face— prime—forward!'—and then *wrang, wr-r-ang*, for three or four hours, or for all day, and the poor, bleeding wounded streaming to the rear. That is a great battle in America."[58]

During these four years the cavalry charge was rendered impotent. "Here, boys," shouted *Morgan*, "are those fools [Federal cavalry] coming again with their sabres, give it to them," and the saddles were emptied. The rifle-cannon came more and more to the fore; for instance, at Gettysburg: "The air was hideous with most discordant noise. The very earth shook beneath our feet, and the hills and rocks seemed to reel like a drunken man. For one hour and a half this most terrific fire was continued, during which the shrieking of shell, the crash of falling timber, the fragments of rocks flying through the air, shattered from the cliffs by solid shot, the heavy mutterings

46

from the valley between the opposing armies, the splash of bursting shrapnel, and the fierce neighing of wounded artillery horses, made a picture terribly grand and sublime."[59] Even in forest fighting we find the gun used if not to hit, then to terrify and dismay. Early in the war in West Virginia, General *Wise* ordered a young artillery lieutenant to open fire. "A dense forest prevented the lieutenant from seeing any of the enemy, and he stated as much to General *Wise*, adding that if he opened fire he would 'do no execution.' The incessant fusilade of rifles and the whistling of minies seemed to emphasize the wisdom of the General's reply, 'D—n the execution, sir, it's the noise that we want.' "[60]

It is in the dethronement of the bayonet, however, that the chief change in tactics is to be sought. Before the advent of the rifle the assault was sometimes a practical operation and, this being so, the bayonet, the successor of the pike, was the superior infantry weapon, the musket being little more than a smoke-producing machine to obscure the bayonet charge. To-day every modern army still thinks in terms of the assault; yet this war proved beyond all doubt that the bayonet was as obsolete as the pike. Here are a few examples: "I don't think a single man of them was bayonetted,"[61] writes one eye-witness. Another, General *Gordon*, says: "I may say that very few bayonets of any kind were actually used in battle, so far as my observation extended. The one line or the other usually gave way under the galling fire of small arms, grape, and canister, before the bayonet could be brought into requisition. The bristling points and the glitter of the bayonets were fearful to look upon as they were levelled in front of a charging line; but they were rarely reddened with blood. The day of the bayonet is passed. . . . It may still serve to

47

impress the soldier's imagination, as the loud-sounding and ludicrous gongs are supposed to stiffen the backs and steady the nerves of the grotesque soldiers of China."[62] *Heros von Borcke* says much the same: "I carefully examined many of the corpses, and found only three or four with bayonet-wounds, and these had been received evidently after the bullets. These accounts of bayonet-fights are current after every general engagement, and are frequently embodied in subsequent 'histories,' so-called; but as far as my experience goes, recalling all the battles in which I have borne a part, bayonet-fights rarely occur, and exist only in the imagination." And again: "The bowie-knife occupied a somewhat conspicuous place in the earlier annals of the war, and we were often told of Louisianians, Mississippians, and Texans who threw away their muskets in the hottest of the fight, and fell upon the enemy with their favourite weapon; but I have always regarded these stories in the same fabulous light with the stories of . . . bayonet conflicts . . . and certainly I have never seen the bowie-knife put to any other than a purely pacific and innocent use."[63] Finally, I will quote Surgeon-Major Albert G. Hart, who writes that he saw few bayonet-wounds "except accidental ones. . . . I think half-a-dozen would include all the wounds of this nature that I ever dressed."[64]

I have gone to this length on the subject of the bayonet, because it is so easy to criticize the tactical ability of Grant, *Lee*, and other generals of this war; yet they had no precedent to guide them, for to all intents and purposes the rifle was a new weapon. And when we do criticize them we might remember this: that to-day ninety out of every hundred professional soldiers still believe in the bayonet, a weapon which proved itself next to useless in this war and in every war since fought. It was because of this same lack of realization that between 1861 and 1865 hundreds of assaults were attempted and over eighty per cent of them failed.

The war which faced Grant and *Lee* was a novel war—the war of the rifle bullet. It was a war which closely resembles the World War of fifty-three years later, so closely that no other war, not even the Russo-Japanese War of 1904-1905, offers so exact a comparison. It was a war of rifle bullets and a war of trenches, of slashings and abattis, and even of wire entanglements; the Confederates calling this form of obstacle "a devilish contrivance which none but a Yankee could devise," because at Drury's Bluff they had fallen over it and had been "slaughtered like partridges."[65] It was a war of astonishing modernity: of wooden wire-bound mortars, hand-grenades, winged grenades, rockets, and many forms of booby-traps. Magazine rifles were invented, and also Requa's machine-gun.[66] Balloons were used by both sides, and though the Confederates did not think much of them[67] they manufactured one out of silk dresses. To the sorrow of many a Southern lady, it was speedily captured, "the meanest trick of the war,"[68] so says General *Taliaferro*. Explosive bullets are mentioned,[69] and in June, 1864, General *Pendleton* asked the Chief Ordnance Officer at Richmond whether he could supply him with stink-shell which would give off "offensive gases" and cause "suffocating effect." The answer he got was: ". . . stink-balls, none on hand; don't keep them; will make if ordered."[70] Nor did modernity halt here: armoured ships and armoured trains, land mines and torpedoes[71] were used, also lamp and flag signalling and the field telegraph. A submarine was built by Horace L. Huntley at Mobile—twenty feet long, five deep, and three and a half wide, which was "propelled by a screw worked from the inside by seven or eight men."[72] On February 17, 1864, she sank U.S.S. *Housatonic* off Charleston, and went down with her.

Colonel Lyman is as amusing when writing on war inventions as many a similar writer during the World War. On November 29, 1864, he jotted down in a letter:

"I did not have room to tell you of the ingenious inventions of General Butler for the destruction of the enemy. He never is happy unless he has half a dozen contrivances on hand. One man has brought a fire-engine, wherewith he proposes to squirt on earthworks and wash them all down! An idea that Benjamin [General Butler] considered highly practicable. Then, with his Greek fire, he proposed to hold a redoubt with only five men and a small garden engine [a flame-projector]. 'Certainly,' said General Meade, 'only your engine fires thirty feet, and a minie rifle 3,000 yards, and I am afraid your five men might be killed, before they had a chance to burn up their adversaries!' Also he is going to get a gun that shoots seven miles and, taking direction by compass, burn the city of Richmond with shells of Greek fire. If that don't do, he has an auger that bores a tunnel five feet in diameter, and he is going to bore to Richmond, and suddenly pop up in somebody's basement, while the family are at breakfast! So you see he is ingenious. It is really summer-warm to-day; there are swarms of flies, and I saw a bumble-bee and a grasshopper."[73]

Life in camp and bivouac was equally modern, though a little rougher. Not only were newspaper boys seen behind, but on the battlefields; and certainly one regimental newspaper called *The Rapid Ann* was published.[74] Delousing was a frequent "operation of war," men "seated shirt in hand on the ground, endeavouring to pick the vermin off that garment. . . ."[75] This done, they would open tins of condensed milk[76] and brew their tea or coffee.

The Two Armies

The two causes, the two political ideas and the two ways of living produced two very different kinds of soldiers, as different in many ways as were the soldiers of the French revolutionary armies from those of Austria and Prussia. The fact that the Federals had to fight in an enemy's country, whilst the Confederates mainly fought in their own country, compelled the former towards discipline and the latter towards laxity. Besides, sparsely populated countries always breed self-reliant people—men and women not over-given to obedience.

The Confederacy being immense in size, badly roaded and pre-eminently agricultural, its soldiers naturally took to guerilla warfare as their forefathers had done in the War of the Rebellion. To conquer such a people military operations had to be methodical, for individual valour and initiative are best overcome by discipline and solidarity. Unfortunately for the Federals they sought to establish these conditions on the conventional European pattern; they copied in place of creating, and possessing the army headquarters and the bulk of the small regular establishment, they expanded it not only bodily, but spiritually in the form they found it. General Fry says: "The army was weighed down by longevity, by venerated traditions, by prerogatives of service rendered in former wars, by the firmly tied red-tape of military bureauism, and by the deep-seated and well-founded fear of the auditors and comptrollers of the treasury." Then he says, because of this antiquated professionalism, "in the beginning of the war, the military advantage was on the side of the Confederates, notwithstanding the greater resources

51

of the North, which produced their effect only as the contest was prolonged."[77]   In other words, the less military side was the more soldierlike; free from shibboleths, the Confederate soldier could expand with expanding events, whilst the Federal sought to overcome difficulties by text-book rules.

The men themselves were also different; though in the western theatre of the war this difference was negligible, in the eastern it was marked.   There the Federal troops were very mixed, large numbers of Irish, German and other foreign stock being enlisted. Though these men might have fought well enough in their own countries, many of them had little heart in the Federal cause; in fact, large numbers did not even understand what the war was about, whilst every Southern soldier realized that he was fighting for his home and freedom.   Wilkeson, a private soldier in the Army of the Potomac, was probably unfortunate; anyhow his opinion is interesting.   Of his batch of recruits he writes: "False history and dishonest Congressmen . . . say they were brave Northern youth going to the defence of their country.   I, who know, say they were as arrant a gang of cowards, thieves, murderers and blacklegs as were ever gathered inside the walls of Newgate or Sing Sing."[78] The opposing army was not altogether free of foreign influence.   *Watson*, a private in the Confederate Army, mentions a German recruit who, given the countersign "Natches," shouted out to the first man who approached his post, "Halt! you can't pass here unless you say 'Natches'."[79]

Except for his lack of discipline, the Confederate soldier was probably the finest individual fighter the world has ever seen.   It is important to realize this, for, unless we do so, we shall not fully appreciate the difficulties of the Federal generals; and to show what this exceptional man was like, I will quote the opinions of a Confederate, a Federal, and an Englishman. General *D. H. Hill* says:

"Self-reliant always, obedient when he chose to be, impatient of drill and discipline, he was unsurpassed as a scout or on the skirmish line. Of the shoulder-to-shoulder courage, bred of drill and discipline, he knew nothing and cared less. Hence, on the battle-field, he was more of a free lance than a machine. Who ever saw a Confederate line advancing that was not crooked as a ram's horn. Each ragged rebel yelling on his own hook and aligning on himself! But there is as much need of the machine-made soldier as of the self-reliant soldier, and the concentrated blow is always the most effective blow. The erratic effort of the Confederate, heroic though it was, yet failed to achieve the maximum result just because it was erratic. Moreover, two serious evils attended that excessive egotism and individuality which came to the Confederate through his training, association, and habits. He knew when a movement was false and a position untenable, and he was too little of a machine to give in such cases the whole-hearted service which might have redeemed the blunder. The other evil was an ever-growing one. His disregard of discipline and independence of character made him often a straggler, and by straggling the fruit of many a victory was lost."[80]

As late as May, 1864, Colonel Lyman writes:

"These Rebels are not half-starved and ready to give up—a more sinewy, tawny, formidable-looking set of men could not be. In education they are certainly inferior to our native-born people; but they are usually very quick-witted within their own sphere of comprehension; and they know enough to handle weapons with terrible effect. Their great characteristic is their stoical manliness; they never beg or whimper, or complain; but look you straight in the face, with as little animosity as if they had never heard a gun."[81]

Colonel Fremantle says:

"But from what I have seen and heard as *yet*, it appears to me that the Confederates possess certain great qualities as soldiers, such as individual bravery and natural aptitude in the use of fire-arms, strong, determined patriotism and boundless confidence in their favourite generals and in themselves. They are sober of necessity, as there is literally no liquor to be got. They have sufficient good sense to know that a certain amount of discipline is absolutely necessary; and I believe that instances of insubordination are extremely rare. They possess the great advantage of being led by men of talent and education as soldiers who thoroughly understand the people they have to lead, as well as those they have to beat. These generals, such as *Lee, Johnston Beauregard*, or *Longstreet*, they would follow anywhere, and obey implicitly. But, on the other hand, many of their officers, looking forward to future political advancement, owing to their present military rank, will not punish their men, or are afraid of making themselves obnoxious by enforcing rigid discipline. The men are constantly in the habit of throwing away their knapsacks and blankets on a long march, if not carried for them, and though actuated by the strongest and purest patriotism, can often not be got to consider their obligations as soldiers. In the early part of the war they were often, when victorious, nearly as disordered as the beaten, and many would coolly walk off home, under the impression that they had performed their share.

"After having lived with the veterans of *Bragg* and *Lee*, I was able to form a still higher estimate of Confederate soldiers. Their obedience and forbearance in success, their discipline under disaster, their patience under suffering, under hardships, or when wounded, and their boundless devotion to their country under all circumstances, are beyond all praise."[82]

The methods of fighting in the two armies were as different as the men composing them. The Southern soldier marched light, carrying from thirty to forty pounds weight,[83] a rifle, a cartridge-box, an old rug and a "tooth-brush stuck like a rose in his buttonhole"; the Northern, more heavily laden, carrying about sixty pounds,[84] which made all the difference in marching, for the economic load is one-third of the body weight. The Federals, far more so than the Confederates, maintained shoulder-to-shoulder formations, which were fatal under rifle fire. "I was wonderfully impressed," writes Colonel *Taylor*, ". . . by the Southern soldier and his independent action in battle [Chancellorsville] as contrasted with the mechanical movement of the machine soldier. . . .

First one man went forward, then another, then at intervals two or three; then there would be a wavering and falling back when the fire became hot; then there would be a repetition of this; one or two at a time, encouraging the others, then small parties advanced, the officers waved their swords and called the men 'forward,' and then with a yell the whole line rushed rapidly forward without precision or order, but irresistibly, sweeping everything before them."[85] *Watson*, as a private soldier, gives us much useful information. He says: "I have sometimes thought that one of the chief causes of the success of the Confederate troops was the alacrity with which they would form up into line, in a temporary rough-and-ready way after being driven into confusion by some sudden cause or movement in a rough or rugged country, and maintain the battle in that position, while as soon as opportunity offered, every man would fall into his place in the company, the company to its place in the battalion, and the battalion to its place in the brigade, and order regained in a short time."[86] Further, he says, as regards the Federal soldiers: "What told most against them was their strict adherence to military rigidity and form of discipline, by standing up close and maintaining their line in the open field, making themselves conspicuous marks for the fire of their opponents, who fought in open ranks and kneeled down, forming a less prominent mark." . . . "They [the Federals], knowing the superiority of their arms over ours, kept falling back to keep us at long shot, while we followed them up to keep at close range. This was a considerable advantage to us. Our advancing upon them kept us enveloped in the dense smoke, while their falling back kept them in the clear atmosphere where they could be easily seen. Our men squatted down when loading, then advanced and squatted down again, and looking along under the smoke could take good aim; while the enemy, firing at random into the smoke, much of their shot passed over our heads."[87]

I think I have now quoted sufficiently to show the main difference between the two armies. The one was semi-regular and the other semi-guerilla. The one strove after discipline, the other unleashed initiative. In battle the Confederate fought like a Berserker: out of battle he ceased to be a soldier. For instance, *Robert Stiles* tells us that on the way to Gettysburg he rode up to a house, asked for a drink of water, rested there, chatted, wrote a letter, and after wasting an hour or two, rejoined his unit.[88] In the Confederate Army straggling was in fact as inalienable a right as State Rights were in the Confederate Government.

CHAPTER II

THE PERSONALITY OF GRANT

Grant—the Enigma

IN all of us, however common-place we may be, there
lurks an enigma, something which neither we nor
others understand.   We call it personality, a vague
word meaning many things—courage, common sense,
quick wit, frankness, determination, self-command,
and many other qualities, none of which can openly
express themselves unless occasion is propitious and
circumstances are favourable.   Most of us live and
die in a dungeon, and the enigma dies with us; a
few of us escape, mostly by chance, and then, if our
personality is strong, we accomplish something worth
accomplishing, and by doing so the enigma is more
often than not transformed into a myth.   We cease to
be what we really were, and become something we
never could be—something which flatters the common
mind.

This was the fate of *Robert E. Lee*, as I will show in
the next chapter, but not of Ulysses S. Grant.   In the
Pantheon of War he has remained uncanonized, and
not only in the common opinion of his fellow-country-
men does *Lee* rank far above him, but not a few
consider that Sherman, *Joseph E. Johnston, Jeb. Stuart*
and *Stonewall Jackson* showed superior generalship.
Yet what did he do?   He won the Civil War for the
North, and so re-established the Union which to-day
has grown into the vastest consolidated power since

57

the fall of Rome. He fought some of the greatest campaigns in history; was never defeated, and after the war was twice chosen by his countrymen as their President. If there is not food for myth here, where shall we seek it? His story is as amazing as Napoleon's, and as startling as Lenin's; yet enigma he lived and enigma he died, and though occasion was propitious and circumstances were favourable, enigma he remains.

Why is this? There must be some reason for it? He was not a quick-witted charlatan who for a period bewildered the common folk and was then found out. Was he then a fortunate general, a nonentity, who grasping "the skirts of happy chance" was whirled on to the footboard of fame, to cling to greatness, to be rushed by events over battlefield and through White House, and then to be slued off into the dust of oblivion? No—he was one of those inscrutably simple men who from time to time appear in history, who manifest at some critical moment, and who being oblivious of their own greatness and desiring no renown, set fire to an epoch; not by spectacular volcano belchings, but like a grey ember which is red hot at the centre.

The popular idea of Grant has always been a depressing one, a leaden man of no great spirit, of no imagination and of little thought. A force which rolled forward, which crushed by weight of numbers; true, a man brave and determined, but utterly lacking in those qualities which give brilliance to human affairs. "During his whole connection with the regiment [the Fourth Infantry] he would have been considered, both by his brother officers and himself, about as likely to reach the position of Pope of Rome, as General-in-Chief, or President of the United States. . . . He was modest and unambitious—such a man as in our land of pretension and bluster could not be expected to go far."[1] Thus wrote a brother officer of him long after the Civil War as he appeared long before it, in 1852.

In 1858 he was a down-and-out, selling cord-wood in St. Louis; in 1859 a partner of one Henry Boggs, a real estate agent; in 1860 a clerk in his brothers' leather store in Galena, and there he was when the war broke out. Describing him as he appeared in 1858, Mrs. Boggs said: "He had no exalted opinion of himself at any time, but in those days he was almost in despair. He walked the streets looking for something to do. He was actually the most obscure man in St. Louis. Nobody took any notice of him."[2] In May, 1861, Grant said to a friend: "To tell you the truth, I would rather like a regiment, yet there are few men really competent to command a thousand soldiers, and I doubt whether I am one of them."[3] A little after, Governor Yates of Illinois placed him in command of the 21st Illinois Regiment, and he appeared on his first parade almost in rags. About this time *Ewell*, in Richmond, discussing the merits of the officers of the old army with a friend, said: "There is one West Pointer, I think in Missouri, little known, and whom I hope the Northern people will not find out. I mean Sam Grant. I knew him well at the Academy and in Mexico. I should fear him more than any of their officers I have yet heard of. He is not a man of genius, but he is clear-headed, quick and daring."[4] Then three years later, in March, 1864, the victor of Donelson, Vicksburg and Chattanooga came to Washington to take over command of the entire land forces of the United States; accompanied by his small son and carrying a portmanteau he entered Willard's Hotel, signing the register, "U. S. Grant and son, Galena, Ill."[5] The clerk, taking him for a captain or a major, showed him up to a fifth floor room, yet Grant saw nothing strange in this. Two months later, on May 10, "while the general-in-chief was out on the lines supervising the afternoon attack, he dismounted and sat down on a fallen tree to write a dispatch. While thus engaged a shell exploded directly in front of him. He looked up from his paper an instant, and then, without the slightest change of countenance, went on writing the message. Some of the Fifth Wisconsin wounded were being carried past him at the time, and Major E. R. Jones of that regiment, said . . . that one of his men made the remark: 'Ulysses don't scare worth a d—n.' "[6]

The ember was indeed a dull one, and though not one to catch the popular eye, or to fix the historian's gaze, yet one which glowed warm on close contact. Further still, whenever it flamed up it soon burnt low again. It glowed out of Galena into Donelson, a victory of immense importance, and then passed into eclipse. So it happened after Shiloh, after Corinth, during and after Vicksburg, once again after the Wilderness and Cold Harbor, and then finally, because of the rascality of Ferdinand Ward, Grant found himself at the very end of his life's journey once again on the high road of misfortune.

So it seems to me these successive eclipses have somehow or another in the popular mind shrouded the glowing periods, denying greatness to Grant by making him appear a lucky general, a general who, though he could weather storms, could never sail clear of them. Yet when we examine these glowing moments we find that under the clouds of gloom begotten by Halleck and his stupidities, a venal, sensation-loving Press, an uninstructed and eager popular opinion, and the ignorance of unstrategically-minded politicians, they are in fact one continuous blaze of genius seldom seen in military history. Donelson flames into Shiloh, Shiloh into Corinth and Iuka, these battles into Vicksburg, Chattanooga, the Wilderness, Petersburg, until the fire burns out at McLean's house on the Appomattox.

"How are you, Sheridan?" said Grant.

"First rate, thank you," answered Sheridan, "how are you?"

"Is General *Lee* up there?" asked Grant.

"Yes," replied Sheridan.

"Well, then, we will go up."[7]

Thus ended the greatest of civil wars, as ends an everyday call on some small matter of business. Grant went up the wooden steps leading into the house, and there brought about the most magnanimous surrender in history: a capitulation which might well have been followed by an equal political magnanimity. Then he came down those wooden steps, and all were expectant to hear what he had to say. Turning to General Rufus Ingalls, he queried: "Ingalls, do you remember that old white mule that so-and-so used to ride when we were in the city of Mexico?"[8]

Was this a mere pose, a striving after effect? Not for a moment do I think so. The war was over, why bother about it; why not talk of something else? Why not let it pass into an eclipse out of which never again such a war would emerge. Some stray mule outside the house may have suggested its brother of Mexico, this was all, a perfectly common-sense solution; for, as I will show later on, Grant was nothing if not a common-sense man. The greatness of the event meant no more to him than the last page of a story, the greatness of which lived in its conception, in its writing, and not in its finished print.

61

Nevertheless Grant was not an unemotional man. It is true that he hid his emotions, most great men do; yet as General *Longstreet*, one of his old opponents, said, "the biggest part of him is his heart."[9] He had received with joy *Lee's* letter proposing the meeting, for it meant the end of this fratricidal conflict; and then when he entered McLean's house he crept into his heroic adversary's shoes, and as he himself says: "What General *Lee's* feelings were I do not know. But my own, which had been quite jubilant on the receipt of his letter, were sad and depressed. I felt like anything rather than rejoicing at the downfall of a foe who had fought so long and valiantly, and who had suffered so much for a cause."[10] When General McPherson was killed he was so overcome with grief that he retired to his tent and wept for his departed friend. At McLean's house he considered it an unnecessary humiliation to demand of *Lee's* officers the surrender of their swords; then, at the very apex of his career, his mind wandered back to a long-forgotten mule.

This little incident, I think, shows that there was strangeness in this man; not a man easy to know or to be understood; a deep man who, like deep waters, appeared to run still. One of his biographers truly says: "He mounted to fame on a ladder of desperate situations."[11] Unromantic in outward appearance and behaviour, he was a man more rightly belonging to fiction than to fact, that type of man who is seldom met with, but is always here somewhere. The man who belongs to the earthquake and the storm, who is as steadfast as a mountain, as indolent as a desert, and as active as a volcano. Grant—and there are many like him, for the world is still inhabited by millions of Nature's children—belonged to the age of the Titans, those primeval forces, rather than to that

THE PERSONALITY OF GRANT

of the peace-loving gods. He was a mass of contradictions: loved order, and yet could find no place
in an orderly world. He hated war, and yet found
his place there above all his fellows. No wonder he
is difficult to understand, and no wonder he has not
been more fully appreciated.

Sometimes he must have thought of himself, and
even have analysed his own peculiarities. On one
occasion he said: "One of my superstitions had
always been when I started to go anywhere, to do
anything, not to turn back, or stop until the thing
intended was accomplished. I have frequently started
to go out to places where I had never been and to
which I did not know the way, depending upon
making enquiries on the road, and if I got past the
place without knowing it, instead of turning back, I
would go on until a road was found turning in the
right direction, take that, and come in by the other
side."[12]   Horace Porter, one of his most intimate
staff officers, noticed this peculiarity; on one occasion
during the Wilderness campaign, he says: "When he
[Grant] found he was not travelling in the direction
he intended to take, he would try all sorts of cross-
cuts, ford streams, and jump any number of fences
to reach another road rather than go back and take
a fresh start."[13]

How true of him as a soldier, for Grant seldom
turned back, and even when he did, as in his first
move on Vicksburg, it was only to "come in by
the other side." Yet how untrue of him as a citizen,
for each road he took was a blind alley ending
abruptly in misfortune.

A Master of Predicaments

To seek an answer to these many riddles of personality and character, to me it seems that the only sure course to take is to get back to his early days, for it is a very true saying that the child is father of the man.

Though his childhood was not a joyous one, yet in manhood he remained always a child at heart, gazing out innocently upon things and men, being seen and seldom heard; wearing a pair of thread gloves on the opening day of the Wilderness campaign, as a good child might on a Sunday, and then once again when *Lee* surrendered to him.

Grant's father, Jesse Grant, was a tanner; curiously enough he had been taught his trade by John Brown's father, John Brown—"A cold prayer hardened to a musket-ball," as Stephen Vincent Benét calls him— of Harper's Ferry fame; where also, curiously enough, Colonel *Robert E. Lee* arrested him on October 16, 1859. Ulysses, the son of Jesse, was in a way a sentimentalist; he loathed the tan-yard, its stench and its blood-clotted hides. Here we have the beginnings of his horror of war and of bloodshed. Throughout life the only meat he would eat was beef cooked to a cinder, for the sight of blood destroyed his appetite. He was certainly peculiar in his tastes, for at 4 a.m. on May 6, 1864, that is during the opening struggle in the Wilderness, at breakfast he "took a cucumber, sliced it, poured some vinegar over it, and partook of nothing else except a cup of strong coffee."[14] A meal which may have refreshed the pacifist within him— the man who said, when accepting the nomination for the Presidency, "Let us have peace."[15]

The tan-yard drove him into the fields, into the farm lands, into the arms of Nature. Untouched by home affections, unspoilt by pedantry, shy by instinct, his early years were lived with his thoughts and his work. There his father's horses became his business partners, the only partners he ever really understood. He gave them his care, and in return they gave him courage and self-reliance, self-control and self-command. In the solitude of the fields, where no one was at hand to satisfy the "whys" and "wherefores" which every child delights in, he learned to reason things out in his own way, to solve problems on his own, and to interpret life in terms of material force, just as Nature seemed to do. Of his struggle amongst the bayous around Vicksburg, W. E. Woodward says of him: "There was not another general in the Union army—probably not one alive in any army—as well qualified as Grant for a military operation of this kind. As we watch him in this terribly arduous Vicksburg campaign we see behind him the shadows of his early years . . . the teamster boy of an Ohio settlement, bringing in the heavy logs from the woodcutter's camp . . . the young ploughman, with calloused hands, driving his plough through the tough black soil . . . the conqueror of horses . . . the sweating quartermaster, with his wagon-train of cantankerous mules on the hot plains of Mexico. If Destiny ever brought the man and the hour together, it was when Grant stood before Vicksburg."[16]

Then he went to West Point, not because he longed to be a soldier, but because he was determined to escape the life of a tanner, and West Point enabled him to escape it. There, outside clearing a jump of six feet three inches, he did only one thing of note, and that on the day of his arrival. His correct name was Hiram Ulysses Grant; he did not like it, and had transposed the names Hiram and Ulysses to avoid being called "Hug." Here we catch a glimpse of his sensitiveness. Then on arriving he found that in error his name had been entered in the register as Ulysses Simpson Grant. A difficulty now arose, for Ulysses Simpson had been expected, and in his place had appeared Ulysses Hiram. As this knotty problem was beyond the powers of West Point to solve, it meant that his papers would have to be sent back to Washington. But to Grant the problem was simplicity itself; he dropped the name Hiram and assumed that of Simpson in its stead. Throughout life he never failed to look at every problem from the simplest point of view, and to answer it in the simplest possible manner.

In the composition of what we call "personality" simplicity is not exactly a flood-light, it does not flash and show up; for in the inner man it burns a tiny flame quite unseen by the outer world. It is not a quality which grips like boastfulness. It is not something which editors can catch on to like pugnacity, nor will it magnetize the popular mind like self-assertion. The quiet simple man is always a mystery, but of a kind which does not entice solution.

At West Point Grant spent his spare time in reading books of action—Cooper, Marryat, Scott, Washington Irving; he liked romances, but he was frankly indolent; life there was too complicated and artificial for him. In this there is nothing extraordinary, but to me it is somewhat curious, that when later on sitting in the leather store of Grant Bros., Galena—for to the tan-yard he returned, every other occupation having failed—though he had no liking for war he would study Napoleon III's campaign in Italy, which was being fought at this time—1859. He read the newspapers, pored over their maps, and would say: "This movement was a mistake. If I commanded the army, I would do thus and so."[17] Even before this date, when stationed at Fort Vancouver in 1853, "his comrades did not fail to notice the singular vividness and comprehensiveness with which he narrated the stirring engagements of the [Mexican] War, and how accurately his memory, like an open book, reproduced not detached incidents, but the action of the whole army as a unit—what it tried to do, what it accomplished or failed in, and what errors weakened its plan. After one of these talks, they would remark: 'How clear-headed Sam Grant is in describing a battle! He seems to have the whole thing in his head.' "[18] When in the spring of 1864 he came to the East to take over the supreme command, he turned to Horace Porter and said: "I have watched the progress of the Army of the Potomac ever since it was organized, and have been greatly interested in reading the accounts of the splendid fighting it has done."[19] This is an illuminating remark, for few generals who had had to face his problems would have troubled to find the time to examine those of others hundreds of miles away. Long after the war, when he travelled round the world, John Russell Young, who accompanied him, tells us that one day, "walking up and down the deck, Grant went on to describe all of Napoleon's campaigns, from Marengo down to Leipsic, speaking of each battle in the most minute manner— the number of men engaged on either side, even the range of their guns and the tactics of both sides; why victory came and why defeat came—as thoroughly learned as a problem in mathematics. Then back to the battles of Frederick the Great; Leuthen, the campaigns of the Thirty Years' War; back to the campaigns of Caesar, and always illustrating as he talked the progress and change in the art of war, and how machinery, projectiles, and improvements in arms had made what would be a great victory for

Napoleon almost impossible now. . . . It is the only occasion on which I ever heard Grant speak of the art of war, because it was a subject to which he had an aversion. You might have known him for a year and never learned that he had fought a battle in his life."[20]

These various quotations, even if some appear a little highly coloured, reveal the fact that though Grant disliked war, what he really loathed was its tactical side—the actual slaughter; but that the strategical side fascinated him. He loved pitting his will against seeming impossibilities—a buck-jumping circus pony, leaping over a battery of six guns in succession, fighting with the bayous round Vicksburg, creating cosmos out of chaos at Chattanooga, and pursuing *Lee* over bottomless road to Appomattox Court House.

It was the Titan within him which called forth this affection, the old pioneer spirit of his forefathers, of Matthew Grant and Priscilla his wife who set out from England, on March 20, 1630, in the good ship *Mary and John* to seek a new life in the New World. Those ancestors of his who moved westwards into Ohio, never to turn back but to fight onwards, never to falter but to dare. It was this spirit, the spirit which founded the United States and upon which it now stands, which made him the soldier he was, and which when a statesmen led him to dream dreams of world federation, of Anglo-Saxon unity, and of the final abolition of war. All great and simple visions of will, with none of that trickery in their composition which politics demand. He failed in the dodges of peace, in war he was not a great tactician, and in both cases it seems to me the reason was that he was in no sense of the word a crafty man.

Though few soldiers have shown such resolution as

Grant, have accepted such risks, and have been faced by so many difficulties and disappointments, he was in no sense a pushing, self-assertive man. The reason for this is clear when his whole life is reviewed in panorama. He was the master of predicaments and the plaything of conventionalities. When everything was right and normal he shrank into his chrysalis of mediocrity; when all was in chaos, or when the occasion demanded desperate action, like the jinn in the *Arabian Nights*, he emerged from his bottle, and nothing would induce him to withdraw into it again until normality had been re-established.

We see this metamorphosis clearly during the first few months of the war. On May 30, 1861, he writes: "During the six days I have been at home I have felt all the time as if a duty was being neglected that was paramount to any other duty I ever owed." Yet he was doubtful whether he was competent to command a regiment, and when Governor Yates offered to recommend him to Washington for a brigadier-generalship, he answered saying, "he didn't want office till he had earned it."[21] Most men would have jumped at such an offer, even had they felt themselves incompetent to fill it, but not so Grant, who on account of his innate honesty, failed to see that the question was not whether he would make an ideal brigadier, but would he be as efficient as any other man Yates might select? This honesty, which I think may be traced to his primitive nature, separated him from ordinary men and ordinary circumstances, making him suspicious of his own abilities; a moral lag he was never able to shake off voluntarily, but which was shaken off by outward circumstances directly these became abnormal. Then this honesty was replaced by a heroism which recognized no limit, which accepted risks, and by accepting them was not restricted by their dangers. Throughout life Grant's enemy was his inner self, an enigma he could not solve, something which always held him back as long as conditions were such that he was unable to break away from its grasp. As long as he was conscious of himself he remained a child; but directly a turmoil arose which drowned this consciousness he became a Titan. For example, when working in his brothers' store at Galena he was a complete nonentity because his surroundings were normal and mediocre. Then one day a debtor of the firm locked himself up in his house and threatened to shoot the deputy-sheriff if he attempted to break in and serve a writ. Grant appeared on the scene, and at once the Grant of Donelson emerged from out the Grant of Galena; he broke the door open and effected an immediate and unconditional surrender. As Church says: "Had the business of dealing with warlike clients been sufficient to occupy his time, Grant would have been a brilliant success as a tanner's clerk."[22]

Fortunately for Grant, Yates was a man of common sense, and a good judge of character. Meeting a book-keeper from the Galena store, he turned to him and said: "What *does* he want?" "The way to deal with him," replied the book-keeper, "is to ask him no questions, but simply order him to duty. He will obey promptly." Thereupon Yates sent the following order to Grant: "You are this day appointed colonel of the Twenty-first Illinois Volunteers, and requested to take command at once."[23] Had this unit been disciplined and well conducted, Grant would have remained in pupa stage, but fortunately it was not— it was a band of toughs.

General John E. Smith describes his first visit to his regiment:

"I went with him to camp, and shall never forget the scene when his men first saw him. Grant was dressed in citizen's clothes, an old coat worn out at the elbows, and a badly damaged hat. His men, though ragged and barefooted themselves, had formed a high estimate of what a colonel should be, and when Grant walked in among them, they began making fun of him. They cried in derision, 'What a colonel!' 'D——n such a colonel,' and made all sorts of fun of him. And one of them, to show off to the others, got behind his back and commenced sparring at him, and while he was doing this another gave him such a push that he hit Grant between the shoulders."[24]

One of Governor Yates's aides, growing nervous, said: "They're an unruly lot. Do you think you can manage them?" "Oh, yes, I think I can manage them," replied Grant, and he did. The boys called for a speech, and he gave them one, to wit: "Go to your quarters!" When a man got drunk, he knocked him down, bound and gagged him, and had him thrown into the guardroom. "Howdy, Colonel?" said a sentry nodding at him. "Hand me your piece," quietly answered Grant. Then facing the somewhat astonished warrior he came to the "present arms," and handing him back his musket, said: "That is the way to say 'How do you do' to your Colonel."[25] Men who were insolent were tied to posts; men who rose late got no food all day. Thus, within a few weeks did Grant discipline the 21st Illinois.

Though he was rougher than his men when action demanded roughness, he had complete control over his temper. Only on one occasion does he appear to have lost it. When crossing the Pamunkey, in 1864, he came upon a teamster brutally beating his horse. "What does this conduct mean, you scoundrel?" he shouted. "This," says Horace Porter, "was the one exhibition of temper manifested by him during the entire campaign, and the only one I ever witnessed during my many years of service with him."[26]

71

His Simplicity and Self-Reliance

"He could not only discipline others, but he could discipline himself,"[27] which gave him complete control over himself, and because of this self-control, again and again was he able to establish self-control in others. At Fort Donelson, his first great battle, he was away from the field discussing the situation with Flag-Officer Foote, when the Confederates attacked. On his return he found that his 1st Division (McClernand's) had been badly defeated, and he was met by a staff officer "white with fear." How did he comport himself? General Lewis Wallace, who was present, says:

> "In every great man's career there is a crisis exactly similar to that which now overtook General Grant, and it cannot be better described than as a crucial test of his nature. A mediocre person would have accepted the news as an argument for persistence in his resolution to enter upon a siege. Had General Grant done so, it is very probable his history would have been then and there concluded. His admirers and detractors are alike invited to study him at this precise juncture. It cannot be doubted that he saw with painful distinctness the effect of the disaster to his right wing. His face flushed slightly. With a sudden grip he crushed the papers in his hand. But in an instant these signs of disappointment or hestitation—as the reader pleases—cleared away. In his ordinary, quiet voice he said, addressing himself to both officers [McClernand and Lewis Wallace], 'Gentlemen, the position on the right must be retaken' . . ."[28]

Then galloping down the line he shouted: "Fill your cartridge-boxes quick, and get into line; the enemy is trying to escape, and he must not be permitted to do so. . . ." "This," as he says, "acted like a charm. The men only wanted someone to give them a command."[29] It was not his presence only which established order, but his self-control. The presence of a general, especially in the face of danger, at once establishes confidence, for his personality is fused into the impersonal crowd, and the higher his self-control the higher does this confidence grow—it magnetizes his men and morally re-unifies them.

Grant's methods were always simple, direct and to the point. So much so that to the common mind it seemed impossible that a man who appeared so ordinary could possibly accomplish what he did on his own initiative. It has more than once been suggested that men like Rawlins, his chief-of-staff, were his brains, as Gneisenau was the brains of old Blücher. There is nothing to prove this, and everything to disprove it. For instance, Colonel Lyman says: "With two or three exceptions, Grant is surrounded by the most ordinary set of plebeians you ever saw. I think he has them on purpose (to avoid advice), for he is a man who does everything with a specific reason; he is eminently a *wise* man."[30] Though in May, 1864, when as General-in-Chief he commanded in all 533,000 men, his staff "consisted of fourteen officers only, and was not larger than that of some division commanders."[31] He did not rely on his staff, he relied upon himself. At Chattanooga, "as throughout his later career, he wrote nearly all his documents with his own hand and seldom dictated one, even the most important dispatch."[32] Of his orders General Meade said: "There is one striking feature . . . no matter how hurriedly he may write them on the field, no one ever has the slightest doubt as to their meaning, or ever has to read them over a second time to understand them."[33] Richardson says: "Two qualities were strongly marked: (1) Whatever he did was done on *his own* judgment. He showed unusual modesty of opinion and unusual confidence of action. He heard all friendly suggestions with unvarying politeness, and then did—exactly as he

73

saw fit. (2) He trusted subordinates thoroughly, giving only general directions, not hampering them with petty instructions."[34] He relied on his staff for detail and not for ideas. "He studiously avoided performing any duty which someone else could do as well as or better than he, and in this respect demonstrated his rare powers of administration and executive methods. He was one of the few men holding high position who did not waste valuable hours by giving his personal attention to petty details. He never consumed his time in reading over court-martial proceedings, or figuring up the items of supplies on hand, or writing unnecessary letters or communications. He held subordinates to a strict accountability in the performance of such duties, and kept his own time for thought."[35]

An interesting and unrecorded example of how Grant tackled his problems has been given me by Mr. O. E. Mack, of Oakland, California. Shortly after Grant was made General-in-Chief he "came to Fort Monroe one forenoon. Asking that no one be permitted to follow him, he went around the warehouse [of the Adams Express Company] to the far end of the walk and sat down on the end of a pile. Placing his elbows on his knees and his chin in his hands, he sat there until long in the afternoon. . . . It may reasonably be inferred what he was thinking about. Grant was reputed to be able to carry in mind a clear picture of the topography of the country he operated in. This would enable him to work out a strategic problem mentally with more certainty than could one who did not have this ability."

This is probably a correct conclusion, nevertheless: Grant could work in all circumstances, never being perturbed physically or morally. His final plan in the Vicksburg campaign was worked out by him in the saloon of the headquarters ship, in which had assembled a lively gathering of officers and ladies—"cards and music were the order of the evening." In this gay turmoil General McPherson offered him a glass of liquor. Looking up and smiling Grant said: "Mac, you know your whisky won't help me to think; give me a dozen of the best cigars you can find. . . . I think by the time I have finished them I shall have this job pretty nearly planned."[36]

The lack of being able to do what others found easy, and of accomplishing what others found difficult and frequently impossible, is the key to Grant's genius, without which the enigma must remain concealed. As I have already pointed out, at Donelson he was at his best when things were at their worst. It was not so much that he could think more clearly when chaos surrounded him, but that he could think just as clearly as when it did not. When others were at their wits' ends Grant was perfectly calm and collected. No general can have ever beheld a more depressing scene than faced him at Shiloh. When he hobbled on crutches off his ship—he had been thrown from his horse a day or two before—he was met by a terrifying spectacle—5,000 panic-stricken stragglers in utter confusion. All appeared lost, but to Grant no battle was ever lost. He at once organized ammunition trains and fell in the stragglers. At 2.45 p.m. the next day General *Jordan* turned to General *Beauregard*, then in command of the Confederate forces, and said: "General, do you not think our troops are very much in the condition of a lump of sugar thoroughly soaked with water, but yet preserving its original shape, though ready to dissolve?"[37] Once Grant took control it was the enemy who was lost, because confusion had no terror for him. He seems to have realized this, for at breakfast, on May 7, 1864, Horace

Porter asked him: "In your battles up to this time, when do you think your presence upon the field was most useful in the accomplishing of results?" He replied: "Well, I don't know"; then after a pause, "Perhaps at Shiloh."[38]

At Chattanooga it is the same. On October 16, 1863, Dana, the Assistant-Secretary of War, then in the besieged town, wrote to the War Department: "I never saw anything which seemed so lamentable and hopeless."[39] On the 23rd Grant arrived, and on the 29th the starving army was wildly cheering: "The Cracker line open. Full rations, boys! Three cheers for the Cracker line"; and an eye-witness adds, "as if we had won another victory, and we had."[40] Again on May 6, 1864, during the battle of the Wilderness, there was a panic. An excited officer rushed up to where Grant was sitting and said: "General, wouldn't it be prudent to move head-quarters to the other side of the Germanna road?" To which came the reply: "It strikes me it would be better to order up some artillery and defend the present location."[41]

During this desperate battle, "while the most critical movements were taking place, General Grant manifested no perceptible anxiety, but gave his orders, and sent and received communications, with a coolness and deliberation which made a marked impression upon those who had been brought into contact with him from the first time on the field of battle. His speech was never hurried, and his manner betrayed no trace of excitability or even impatience. . . . In the darkness of the night, in the gloom of a tangled forest, and after men's nerves had been racked by the strain of a two days' desperate battle, the most immovable commander might have been shaken. But it was in just such sudden emergencies that

General Grant was always at his best." He quietly questioned, sorted truth from falsehood, and "gave directions for relieving the situation with the marvellous rapidity which was always characteristic of him. . . ." His sense of proportion never deserted him. It was at this time, when *Lee* counter-attacked him on the evening of May 6, that in great excitement a general officer said to him: " 'General Grant, this is a crisis that cannot be looked upon too seriously. I know *Lee's* methods well by past experience; he will throw his whole army between us and the Rapidan, and cut us off completely from our communications.' The General rose to his feet, took his cigar out of his mouth, turned to the officer, and replied, with a degree of animation which he seldom manifested: 'Oh, I am heartily tired of hearing about what *Lee* is going to do. Some of you always seem to think he is suddenly going to turn a double somersault, and land in our rear and on both of our flanks at the same time. Go back to your command, and try to think what we are going to do ourselves, instead of what *Lee* is going to do.' "[42]

Then at the very end, when Ferdinand Ward swindled him out of his entire fortune and left him in debt to Mr. W. H. Vanderbilt to the sum of $150,000, in order to pay his way Grant began to dictate his "Memoirs," and when the cancer in his throat choked his voice, in agony he wrote on. It was a race with death, and in this greatest predicament which ever faced him, once again he rose with the occasion, and with that dauntless spirit of resolution which won him Donelson, Vicksburg, Chattanooga and Appomattox Court House, he won this his final victory. The book was finished about a week before he died, and in royalties brought in to his widow $450,000.

His Modesty and Common Sense

Simplicity was the mainspring of his nature. His faith in the goodness of mankind was unbounded. At the age of eight he wanted to own a horse. What did he do? He called on its owner and said: "Papa says I may offer you twenty dollars for the colt, but if you won't take that, I am to offer twenty-two and a half, and if you won't take that to give you twenty-five."[43] What is remarkable in this story is not that little Ulysses paid the full price, but that this story in itself is an epitome of his dealings throughout life with his fellowmen. In none could he see guile, because he believed everyone to be as honest as himself—no wonder he failed in every business venture. Yet as a soldier this simplicity was his guardian angel. Whilst as a general McClellan could see nothing beyond his own operations, and Halleck nothing outside of the text books, he saw things as they were, uncontaminated by his ideas or anyone else's. He saw the war in its simplest form, that is as a whole, because he did not see the difficulties in winning it until they arose, and those who did lost their faith in doubts. His strategy was simple—hold *Lee* in Virginia and move Sherman through Georgia to attack him in rear. His theory of war was simplicity itself; he says: "The art of war is simple enough. Find out where your enemy is. Get at him as soon as you can. Strike at him as hard as you can and as often as you can, and keep moving on."

He disliked figures of speech and exaggeration. When towards the end of the Appomattox campaign he caught up with Sheridan and said to him: "*Lee* is in a bad fix. It will be difficult for him to get away," that wild little cavalry leader shouted out:

78

"D—n him, he *can't* get away. We'll have his whole army, we'll have every——of them!" To which Grant quietly replied: "That's a little too much to expect. I think if I were *Lee* I could escape at least with some of my men."[44]

Not understanding why a man should want to be dishonest, for honesty seemed to him to be always the best policy, he should never have become a politician. In 1864, Sherman urged him saying: "For God's sake and your country's sake, come out of Washington," for he knew Grant's honest simplicity, and was afraid of political cunning. Then, after the war, Grant went as President to Washington utterly lacking that insight into men which once led Lincoln to exclaim: "Honest statesmanship is the employment of individual meanness for the public good." Yet in spite of his inexperience in government, he was always plain and practical and did not seek to influence men by unworthy motives, nor did he rely upon popular emotionalism to benefit his party. Thus we see that whilst as a soldier he was a realist moved solely by external situations, as a citizen he was an idealist, and this I think explains his many failures before the war and after it. The simplicity and honesty of war unconsciously appealed to him, whilst the complexity and dishonesty of peace, being so alien to his nature, he left to be entangled rather than disentangled by others.

His simplicity was the foundation of his honesty and his modesty. He could not bear shams, pretensions and humbug. He despised after-dinner speeches and such-like orations, because he felt they were humbug; he simply could not deliver them. His relationship with President Lincoln was always modest and understanding. When, in August, 1864, Lincoln wrote to him: "The particulars of your plans I

79

neither know nor seek to know. . . . I wish not to obtrude any restraints or constraints upon you."[45] He answered: "Should my success be less than I desire or expect, the least I can say is, the fault is not with you."[46] Here is a man who is not only capable but self-reliant, and it is self-reliance which nearly always wins over a superior, because it relieves him of the onus of a work which he himself cannot control. This self-reliance was the child of his modesty, for modesty taught him self-control, and his sense of duty towards himself in its turn pointed the way to duty towards his country.

His honesty and modesty towards himself endowed him with wisdom; he could discover his own mistakes, and was never stampeded by his successes. He was not content to do just what other people did. He was no copyist, but in place a student, not only of events and of others, but of himself. This wisdom is nothing more than common sense, action adapted to circumstances, refusal to live, or think, in a rut; refusal to be stampeded by events however depressing or elating. His common sense was such that he possessed the inestimable gift of being able to learn from his own mistakes, as well as from the mistakes of others. He was in no way bound by traditions, and had a horror of precedents and formalities.

One of his biographers says: "His success was the success of sheer common sense—which is almost the same thing as generalship—and of American democracy."[47] For instance, when, in March, 1863, Halleck wrote a letter to Grant and Rosecrans offering a major-generalship to whomever of the two first gained a decisive victory, Rosecrans adopted the conventional attitude: he felt "degraded at such an auctioneering of honours." Otherwise Grant: he folded up his copy, put it into his pocket, and went on with his plan of campaign. Grant's action saved time, Rosecran's only increased friction.

His common sense was due to his reasoning nature; he always had a reason for what he did; chance and luck he did not believe in. He never entered into recriminations, and as Greene writes: "He was accustomed to take things as they were and to devote his whole energies to making the best of them."[48] Richardson says, "he never complained, he never once asked for re-enforcements, but always did cheerfully the best he could with whatever the Government saw fit to give him."[49] And General James B. Fry writes: "He had no readiness in showing off his acquirements; on the contrary, his acquirements did not appear until forced to the front, and then they showed him off without his knowing it. . . . He did not hesitate in choosing the best course, no matter who proposed it; and in military affairs he would execute a plan prescribed by higher authority with as much vigour and fidelity as if it had been his own. . . . Neither responsibility, nor turmoil, nor danger, nor pleasure, nor pain, impaired the force of his resolution, or interrupted the steady flow of his intellect. . . . He could not dwell upon theories, or appear to advantage in hypothetical cases, and even in practical matters his mental processes were carried on beneath the surface. Until he was ready to act he gave no sign by word or expression of his own train of thought, or the impression made upon him by others, though they might make him change his mind and induce action different from what he had intended. He generally adhered to his first convictions, but never halted long between two opinions. When he changed he went over without qualification or regard of consequences, and was not disturbed by lingering doubts or regrets."[50]

His outlook on war was a purely common sense one. I have already noted his views on tactics; here I will give an example of his opinion on military history:

"Some of our generals," he says, "failed because they worked out everything by rule. They knew what Frederick did at one place, and Napoleon at another. They were always thinking about what Napoleon would do. Unfortunately for their plans, the rebels would be thinking about something else. I don't underrate the value of military knowledge, but if men make war in slavish observances to rules, they will fail. No rules will apply to conditions of war as different as those which exist in Europe and America. Consequently, while our generals were working out problems of an ideal character, problems that would have looked well on a blackboard, practical facts were neglected. To that extent I consider remembrances of old campaigns a disadvantage. Even Napoleon showed that, for my impression is that his first success came because he made war in his own way, and not in imitation of others. War is progressive. I do not believe in luck in war any more than luck in business. Luck is a small matter, may affect a battle or a movement, but not a campaign or a career."[51]

Conditions and not rules governed his actions. He did not resist circumstances, neither did he seek a justification for failure, nor did he blindly repeat methods which had led to success. In place he analysed circumstances and acted accordingly. He learned something of importance from each operation he undertook. From these lessons—and every engagement was a lesson, and not merely a victory or a defeat—he built up his art of war.

His Physical and Moral Courage

In all these many qualities there was little of the spectacular. He was an "ordinary scrubby-looking man with a slightly seedy look," says Richard Henry Dana, eyeing him at Willard's Hotel in March, 1864.

But I prefer Colonel Lyman's description of him in his delightful letters to his wife. On March 5, at Willard's, "General Grant came in, with his little boy," he writes, "and was immediately bored by being cheered, and then shaken by the hand by the οἱ πολλοί! He is rather under middle height, of a spare strong build; light-brown hair, and short, light-brown beard. His eyes of a clear blue; forehead high; nose aquiline; jaw squarely set, but not sensual. His face has three expressions: Deep thought; extreme determination; and great simplicity and calmness."[52] On April 12 he says: "Grant is a man of a good deal of rough dignity; rather taciturn; quick and decided in speech. He habitually wears an expression as if he had determined to drive his head through a brick wall, and was about to do it. I have much confidence in him."[53] Again, on April 18: "He is a man of a natural, severe simplicity in all things— the very way he wears his high-crowned felt hat shows this: he neither puts it on behind his ears, nor draws it over his eyes; much less does he cock it on one side, but sets it straight and very hard on his head. His riding is the same: without the slightest 'air,' and, *per contra*, without affectation of homeliness; he sits firmly in the saddle and looks straight ahead, as if only intent on getting to some particular point. General Meade says he is a very amiable man, though his eye is stern and almost fierce-looking."[54] Lastly, on June 12, the day the Army of the Potomac began to march to the James River: "He is an odd combination; there is one good thing, at any rate— he is the concentration of all that is American. He talks bad grammar, but he talks it naturally, as much as to say, 'I was so brought up and, if I try fine phrases, I shall only appear silly.' Then his writing, though very terse and well expressed, is full of horrible

83

spelling. In fact, he has such an easy and straight-forward way that you almost think that he must be right and you wrong, in these little matters oʌ elegance."[55]

In these glimpses of Grant we obtain, I think, excellent pen-portraits of the man. There is nothing spectacular in them—the reverse, something reticent and deep. When before Fort Donelson he issued his dramatic terms to *Buckner* of "unconditional and immediate surrender," which were not meant to be dramatic, the press and people cheered him to the echo. But he seldom did these things, for instinctively he crept out of the popular gaze, and not, like the normal general, into it.

His physical courage was acclaimed, for it could be seen and almost felt. As a subaltern, during the Mexican War, at Monterey, he had galloped through the bullet-swept streets in search for ammunition. Of this incident he says: "Before starting I adjusted myself on one side of my horse furthest from the enemy, and with only one foot holding to the cantle of the saddle, and an arm over the neck of the horse exposed, I started at full run. It was only at street crossings that my horse was under fire, but these I crossed at such a flying rate that generally I was under cover of the next block of houses before the enemy fired."[56] At Belmont, the first battle he fought during the Civil War, he was the last man to leave the field. As the transports were pushing out with his retiring little army, his horse "put his fore feet well under him, slid down the bank and trotted aboard the boat, twelve or fifteen feet away, over a single gang plank."[57] When Fort Harrison was captured, on September 29, 1864, Grant as usual was well forward, and came under heavy fire, one shell bursting immediately over him as he was writing a dispatch.

"The handwriting of the dispatch when finished," writes Porter, "did not bear the slightest evidence of the uncomfortable circumstances under which it was indited."[58]

Physical courage is, however, common to most soldiers; in fact, without physical courage a man can scarcely be called a soldier, for it is courage and not uniform or even obedience which is the soldier's first qualification. But when courage is faced not by danger only but by physical suffering, it begins to assume a moral form. Thus, when Grant hobbled off his ship at Shiloh, he was not only confronted by a ruined army, but was crippled by an injured leg. His ride to Chattanooga was an equal test of endurance. He travelled over wretched roads, or "rather bridle-paths, over the mountains, and the severe injury to his leg which had been caused by a fall of his horse" was such that over the roughest places the soldiers had to carry him in their arms. "When he arrived he had to be lifted from his saddle, and was evidently experiencing much pain."[59] Though soaked by the rain, he refused to change his clothes, drew a chair up to the fireside, and after listening to what General Thomas had to say, he fired "whole volleys of questions at the officers present," and early the next morning he reconnoitred the Brown's Ferry position.

A deeper moral courage than the overcoming of suffering lay within him, a courage which could not be seen or measured. A little before the battle of Belmont, fought on November 7, 1861, Grant was ordered with his regiment to Salt River, Missouri, to round up a certain *Thomas Harris* who there had established his camp. In his "Memoirs" Grant says: "As we approached the brow of the hill from which it was expected we could see *Harris's* camp, and

85

possibly find his men ready formed to meet us, my heart kept getting higher and higher until it felt to me as though it was in my throat. I would have given anything then to have been back in Illinois, but I had not the moral courage to halt and consider what to do; I kept right on. When we reached a point from which the valley below was in full view I halted. The place where *Harris* had been encamped a few days before was still there and the marks of a recent encampment were plainly visible, but the troops were gone. My heart resumed its place. It occurred to me at once that *Harris* had been as much afraid of me as I had been of him. This was a view of the question I had never taken before; but was one I never forgot afterwards. From that event to the close of the war, I never experienced trepidation upon confronting the enemy, though I always felt more or less anxiety. I never forgot that he had as much reason to fear my forces as I had his."[60]

The remarkable point in this confession is not that Grant overcame his fears and "kept right on," but that he analysed his fears. For a brief moment fear had mastered him, then he mastered fear, and having done so at once examined why it had mastered him. Having discovered the reason, he learned one of the most important lessons in generalship, namely, that he who fears the least holds the initiative, and that he who can make his adversary fear more than he does himself has already defeated him morally. It was because Grant could learn such lessons as this one, and not because he possessed a genius for war, that he commands our admiration.

The most remarkable example, I think, of his moral courage is to be found in his Vicksburg campaign. As the weather improved and the floods subsided, Grant determined to move down the

Mississippi and attack Vicksburg from the south. His leading generals, Sherman, McPherson, Logan and Wilson, strongly opposed this move. Sherman, the ablest of them, pointed out that the army could not be supplied by a single road. "Stop all troops till your army is partially supplied with wagons, and then act as quickly as possible, for this road will be jammed, as sure as life."[61] But Grant had no intention of relying on this road; in place he had determined to accept a risk few generals have ever taken, namely, to cut loose from his base of supply and to live on the country. His moral courage here has seldom been equalled; not only did his generals oppose this move, believing it to be suicidal; not only did he know that should Halleck, at Washington, learn of it than he would at once order its cancellation, but the move itself was obviously an extremely risky one. If it failed, it would fail utterly. Grant realized this, and such a failure meant the loss of the entire Mississippi valley except for New Orleans. It is not too much to say that had Grant been decisively defeated the South would have won the war. To-day we know that the fall of Vicksburg was the deciding factor in the war. Which was it to be? Grant could not possibly tell, yet single handed he accepted the risk, because he had carefully thought out his plan and the object was of such tremendous importance.

Well may Badeau, one of his staff officers, say:

"So Grant was alone; his most trusted subordinates besought him to change his plans, while his superiors were astounded at his temerity and strove to interfere. Soldiers of reputation and civilians in high places condemned, in advance, a campaign that seemed to them as hopeless as it was unprecedented. If he failed the country would concur with the Government and the Generals. Grant knew all this, and appreciated his danger, but was as invulnerable to the apprehensions of ambition as to the entreaties of friendship, or the anxieties even of patriotism. That quiet confidence in himself which never forsook him, and which amounted indeed almost to a feeling of fate, was uninterrupted. Having once determined in a matter that required irreversible decision he never reversed, nor even misgave, but was steadily loyal to himself and his plans. This absolute and implicit faith was, however, as far as possible from conceit or enthusiasm; it was simply a consciousness or conviction, rather, which brought the very strength it believed in; which was itself strength, and which inspired others with a trust in him, because he was able thus to trust himself."[62]

In the history of war such self-reliance is certainly as rare as genius.

This moral courage and close reasoning the people could not see. They could not see it at Salt River, and they could not see it at Vicksburg, and few military historians have troubled to see what Sheridan saw when he wrote in his "Memoirs": "When his military history is analysed after the lapse of years, it will be shown even more clearly than now, that during these [the final campaigns] as well as his previous campaigns, he was the steadfast center about and on which everything else turned."[63]

His Magnanimity and Fellow-Feeling

Unlike nearly every other general in this war, or any other war, Grant always accepted things as they were, devoting the whole of his energies in making the best of them. He accepted failure without recrimination, but never allowed himself to become resigned to it. Because he was always ready to act, and because he was not afraid to fail, the psychological moment when to act was never missed by him. McClellan was never ready to strike, he was always asking for something he had not got, in fact he was never sure of himself. *Lee* was always asking for advice or supplies, and Thomas, of Chickamauga fame, a fine fighting general, delayed and delayed to engage *Hood* at Nashville because he was not certain of victory, and wanted to make sure of it before he struck.

Lincoln, who possessed that wonderful gift of looking into the hearts of men, said: "Grant is the first general I have had. You know how it has been with all the rest. As soon as I put a man in command of the army, he'd come to me with a plan of campaign and about as much as to say, 'Now, I don't believe I can do it, but if you say so, I'll try it on,' and so put the responsibility of success or failure on me. They all wanted me to be the General. Now, it isn't so with Grant. He hasn't told me what his plans are. I don't know and I don't want to know. I am glad to find a man that can go ahead without me. When any of the rest set out on a campaign, they would look over matters and pick out some one thing they were short of and they knew I couldn't give 'em and tell me they couldn't hope to win unless they had it; and it was most generally cavalry. Now, when Grant took hold, I was waiting to see what his pet impossibility would be, and I reckoned it would be cavalry, of course, for we hadn't horses enough to mount what men we had. There were fifteen thousand or thereabouts up near Harper's Ferry and no horses to put them on. Well, the other day, Grant sends to me about those very men, just as I expected; but what he wanted to know was whether he could make infantry of them or disband 'em. He doesn't ask impossibilities of me, and he's the first general I have had that didn't."[64]

By not asking his difficulties remained unknown; by not quarrelling with the Government and damning the politicians he made no spectacles, creating few problems in which the newspapers and the populace could take sides and advertise their own views. He did not light up the gloom of the war with the fireworks of abuse. He did not quarrel with his subordinates or his staff. Possessed of a boundless capacity to forget and forgive, personal or public quarrels, which are so magnetic to the human desire for sensation, never blemished his history or threw it into the limelight.

His regard for others and his relationship with his fellow-men were exceptional. He was "always more concerned about preventing disasters to the armies of his distant commanders than to the troops under his own personal direction,"[65] says Horace Porter; and General Burnside once said of him: "If there is any quality for which General Grant is particularly characterized, it is that of magnanimity. He is one of the most magnanimous men I ever knew. He is entirely unambitious and unselfish."[66] "It was a principle with him never to abandon a comrade 'under fire'; and a friend in disgrace, as well as a friend in trouble, could depend upon him until Grant himself found him guilty."[67] When, on April 8, 1863, Sherman wrote to Rawlins objecting to Grant's move south of Vicksburg, Grant folded up the letter without comment and never mentioned its existence.[68] Similarly, when in September, 1864, he hurried to Charlestown, Va., with a plan in his pocket for Sheridan, finding him so thoroughly ready to move, as he said to Badeau, in 1878, "so confident of success when he did move, and his plan so thoroughly matured, that I did not let him know this, and gave him no order whatever except the authority to move. . . . I was so pleased that I left, and got as far as possible from the field before the attack, lest the papers might attribute to me what was due to him."[69] Again, on

May 12, 1864, when General *Edward Johnson* was sent a prisoner to Grant's headquarters, "Grant, out of consideration for his feelings, passed round the dispatches from Hancock instead of reading them aloud."[70]

Thus to his enemies he was the same as to his friends. He fought to win a cause and not solely to defeat those who were opposed to it; it was the Confederate cause he was fighting, and not the Confederate soldiers and people. "Why humiliate a brave enemy?" he asked after Donelson and after Vicksburg, and when *Lee* finally surrendered it was the same—why humiliate?[71] What sense was there in doing so? Was not the object of the war to re-establish the Union, a union of the North and the South, and would not this union be more perfectly established by showing the people of the Confederacy that it was their cause which was at fault, and that once they abandoned it all were again one people—Americans?

Here, once again, the outlook is spiritual rather than material, something which can be sensed and not grasped, something which eludes the common eye, and a voice too still for the common ear.

He went to work without quarrelling with himself, or with his friends or foes, surely and silently overcoming difficulties, never losing faith in his cause, in his men or in himself. This amazing trust led him on from Donelson to Shiloh, to Vicksburg, to Chattanooga and through the Wilderness to the end which was haloed by his magnanimity to his great opponent.

His imperturbability was the stability of his army; his fearless decisions were its motive force. From the tangled depths of the Wilderness, Pope, Burnside, Hooker and Meade had turned back in dismay. By

the evening of May 6, 1864, both sides were fought
to a standstill, yet Grant's one idea was to advance.
The hour of this decision was, in Sherman's judgment,
the supreme moment in Grant's life: "Undismayed,"
he writes, "with a full comprehension of the importance
of the work in which he was engaged, feeling as
keen a sympathy for his dead and wounded as anyone, and without stopping to count his numbers, he
gave his orders calmly, specifically and absolutely:
'Forward to Spottsylvania.'"[72]   The effect of this
decision upon the Army of the Potomac was electric.
"At the Chancellorsville House we turned to the
right," writes Frank Wilkeson, "instantly all of us
heaved a sigh of relief. We marched free. The men
began to sing. The enlisted men understood the
flanking movement. That night we were happy."[73]

His pertinacity led his men over every obstacle.
Once at Vicksburg he stopped at the house of a
Confederate woman for a drink of water. This woman
taunted him, asking him if he ever expected to take
the fortress: "Certainly," he replied. "But when?"
"I cannot tell exactly when I shall take the town,
but I mean to stay here till I do, if it takes me thirty
years." At Spottsylvania on May 11, 1864, though
his losses had been severe, he wrote to President
Lincoln, saying: "I propose to fight it out on this line
if it takes all summer,"[74] and he did. After the battle
of Five Forks, towards the end of March, 1865, when
the roads were reduced to a porridge of mud, and
when elation turned to gloom, for all thought that the
army would founder, Grant once again rose with
the occasion. He saw horses sinking to their bellies,
and wagons half-submerged on the roadside and in
the fields, many of which were churned up to quick-
sands;[75] but he knew that the decisive hour had
struck, so in place of calling a halt he kept right on

to the very end, "right on" as he had done at Salt River.

Lincoln understood this strange man who moved his army ever forwards, silently and surely, as a dynamo moves some great machine. Once when urged to dismiss him, and this was frequently suggested, he turned round and earnestly replied: "I can't spare this man; he fights!"[76] Few others understood him, and least of all the multitudes of his generation. They would shout themselves hoarse when he gained some victory, but how he gained it was beyond their comprehension. He said very little, and was seemingly commonplace in his everyday life, a curious mask of a man whose soul was as unfathomable to them as was the soul of his great namesake, Ulysses of the Odyssey, of whom Fénélon wrote: "His heart is an unfathomable depth; his secret lies beyond the line of subtlety and fraud; he is the friend of truth; saying nothing that is false, but, when it is necessary, conceding what is true; his wisdom is, as it were, a seal upon his lips which is never broken but for an important purpose." No wonder he remained an enigma in the popular mind.

Thus it happened, when his work was finished, and his simplicity was obliterated by the majesty of a stupendous mausoleum, the spirit that was in him was hidden behind the mask, and a mummy of the man was left to be gazed upon by the curious. This enigma never gave way to the myth, and it is mythological men, men who have become deified and not petrified in the minds of the people who attract historians; conversely it is the enigmatic man who so frequently repels them. Hence Grant is still so little understood. Though the greatest general of his age, and one of the greatest strategists of any age, he is little quoted in military histories and text-books.

Still has it to be realized that as Sherman said of this simple and modest friend: "Each epoch creates its own agents, and General Grant more clearly than any other man impersonated the American character of 1861-65. He will stand, therefore, as the typical hero of the Great Civil War."

CHAPTER III

THE PERSONALITY OF LEE

Lee—the Virginian

ON the tombstone which marked the final resting-place of two brothers, one a Federal and the other a Confederate, a Kentucky father cut these words: "God knows which was right." Such also was the doubtful state of Colonel *Robert E. Lee's* mind in December, 1860, when in a letter he wrote: "While I wish to do what is right, I am unwilling to do what is wrong at the bidding of the South or of the North."[1] Here began that battle between his heart and his head. The one represented the Virginian within him, the other the American. "As an American citizen," he wrote from Fort Mason, Texas, on January 23, 1861, "I take a great pride in my country. . . . I can anticipate no greater calamity . . . than a dissolution of the Union. . . . Secession is nothing but revolution. . . . Still, a Union that can only be maintained by swords and bayonets, and in which strife and civil war are to take the place of brotherly love and kindness, has no charm for me."[2] As regards slavery, his views are as definite: "There are few, I believe, in this enlightened age," he wrote in 1856, "who will not acknowledge that slavery as an institution is a moral and political evil in any country. It is useless to expatiate on its disadvantages. I think it a greater evil to the white than to the black race";[3] and again on another occasion: "I have always

95

observed that wherever you find the negro, everything is going down around him, and wherever you
find the white man, you see everything around him
improving."[4]   Yet to oppose this institution was
contrary to *Lee's* principles; this question must be
left to Providence, "we must leave the progress as
well as the result in his hands, who sees the end and
who chooses to work by slow things, and with whom
a thousand years are but as a single day."[5]   Thus was
waged that battle of heart and head in which the
former won, though the head was convinced from the
beginning that if it came to a clash of arms the cause
was lost.   On April 7, 1865, two days before his
surrender to Grant, he said to General *Pendleton*:
"I have never believed we could, against the gigantic
combination for our subjugation, make good in the
long run our independence unless foreign powers
should, directly or indirectly, assist us. . . . But such
considerations really made with me no difference.
We had, I was satisfied, sacred principles to maintain
and rights to defend, for which we were in duty bound
to do our best, even if we perish in the endeavour."
Then in this conversation shoots forth another beam of
inner light.   General *Pendleton* had been deputed by a
number of principal officers to explain to him that
further resistance was hopeless, and that negotiations
should be opened for a surrender.   On hearing this
Lee exclaimed: "Oh, no, I trust it has not come to
that"; and then added, "General, we have yet too
many bold men to think of laying down our arms.
The enemy do not fight with spirit, while our boys
still do. Besides, if I were to say a word to the Federal
commander he would regard it as such a confession
of weakness as to make it the condition of demanding
unconditional surrender—a proposal to which I will
never listen."[6]

Here we have revealed to us the personal pride of the soldier, the true soldier, the man who cannot and will not follow in the footsteps of such lesser men as *Buckner* and *Pemberton,* who though his heart is ever willing to surrender to Providence, his pride will surrender to no man. Illogical, perhaps, but one of those contradictions which is the essence of human nature, and which made *Lee* what he was—at one and the same time a humble Christian and a proud aristocrat. In his last interview with General Scott he is reputed to have said: "I can not raise my hand against my children,"[7] and after the war he exclaimed: "I did only what my duty demanded. I could have taken no other course without dishonour. And if it were all to be done over again, I should act in precisely the same manner."[8]

Deep in *Lee's* soul it was the voice of his ancestors that was speaking. Richard Lee who, in 1641, came from Stratford-Langton, in England, to Virginia, who had assisted Sir William Berkeley its governor in keeping this State in allegiance to the Crown when Cavalier fought Roundhead and Charles I went down before Cromwell and his Ironsides. Above all the voice of his father—Harry Lee, Light-horse Lee, the friend and trusty henchman of Washington, the same Lee who wrote to Joseph Reed, in 1780, saying: "However, I have learned the art of being happy under distress. I have done my duty, so far as I know, faithfully."[9] The blood of his ancestors called him, and sorrowfully looking down from the heights of Arlington upon the capital of the Union, he unsheathed his sword in defence of his native State, his home, his children, his traditions and his God. In one of his first general orders he says: "They [the Confederate soldiers] cannot barter manhood for peace nor the right of self-government for life or property. . . . Let us oppose constancy to adversity, fortitude to suffering, and courage to danger, with the firm assurance that He who gave freedom to our fathers will bless the efforts of their children to preserve it."[10]

From this it will be seen that *Lee* was no ordinary man; a strange man, not the last of his race but the last of an epoch—a pious age of Christian men, followers of Knox, Cranmer, Wesley and Bunyan. A knight-errant and one of the greatest of this fraternity. When on September 17, 1862, the remnants of *Hood's* division passed him, he exclaimed: "Great God! where is the splendid division you had this morning?" And when told that its men were lying on the field of battle, he said: "Gentlemen, we will not cross the Potomac to-night. . . . If McClellan wants to fight in the morning, I will give him battle again. Go!"[11] Rightly he belonged to feudal times, those days in which the blood of the few was the driving-force of the many. "He loved the old country-houses of old Virginian families, simple-minded and honourable folks, attached, like himself, to the soil of Virginia,"[12] writes his nephew. Had not his father said: "Virginia is my country, her will I obey, however lamentable the fate to which it may subject me,"[13] and how could he do otherwise but follow in his footsteps? A Virginian at heart, far more so than an American, *Lee* strode into the war never forgetting that he was a Virginian, and though he led the Confederate cause, it was in Virginia he fought and for Virginia that spiritually he died. When he marched to Sharpsburg (Antietam), it was Virginia which called him; when he marched to Gettysburg it was the same.[14] After the war, when the great illusion had vanished, he turned to a lady who had brought to him her two sons, and said: "Madam, don't bring up your sons to detest the United States Government. Recollect that we form but one country, *now*. Abandon all these local animosities, and make your sons Americans."[15]

What it must have cost him to effect this inward change it is impossible to know, for *Lee* was a proud man yet a man who hid his pride. He would talk of the enemy as "those people," and of his adversary Grant as "that man," but only when agitated. Outwardly he was humility itself. In June, 1864, when pinned down at Petersburg by Grant, he wrote to his wife: "God has been very merciful and kind to us, and how thankless and sinful I have been."[16] Such sentences teem throughout his letters, yet he was a man of hot temper and strong passions; but with few exceptions he kept them under control, maintaining a mien of calm dignity. When a question concerned him directly he could be severe; for instance, when he heard that some of *Mosby's* troopers had been hung by Sheridan, in retaliation he ordered a number of Custer's men to be shot.[17] On one occasion he spoke roughly to Colonel *Venable*, one of his staff, and then when this officer had made his report and had thrown himself on the ground and was asleep, *Lee* took an oil-cloth poncho from his own shoulders and lightly drew it over his sleeping aide.[18] On another he spoke very angrily to a scout, *Goode* by name, but upon finding that he had committed an injustice, he came out of his tent, "commanded his orderly to have supper with hot coffee put on the table for *Goode*, made him sit in his own camp-chair at the table, stood at the fire near by, and performed all the duties of a hospitable host. . . ." Well may General *Long* write: "Few generals ever made such thorough amends to a private soldier for an injustice done him in anger."[19]

He was very generous and amazingly gentle. At
Gettysburg he passed a wounded Federal who, seeing
him, raised himself up and shouted in defiance:
"Hurrah for the Union!" Then this man says: "The
general heard me, looked, stopped his horse, dismounted, and came towards me. I confess that I at
first thought he meant to kill me. But as he came up
he looked down at me with such a sad expression
upon his face that all fear left me, and I wondered
what he was about. He extended his hand to me, and
grasping mine firmly and looking right into my eyes,
said: 'My son, I hope you will soon be well.' . . . As
soon as the general had left me I cried myself to
sleep there upon the bloody ground."[20]

The Man and the Legend

Born on January 19, 1807, at Stratford, the ancient
manor-house of the Lees of Virginia, *Robert E. Lee*
owed much of his nobility of nature to his mother.
His father died when he was still a small boy, yet he
seems never to have forgotten a brief sentence written
by him in a letter dated September 3, 1817. It was as
follows: " 'A man ought not only to be virtuous in
reality, but he must also always appear so'; thus said
to me the great Washington,"[21] and on this text *Lee*,
the man, modelled himself. Left with his mother he
was always watchful over her; doing the marketing,
attending to household duties, looking after the
horses and acting the "little man" with a discretion
unusual in a boy of his age. She taught him self-
denial, and unconsciously self-sacrifice, and there can
be little doubt that she softened his proud nature,
and perhaps over-much so. Early in the war he
writes: "To-day my tent came up, and I am in it,

yet I fear I shall not sleep for thinking of the poor men."[22] Again: "My heart bleeds at the death of every one of our gallant men."[23] He loved the gentleness of young girls, was an advocate of early matrimony, liked writing about it, was at ease in the society of women, "honouring a woman as a woman," and consequently seldom appealed to them as a man normally does. For instance, Mrs. Chesnut says: "All the same, I like *Smith Lee* better, and I like his looks too. I know *Smith Lee* well. Can anybody say they know his brother? I doubt it. He looks so cold, quiet, and grand."[24] Another spritely lady, Mrs. Pickett, said much the same: "*Lee*," she writes, "was a great soldier and a good man, but I never wanted to put my arms round his neck, as I used to want to do to *Joe Johnston*."[25]

On March 10, 1868, he writes to a young niece and tells her he has received "a very pretty picture from a young lady in Baltimore," and two days later to his son Robert, saying: "A farmer's motto should be *toil and trust*."[26] Nearly all his letters are like these two, full of commonplaces and good advice. In them his nature appears distinctly soft and proper, and because of this I think we can trace many of his failures as a general, which on account of his self-sacrificing dignity and austerity were lost to sight in that sanctity which soon began to envelop him, until the man was frozen into the saint. Yet in spite of this unsought halo, *Lee was* a man.

In 1825 he went to West Point, and at once became, anyhow to historians, the "blue-eyed" boy of the Academy. There, we are told by his nephew *Fitzhugh Lee*, he was "a model cadet . . . his . . . trousers were as white as the driven snow mounting guard upon the mountain top. . . . He never 'ran the sentinel post,' did not go off the limits to the 'Benny

Havens' of his day, or put 'dummies' in his bed to deceive the officer in charge as he made his inspection after taps. . . ."[27] In short, he never behaved like a boy should. He was tall and of fine figure, and later on in life he was reputed to be "the handsomest man in the army."[28]

As a young man he was far more human than towards the close of his life. His letters during the Mexican War possess some life; even in one of them he asks his naval brother to obtain for him "a box or two of claret, one of brandy, and four colored shirts," but our rising enthusiasm is at once damped when we are told by his nephew that "it seems he wanted some liquors, in all probability, for his guests."[29] But when he became an old man and President of Washington College, so little humanity was left in him that he cut down the one week's holiday at Christmas to Christmas day itself. No wonder he was respected rather than loved by his students.

In 1831 he married Mary Randolph Custis, great-granddaughter of Martha Custis, the wife of George Washington. This marriage, so I think, had a marked moral influence upon him, for in the eyes of the world it made him the representative of the family which had founded American liberty. So, I feel, that when estimating his conduct at the outbreak of the Civil War, this fact should be remembered. More than ever had he now a reputation to live up to—the reputation of Washington, and from this day onwards he became his representative on earth.

In the Mexican War he distinguished himself beyond all his brother officers. His pluck and daring were the common topic of the camp. General Scott mentions him in one of his dispatches as "the gallant and indefatigable Captain *Lee* of the Engineers," reporting that "the brilliant victory of Contreras" was made possible "only by Captain *Lee's* service."[30] From this war onwards, more and more did *Lee* become the *beau ideal* of Southern chivalry; the typical country gentleman, rather Victorian, very staid, courteous and kindly, but frozen up in an austere dignity which induced veneration but repelled all emotionalism. Then came the war, and with Stephen Vincent Benét we may say:

"You too are a legend now
And the legend has made your fame and has dimmed that fame,
—The victor strikes and the beaten man goes down
But the years pass and the legend covers them both,
The beaten cause turns into the magic cause."[31]

Lee ceases to be a man of human passions, he becomes the idol of a mythical cause—State Freedom, which, as I have shown in Chapter I, though alive in theory was dead in fact; for in 1861 the age of steam had begun to fuse all States into one whole. He became, as Benét truly says: "The incarnation of a national dream"—

"Of the America we have not been,
The tropic empire, seeking the warm sea,
The last foray of aristocracy
Based not on dollars or initiative
Or any blood for what that blood was worth
But on a certain code, a manner of birth."[32]

As an individual apart from the war there is nothing remarkable in *Lee's* character and personality, except that he was pre-eminently a good man; he possessed no personal ambition, no sense of humour except of a polite bantering type; he was very generous, as I have shown, kind though somewhat austere towards others. Then came the war, and at once these very virtues made him stand out from among his fellows. "He always seemed anxious to keep himself in the background," writes Colonel *Taylor*, "to suppress all consideration of himself, to prevent any notice of himself. A more modest man did not live."[33] General *Long* says:

"It was his constant feeling that he was living and working to an end that constituted the source of General *Lee's* magnanimity and put him far above any petty jealousy. He looked at everything as unrelated to himself, and only as it affected the cause he was serving. This is shown in his treatment of his subordinates. He had no favorites, no unworthy partialities. On one occasion he spoke highly of an officer and remarked that he ought to be promoted. Some surprise was expressed at this, and it was said that that particular officer had sometimes spoken disparagingly of him. 'I cannot help that,' said the general; 'he is a good soldier, and would be useful in a higher position.' As he judged of the work of others, so he judged of his own. A victory gave him pleasure only as it contributed to the end he had in view, an honourable peace and the happiness of his country. It was for this cause that even his greatest victories produced in him no exaltation of spirits: he saw the end yet far off. He even thought more of what might have been done than of what was actually accomplished. In the same way a reverse gave him pain, not as a private but as a public calamity. He was the ruling spirit of his army. His campaigns and battles were his own.

* * * * *

"There was no hestitation or vacillation about him. When he had once formed a plan the orders for its execution were positive, decisive, and final. The army which he so long commanded is a witness for him. He imbued it with his own spirit; it reflected his energy and devotion."[34]

I think this is a very just appreciation. He stood so apart from his men, that in their eyes *he* became the cause for which they were fighting. Colonel *Marshall*, another of his staff officers, notices this and says: "To them he represented cause, country, and all."[35] His bravery magnetized them, for *Lee* had no fear of personal danger. When his plans were working smoothly, generally he was well in rear of the battle-front, but when they were threatened by disaster he immediately rode forward. In General *Long's* opinion, "General *Lee* never unnecessarily courted danger, though he never cautiously avoided it."[36] During the fighting in the Wilderness *Lee* rode forward, and he did so again in the battle for the salient at Spottsylvania. Of this incident General *Gordon* writes:

"*Lee* looked a very god of war. Calmly and grandly, he rode to a point near the center of my line and turned his horse's head to the front, evidently resolved to lead in person the desperate charge and drive Hancock back or perish in the effort. I knew what he meant; and although the passing moments were of priceless value, I resolved to arrest him in his effort, and thus save to the Confederacy the life of its great leader. I was at the center of that line when General *Lee* rode to it. With uncovered head, he turned his face toward Hancock's advancing column. Instantly I spurred my horse across old Traveller's [*Lee's* favourite charger] front, and grasping his bridle in my hand, I checked him. Then, in a voice which I hoped might reach the ears of my men and command their attention, I called out, 'General *Lee*, you shall not lead my men in a charge. No man can do that, sir. Another is here for that purpose. These men behind you are Georgians, Virginians, and Carolinians. They have never failed you on any field. They will not fail you here. Will you, boys?' The response came like a mighty anthem that must have stirred his emotions as no other music could have done. . . . 'No, no, no; we'll not fail him' . . . I shouted to General *Lee*, 'You must go to the rear.' The echo, 'General *Lee* to the rear! General *Lee* to the rear!' rolled back with tremendous emphasis from the throats of my men."[37]

That *Lee* could bring out what was best in others is undoubted, and little by little the valour of his army encircled him like the halo of a saint. He was both a Sidney and a Bayard, a man of high nobility of mind and high bravery of heart. Every soldier of the South turned to him as a devout Catholic turns towards the Virgin Mother. At Gettysburg, though the terrible repulse of the Confederate assault on the third day of this battle was entirely due to his faulty orders, no man blamed him, he alone blamed himself. Colonel Fremantle, an eye-witness, says: "If *Longstreet's* conduct was admirable, that of General *Lee* was perfectly sublime. He was engaged in rallying and in encouraging the broken troops, and was riding about a little in front of the wood, quite alone—the whole of his staff being engaged in a similar manner further to the rear. His face, which is always placid and cheerful, did not show signs of the slightest disappointment, care, or annoyance; and he was addressing to every soldier he met a few words of encouragement, such as: 'All this will become right in the end: we'll talk it over afterwards; but, in the meantime, all good men must rally. We want all good and true men just now,' etc. . . . He said to me, 'This has been a sad day for us, Colonel—a sad day; but we can't expect always to gain victories.' "[38]

When *Lee* surrendered to Grant not a man blamed him, and so deep was their regard for him that they seldom cheered him; in place they would take off their hats and gaze upon him in silent veneration.

Heroism and self-sacrifice, and not generalship, were the foundations of this cult, a cult exalted and fostered by the poverty of the South, and by the very omissions in generalship which, as I shall show, marked *Lee's* career. Though the patriotism of the South was intense, it was also patchy; there was much selfishness as well as self-sacrifice, and not a little shirking and an abundance of weakness and mismanagement. But the myth which arose out of the cult of valour has obscured most of these facts. *Fitzhugh Lee* loves to tell us, that the Southern soldier "was a veritable tatterdemalion, loading and firing his rifle with no hope of reward, no promise of promotion, no pay, and scanty rations,"[39] which is not altogether true. Henderson repeats this description in his *Stonewall Jackson*; and when it comes to Southern generals the myth takes on an exaggerated form: Thus *Jeb Stuart* was not only a Prince Rupert, but a Murat and a Seidlitz rolled into one.[40]

With *Lee* the myth becomes transcendental. Even before the war General Scott had said that he was "the greatest military genius in America,"[41] which may be true enough; and then immediately after the war broke out, and he was appointed Commander-in-Chief of the Virginia forces, at the convention which followed, Mr. Janney, its president, at once compared him with Washington.[42] Thus did the myth begin to sprout, and it grew and grew until every child in the Confederacy knew him though they had never seen him, and tiny tots would run up to him and cry: "We know you are General *Lee!* We have got your picture!"[43]

Of Chancellorsville, for instance, Colonel *Marshall* paints for us this battle icon:

"The fierce soldiers, with their faces blackened with the smoke of battle, the wounded, crawling with feeble limbs from the fury of the devouring flames, all seemed possessed with a common impulse. One long, unbroken cheer, in which the feeble cry of those who lay helpless on the earth blended with the strong voices of those who still fought, rose high above the roar of battle and hailed the presence of the victorious chief. He sat in the full realization of all that soldiers dream of—triumph; and as I looked on him in the complete fruition of the success which his genius, courage, and confidence in his army had won, I thought that it must have been from such scenes that men in ancient days ascended to the dignity of the gods."[44]

Then, when the war was over, this triumphant grandeur was apotheosized. General *Gordon* writes: "*Lee* was never really beaten. *Lee* could not be beaten! Overpowered, foiled in his efforts, he might be, but never defeated until the props which supported him gave way."[45] Benjamin H. Hill exclaims: "He was a foe without hate, a friend without treachery, a soldier without cruelty, and a victim without murmuring. He was a public officer without vices, a private citizen without wrong, a neighbour without reproach, a Christian without hypocrisy, and a man without guilt. He was Caesar without his ambition, Frederick without his tyranny, Napoleon without his selfishness, and Washington without his reward. He was as obedient to authority as a servant and royal in authority as a king. He was as gentle as a woman in life, pure and modest as a virgin in thought, watchful as a Roman vestal, submissive to law as Socrates, and grand in battle as Achilles."[46]

This myth, in which the idol replaced the man, swept over the whole civilized world, until we find so enlightened a writer as Colonel G. F. R. Henderson saying: "At the head of the Confederate Army was General *Lee*, undoubtedly one of the greatest, if not the greatest, soldier who ever spoke the English tongue."[47] This estimate has been accepted as fact by practically every subsequent historian.

From these fulsome and uncritical adulations, which can do justice to no man, it is refreshing to turn to the judgment of one who was never swept off his feet by popular emotions. General Grant, during his voyage round the world, said to J. Russell Young:

"I never ranked *Lee* so high as some others in the army; that is to say I never had so much anxiety when he was in my front as when *Joe Johnston* was in front. *Lee* was a good man, a fair commander, and had everything in his favour. He was a man who needed sunshine. . . . *Lee* was of a slow, cautious nature, without imagination, or humour, always the same, with grave dignity. The illusion that heavy odds beat him will not stand the ultimate light of history. I know it is not true. *Lee* was a good deal a headquarters general, from what I can hear and from what his officers say. He was almost too old for active service—the best service in the field."[48]

Grant's appreciation may not be a faultless one, yet I cannot help feeling that the most fervent admirer of *Lee* must agree that on the face of it it sounds more honest than those others I have quoted. Anyhow, I think it is a good starting-point from where we can begin to disentangle the great man from the great myth.

His Reliance on God

The Duke of Wellington is reputed once to have said, that it was not possible to apply Christian principles to war. Well, he was wrong, for *Lee* did so, and though had he not done so he might have been a greater general, through doing so, and because of his high chivalry and nobility of nature, there can be no doubt that this fact has been obscured. He himself said in a letter to Mr. Seddon, Secretary of War, dated March 6, 1864, "I think it better to do right, even if we suffer in so doing, than to incur the reproach of our consciences and posterity."[49] This high ideal coloured the whole of his generalship.

Lee was a member of the Episcopal Church; he was not so much a religious man as a man absorbed in religion; his every letter shows this, and so do many of his orders. For instance, in September, 1861, having failed in West Virginia, he wrote to his wife: "But the Ruler of the Universe willed otherwise and sent a storm to disconcert a well-laid plan and to destroy my hopes";[50] and on August 13, 1863, he issued the following order to his army: "Soldiers! we have sinned against Almighty God . . . we have relied too much on our own arms for the achievement of our independence. God is our only refuge and our strength. Let us humble ourselves before Him. . . ."[51] To *Lee*, even more so than to Cromwell, God was the giver of victory, consequently to stand in the favour of God was something far more desirable than mere generalship.

When the war broke out Bishop Wilmer said to him: "Is it your expectation that the issue of this war will be to perpetuate the institution of slavery?"

"The future is in the hands of Providence," answered *Lee*. "If the slaves of the South were mine, I would surrender them all without a struggle to avert this war."

"Are you sanguine of the result [of the war]?" asked the Bishop.

"At present I am not concerned with results," replied *Lee*. "God's will ought to be our aim, and I am contented that His designs should be accomplished and not mine." [52]

Lee was in fact a fatalist. In April, 1857, he wrote in a letter: "I feel always as safe in the wilderness as in the crowded city. I know in whose powerful hands I am, and on Him I rely and feel that in all our life we are upheld and sustained by Divine Providence." [53] Of him, during the winter of 1864-1865, his nephew rightly says: "It was the old heathen picture of 'man sublimely contending with Fate to the admiration of the gods, accepting the last test of endurance, and with the smile of a sublime resolution risking the last defiance of fortune'." [54] Then, when he was dead, a writer in the *New York Herald* said: "Even as in the days of his triumph glory did not intoxicate, so when the dark clouds swept over him adversity did not depress. From the hour that he surrendered his sword at Appomattox to the fatal autumn morning [of his death] he passed among men, noble in his quiet, simple dignity, displaying neither bitterness nor regret over the irrevocable past." [55]

"God's will be done," was the text of his life, for as

Gamaliel Bradford writes: "God gives the victory. God permits the defeat. God sends rain to mire the Virginia roads. He sends his sunshine to make them passable again. If God is appealed to passionately enough, devoutly enough, humbly enough, we win. If we lose, it is because we have not honored God sufficiently. . . . So I think we may conclude that the cardinal fact of *Lee's* life was God."[56]

To *Lee*, "duty" was but another word for "the Divine Will." To his son, G. W. Custis Lee, he once wrote: "In regard to duty, let me in conclusion of this hasty letter, inform you that nearly a hundred years ago there was a day of remarkable gloom and darkness, still known as 'the Dark Day'—a day when the light of the sun was slowly extinguished as if by an eclipse. The legislature of Connecticut was in session, and as its members saw the unexpected and unaccountable darkness coming on they shared in the general awe and terror. It was supposed by many that the Last Day, the day of judgment, had come. Someone, in the consternation of the hour, moved an adjournmen.. Then there arose an old Puritan legislator, Davenport of Stamford, who said that if the Last Day had come he desired to be found at his place doing his duty, and therefore moved that candles be brought in, so that the House could proceed with its duty. There was quietness in that man's mind—the quietness of heavenly wisdom and inflexible willingness to obey present duty. Do your duty in all things, like the old Puritan. You cannot do more—you should never wish to do less."[57] Again, upon another occasion: "There is a true glory and a true honor, the glory of duty done, the honor of the integrity of principle."[58] "Duty first," writes Colonel *Taylor* in his *Four Years with General Lee*, "was the rule of his life, and his every thought, word and action was made to square with duty's inexorable demands";[59] yet he was tolerant towards the religious faith of others,[60] he was not only too meek but too just to persecute.

This sense of duty was carried to such an extreme, that as Jefferson Davis said: "He was unwilling to offend anyone who was wearing a sword and striking blows for the Confederacy";[61] consequently, incompetence, if devout, was no blemish in *Lee's* eyes. Without wishing to be ironical, *Lee's* religious outlook may well be compared to that of the darkie minister who exclaimed: "Brethren ef de Lord tell me to jump through a stone wall, I's gwine to jump at it; jumpin' at it 'longs to me, goin' through it 'longs to God."

As regards himself, he avoided all duties which he considered belonged to others. "Be content to do what you can for the well-being of what properly belongs to you," he wrote to his wife, "commit the rest to those who are responsible."[62] This rigid principle controlled the whole of his generalship. "My interference in battle would do more harm than good," he said. "I have, then, to rely on my brigade and division commanders. I think and work with all my power to bring the troops to the right place at the right time; then I have done my duty. As soon as I order them forward into battle, I leave my army in the hands of God";[63] or may I be allowed to suggest—in the hands of his subordinate commanders. Thus it happened that when such men as *Jackson* and *Stuart* were gone, his generalship so often failed. No wonder after Gettysburg he exclaimed: "Had I *Stonewall Jackson* at Gettysburg, I would have won a great victory."

As God was the giver of victory, so also in *Lee's* eyes was Jefferson Davis his chosen servant, a man totally different from himself. As I have shown, Davis was a politician of the overbearing legal type, *Lee* was no politician at all, hence from start to finish of the war that relationship between policy and strategy, which is generally called grand strategy, was all but non-existent.

His Humility and Submissiveness

It may be said that for two brief periods only was *Lee* Commander-in-Chief, and that, consequently, during the greater part of the war, from June 8, 1861, to February 8, 1865, he was not in a position to influence policy. This would be incorrect, for throughout the war, whether as Commander-in-Chief, or in command of the Army of Northern Virginia, as his son tells us, "he advised the President and Secretary of War as to the movements and dispositions of the other armies in the Confederacy."[64]   He was in fact Davis's unofficial Chief of Staff.   Nevertheless *Lee* said: "I must not wander into politics, a subject I carefully avoid."[65]

Politics were not his business, even policy was not his business.   Let others plan, he would carry out; for, as General *Long* says, and in order to compliment him: "If it should be asked, what was General *Lee's* opinion in regard to the defence of Richmond?   It might be said that he was too thorough a soldier openly to question the wisdom of the Government in forming its plan of operations or to employ less than his utmost ability in his efforts to execute them."[66]   Even towards the end of the war, when asked by a leading member of Mr. Davis's Cabinet: "General, I wish you would give us your opinion as to the propriety of changing the seat of Government and going further south," *Lee* replied: "That is a political question . . . and you politicians must determine it.

I shall endeavour to take care of the army, and you must make the laws and control the Government."[67] Yet at this moment it was a question of vital strategical importance, of life or death to the Confederacy, whether Richmond should be held or not—it was essentially a strategic question.

Lee's admiration for Davis was unbounded; it was the attraction of the negative by the positive. "If my opinion is worth anything," he said after the war, "you can *always* say that few people could have done better than Mr. Davis. I know of none that could have done so well"[68]—which is probably true. His relationship with him was intimate, for he was the only soldier who was allowed to enter the Cabinet meetings unannounced.[69] He disagreed with Davis once, and this exception is worth recording as it arose out of a purely military situation, and consequently one which it was the duty of *Lee* to control. It happened before Richmond in 1862. Davis and a cavalcade appeared on the battlefield, *Lee* seeing him, frigidly saluted, and then, turning towards the President's party, he asked in a tone of irritation: "Who are all this army of people, and what are they doing here?"

"No one moved or spoke, but all eyes were upon the President; everybody perfectly understood that this was an order for him to retire to a place of safety, while the roar of the guns, the rattling fire of musketry, and the bustle of a battle in progress, with troops continually arriving across the bridge to go into action, went on. The President twisted in his saddle, quite taken aback at such a greeting—the general regarding him now with glances of growing severity. After a painful pause the President said, deprecatingly: 'It is not my army, General.' 'It certainly is not *my* army, Mr. President,' was the prompt reply, 'and this is no

place for it'—in an accent of command. Such a rebuff
was a stunner to Mr. Davis. . . ."[70]
    Had *Lee* been in the habit of administering these
"stunners" more frequently, so great was his prestige
that it is not too much to suppose that the North
would never have won the war. Politically, however,
he never disagreed with him, this Davis says himself;[71]
he was always dependent upon him. "The President
from his position being able to survey all the scenes
of action, can better decide than anyone else,"[72] he
writes. He nearly always submitted questions to
Davis's decision: "Should you think proper to concentrate the troops near Richmond I should be glad
if you would advise me."[73] He asked Davis to visit
him in the field: "I need not say how glad I should
be," he wrote, "if your convenience would permit
you to visit the army, that I might have the benefit
of your advice and direction."[74] When he does
interfere, when he feels compelled to suggest a course
which has not been suggested to him, he does so in
terms which one would scarcely expect from a junior
clerk. For instance, when in June, 1863, he suggested
greater activity on the part of the army, he ended
his letter as follows: "I earnestly commend these
considerations to the attention of Your Excellency,
and trust that you will be at liberty, in your better
judgment and with the superior means of information
you possess as to our necessities and the enemy's
movements in the distant regions I have mentioned,
to give effect to them, either in the way I have
suggested or in such other manner as may seem
to you more judicious."[75] His subservience is more
utter, more abject, than that of any other noted
general to any other Government in history. Even
when after his surrender, Grant asked him for the
good of the country to meet President Lincoln, he

answered: "General Grant, you know that I am a soldier of the Confederate Army, and I cannot meet Mr. Lincoln. I do not know what Mr. Davis is going to do. . . ."[76] Davis at this moment was in flight and could not possibly do anything. Commenting on this remark, Colonel *Marshall* says: "I think myself, and have always thought, that if General *Lee* and Mr. Lincoln would have met, as General Grant proposed, we could have had immediate restoration of peace and brotherhood among the people of these States."[77]

There can be little doubt, as someone remarked at the time: "*Lee* had got a crick in his neck from looking over his shoulder towards Richmond."[78] To General *Gordon* he said: "I am a soldier. It is my duty to obey orders. It is enough to turn one's hair grey to spend one day in the Congress. The members are patriotic and earnest, but they will neither take the responsibility of action nor will they clothe me with the authority to act for them."[79] Yet, when in February, 1865, he was made to all intents and purposes dictator, with the exception of recommending the enlistment of negroes[80] he did nothing. Of this elevation to power the *Richmond Examiner* said: "This clothes him with great power, and loads him with heavy responsibility. If he is willing to wield that power and shoulder that responsibility, in the name of God, let him have them."[81] But no, Pollard tells us that he "went so far as to declare to several members of the Richmond Congress that whatever might be Davis's errors, he was yet constitutionally the president, and that nothing could tempt himself to encroach upon prerogatives which the Constitution had bestowed upon his designated head."[82]

His Want of Authority and Inexhaustible Tact

As Davis had been entrusted by God with the Presidency, so had God entrusted the army to his own care, for to *Lee* the Army of Northern Virginia was a divine instrument, which, as long as it was tempered by humility and repentance, must cut its way through all opposition.   It was not efficiency which counted, or big battalions, or even discipline, but faith.

What this bootless, ragged, half-starved army accomplished is one of the miracles of history.   It was led by a saint, it was endowed with the sanctity of its cause, and yet had its leader been more of a general and less of a saint, even if this had filched from it a little of its enthusiasm, its hardships would have been vastly reduced.   Its spiritual morale was of the highest, its discipline of the lowest.   It was full of young men full of life and quarrels, men who needed some show of severity to curb their discordant spirits.   "Army of Northern Virginia, fabulous army," cries Stephen Vincent Benét:

> "Strange army of ragged individualists,
> The hunters, the riders, the walkers, the savage pastorals,
> The unmachined, the men come out of the ground,
> Still, for the most part, living close to the ground
> As the roots of the cow-pea, the roots of the jessamine,
> The lazy scorners, the rebels against the wheels,
> The rebels against the steel combustion chamber
> Of the half-born new age of engines and metal hands."[83]

Physically such an army was beyond *Lee's* control. He could not be severe, he could not punish, he could only accept blame himself and shame it into some sort of discipline—set it an example.   He sought discomfort, as once upon a time a Christian saint sought his hair shirt. Lord Wolseley informs us that his headquarters "consisted of about seven or eight pole-tents, pitched with their backs to a stake fence, upon a piece of ground so rocky that it was unpleasant to ride over it. . . . In front of the tents were some three four-wheeled wagons, drawn up without any regularity, and a number of horses roamed loose about the field. . . . No guard or sentries were to be seen in the vicinity; no crowd of aides-de-camp loitering about, making themselves agreeable to visitors. . . . A large farmhouse stands close by, which, in any other army, would have been the general's residence *pro tem.*; but, as no liberties are allowed to be taken with personal property, in *Lee's* army, he is particular in setting a good example himself. His staff are crowded together, two or three in a tent; none are allowed to carry more baggage than a small box each, and his own kit is but very little larger."[84] The covering of the commander-in-chief was the same as that of the private soldier, his food generally inferior, as all dainties were sent to the sick and wounded; for as his nephew Edward Lee Childe tells us: "His guiding principle was that of setting his officers an example of not faring better than their soldiers."[85]

That his example did influence his army is beyond doubt—it sanctified it and him; yet its discipline remained beneath contempt. Towards it he acted like a soft-hearted father; he was its exalted leader, its high priest, but not its general. "Colonel," he said to an officer who begged for a visit, "a dirty camp gives me nausea. If you say your camps are clean, I will go."[86] A normal general would not have avoided dirty camps, but would have sought them out, so that the officers in charge might suffer for their uncleanliness. But *Lee* was not a normal general; in place of the hot word he relied upon the half-disguised censure. He was always tolerant, even when tolerance was little short of criminal. "His one great aim and endeavour," writes Colonel *Taylor*, "was to secure success for the cause in which he was enlisted; all else was made subordinate to this."[87] The cause was God's: who was he then to judge the soldiers of the Almighty? So deep was his horror of friction and dissensions that after the battle of Gettysburg he asked General *C. E. Pickett* to "destroy both copy and original" of his report, "substituting one confined to casualties merely."[88]

The essential weaknesses of his character have been so slurred over, rather than unobserved, by historians, that I will record them as fully as space permits. *John Tyler* says he was "almost unapproachable, and yet no man is more simple."[89] *Joseph E. Johnston* says: "He was the only one of all the men I have known who could laugh at the faults and follies of his friends in such a manner as to make them ashamed without touching their affection."[90] These may seem high virtues, but in fact they are weaknesses, for they were carried to extremes. "The summary methods of *Jackson* did not appeal to *Lee*, who, instead of the guard-house, employed tact as soothing as it was inexhaustible."[91] These words of Gamaliel Bradford ring true, for it was *Lee's* inexhaustible tact which ruined his army. To support them I will quote the evidence of eye-witnesses:

Colonel Fremantle says: "His only faults, so far as I can learn, arise from his excessive amiability."[92] Lord Wolseley writes: "His nature shrank with such horror from the dread of wounding the feelings of others, that upon occasions he left men in positions of responsibility to which their abilities were not equal. This softness of heart, amiable as that quality may be, amounts to a crime in the man entrusted with the direction of public affairs at critical moments."[93] Colonel Mangold, a German officer, says, that his two defects were "an indifference to discipline and a too kindly consideration for incompetent officers."[94] And Colonel *Taylor*, of his staff: "First, that he was too careful of the personal feelings of his subordinate commanders, too fearful of wounding their pride, and too solicitous for their reputation. In the next place it may be said that he was too law-abiding, too subordinate to his superiors in civil authority, those who managed the governmental machinery. . . . Obedience to orders was, in his judgment, the cardinal principle with all good soldiers of every grade. As a rule, no one can deny the correctness of this view; but those were extraordinary times, and, in some matters, ordinary rules were extraordinary evils."[95] Finally Jefferson Davis himself remarked that, "his habit of avoiding any seeming harshness . . . was probably a defect."[96]

His patience and long-suffering were not only heroic but fanatical, not openly so but inwardly so. In his first campaign in West Virginia, in place of dismissing *Floyd* or *Wise*, who were daggers drawn, he spent his time, as Henry A. White informs us, "in pouring oil upon troubled waters that should have dashed their united volume against the enemy";[97] and what was the result? This campaign ended in a complete fiasco. Here at the very opening of the war, his "reluctance to oppose the wishes of others, or to order them to do anything that would be disagreeable and to which they would not consent"[98]—and these are the words of his nephew *Fitzhugh Lee*—ruined his generalship.

What was the result? The Army of Northern Virginia was not only, as White says, "The worst-clad and the worst-fed army, perhaps, ever mustered into service,"[99] but one of the worst disciplined. "Scores of them," writes Colonel *Taylor*, "wandered about the country like locusts, and were only less destructive to their own people than the enemy."[100] On September 23, 1862, *Lee* wrote to President Davis: "Our stragglers are being daily collected, and that is one of the reasons of my being now stationary."[101] On turning to the Official Records what do we find? On September 22, that is the day before the above was written, in *Ewell's* division, out of a total of over 11,000 men less than 4,000 were present for duty.[102] Of this heinous military vice Colonel Fremantle writes: "The straggling of the Georgians was on the grandest scale conceivable; the men fell out by dozens, and seemed to suit their own convenience in that respect, without interference on the part of the officers."[103] And Colonel Grenfell, another English witness, says: "The only way in which an officer could acquire influence over the Confederate soldier was by his personal conduct under fire. . . . Every atom of authority has to be purchased by a drop of your blood."[104] *Lee* knew of this desperate state of affairs as well as any man. On March 21, 1863, he wrote to Davis: "The greatest difficulty I find is in causing orders and regulations to be obeyed."[105] Why then did he not enforce discipline? The answer is: he could not; each man to him was a hero, a soldier of God. Thus through lack of severity, of generalship, of soldiership, this "Aristo-democracy armed with a forlorn hope," performing miracles of heroism as it did, straggled under the banner of *Lee's* sanctity to its doom.

Colonel *Taylor* tells us that "excessive generosity and perfect subordination, while they adorned the life of General *Lee*, are not compatible with the generally accepted notions of perfection in a revolutionary leader,"[106] and Lord Wolseley says: "He appears to have forgotten that he was the great Revolutionary Chief engaged in a great Revolutionary war; that he was no mere leader in a political struggle of parties carried on within the lines of an old, well-established form of government. It was very clear to many at the time, as it will be commonly acknowledged now, that the South could only hope to win under the rule of a Military Dictator."[107] The Hon. B. H. Hill, of the Confederate Government, apparently thought so, for shortly before the end of the war he urged *Lee* to form and express political opinions, saying: "If we establish our independence the people will make you Mr. Davis's successor." "Never," answered *Lee*, ". . . I shall not do the people the injustice to accept high civil office with whose questions it has not been my business to become familiar." The rest of the conversation is illuminating:

"Well, but, General," said Hill, "history does not sustain your view. Caesar and Frederick of Prussia and Bonaparte were great statesmen as well as great generals."

"And great tyrants," he promptly responded. "I speak of the proper rule in republics, where, I think, we should have neither military statesmen nor political generals."

"But Washington was both, and yet not a tyrant."

With a beautiful smile he responded, "Washington was an exception to all rule, and there was none like him."[108]

He simply could not realise that the occasion demanded, if not a military dictator, then the strongest military hold over the Government and the political situation; consequently, though Commander-in-Chief for two short periods, never once during them did he show the slightest aptitude for such a command. On the second occasion, when dictatorial powers were offered to him, "he accepted the office only as the subordinate of the President,"[109] though he understood clearly that the intention of Congress was to take military control out of Davis's hands. He could have done this, could have evacuated Richmond, and joining up with *Joseph E. Johnston* have concentrated a formidable force against Sherman in North Carolina. His prestige alone would have overcome all opposition, for in February, 1865, the Army of Northern Virginia was heart and soul *Lee's* army, and *the* cause of the South—*Lee's* cause. He had become a St. Francis, a St. Bernard in the eyes of the Confederacy, he had led a Crusade and was all but a god; yet he could not bring himself to act as a revolutionary general should, because to have ousted Davis would have infringed the prerogative of God. Grant said: "All the people except a few political leaders in the South will accept whatever he does as right and will be guided to a great extent by his example."[110] But no, *Lee* could not act against his convictions. Because of them he was incapacitated from being a true Commander-in-Chief, even a true commander, as this word is generally understood, of his own army, for his convictions ruined discipline, and added infinitely to the misery of his officers and men.

"An army," so said Napoleon, "marches upon its belly"; but *Lee*, though a saint, and because he was a saint, was no quartermaster. He said: "I am content to share the rations of my men." On one occasion he wrote to Richmond: "Nothing prevented my continuing in his [the enemy's] front but the destitute condition of my men, thousands of whom are barefooted, a greater number partially shod, and nearly all without blankets, overcoats, or warm clothing. I

123

think the sublimest sight of the war was the cheerfulness and alacrity exhibited by the army in the pursuit of the enemy under all the trials and privations to which it was exposed."[111]

It *was* sublime, one of the grandest pictures in history, this all-gripping misery of his men. But it was a picture of which he was the artist. Though again and again he pleads for supplies, his pleadings are so tactful that they are disregarded. He never thunders for them, they are not his personal concern; even at the beginning of the war, when Commander-in-Chief, he never insisted upon their collection or economy. General *Long* informs us: "Besides the want of money and men the Army of Northern Virginia was deficient in clothing, shoes, blankets, tents, provisions; in fact, everything needful was wanted except arms and ammunition. The abundant supplies with which the country teemed at the beginning of the war, instead of being collected and preserved for future use, were allowed to be dissipated, and in less than two years one of the most fruitful countries known was reduced to the condition of being barely able to afford a scanty subsistence for armies whose effective strength did not exceed 200,000 men."[112]

Time and again he almost sobs for supplies. By the beginning of 1865 the position is desperate, and a most heartrending appeal is endorsed by Jefferson Davis: "This is too sad to be patiently considered, and cannot have occurred without criminal neglect or gross incapacity. Let supplies be had by purchase, or borrowing, or other possible mode."[113] Yet nothing happens, and the army founders through starvation and its consequent—desertion. *Lee's* subservience was so complete that it was constantly taken advantage of. At the time of Chancellorsville we find him writing: "I have understood, I do not know with what truth, that the armies of the West and that in the Department of South Carolina and Georgia are more bountifully supplied with provisions. . . . I think that this [his] army deserves as much consideration as either of those named, and, if it can be supplied, respectfully ask that it be similarly provided."[114] And again a little later on: "I have been mortified to find that when any scarcity existed, this was the only army in which it is found necessary to reduce the rations."[115]

Not only did he refuse to exert his full authority to obtain supplies, but instinctively he had a horror of the whole question. Unconsciously, trading was antipathetic to his aristocratic nature; besides, to compel the people to part with their food stocks was abhorrent to him, he looked upon them as an heroic race, almost as God's chosen people, who must be appealed to only through the heart. Colonel *Taylor* tells us that: "He did not enjoy writing; indeed he wrote with labor, and nothing seemed to tax his amiability so much as the necessity for writing a lengthy official communication."[116] Also that he "could not bear to be annoyed with the considerations of . . . matters of routine,"[117] and: "He had a great dislike to review army communications."[118] How could he then hope to succeed? Through faith alone; for the cause was God's. He was the sole referee in this stupendous war. He would award the laurels as He saw fit.

This lack of thunder; this lack of appreciation that administration is the foundation of strategy; this lack of interest in routine, and his abhorrence to exert his authority, maintained his army in a state of semi-starvation and were the causes of much of its straggling and ill-discipline. And though we must stand amazed at what he was able to accomplish through spiritual force, lack of material necessities ultimately brought the Confederacy to its knees; for his army and his

cause were starved into surrender, and this in spite of
the fact that at this time four months' supplies were
stacked in the neighbourhood of Richmond!

His Audacity and Resignation

To consider now the influence of his personality
upon his generalship, a question we can at once
answer is that *Lee* was no grand-strategist, for he
refused to be influenced by policy or to influence it.
His theory of war was based upon the spirit of his
army which he considered to be invincible. He under-
valued the valor of his adversaries, though he read
like a book the character of many of their generals, and
on the whole had the highest contempt for their
abilities. His cause was a moral one, and his attacks
were also moral ones. He struck at Washington
because this city was the nervous base of the several
Federal commanders who crossed swords with him.
Henderson is right when he says: "Far away to the
north, beyond the Potomac, beneath the shadow of
the Capitol at Washington, was the mainspring of the
invader's strength. The multitude of armed men that
overran Virginia were no more than the inanimate
pieces of the chess-board. The power which controlled
them was the Northern President. It was at Lincoln
that *Lee* was about to strike, at Lincoln and the Northern
people, and an effective blow at the point which
people and President deemed vital might arrest the
progress of their armies as surely as if the Confederates
had been reinforced by a hundred thousand men."[119]
And again: "He knew McClellan and he knew Lincoln.
He knew that the former was over-cautious; he knew
that the latter was over-anxious,"[120] and on this
psychological knowledge he founded his strategy.

He relied on manoeuvre more than on attack. Manoeuvre he understood, and he was a past-master in field movements; attacking he did not, and most of his offensive battles failed. Grant, understanding this, understood *Lee* so well that at the outset of the Wilderness campaign he said that he did not intend to manoeuvre; he refused to dance to *Lee's* pipe. Once *Lee* was cooped up behind the Richmond defences he could no longer indulge in his favourite pastime of turning the Valley of Virginia into a race-course. The only time he attempted to do so was when *Early* raided up to Washington; yet on this occasion, in spite of all his psychological insight, *Lee* failed to gauge the temper of the North. There was no panic as in 1862, Lincoln quietly saying: "Let us be vigilant, but keep cool."[121]

As a general *Lee* was a mixture of caution and audacity. His theory of war was that "in planning all dangers should be seen, in execution none, unless very formidable."[122] At Richmond, on June 15, 16 and 17, he did nothing to support *Beauregard*, at Chancellorsville he acted like lightning, and, I suspect, because *Jackson* provided the "sunshine" he so needed. *Taylor* says: "This battle illustrates most admirably the peculiar talent and individual excellence of *Lee* and *Jackson*. For quickness of perception, boldness in planning and skill in directing, General *Lee* had no superior: for celerity in his movements, audacity in the execution of bold designs and impetuosity in attacking, General *Jackson* had not a peer."[123] *Lee's* initial moves were frequently bold in the extreme; his methods few could foresee, least of all men such as Pope, Burnside and Hooker. Whilst at Chancellorsville he struck with startling speed, at Fredericksburg he let the decisive moment slip away. There, on the morning of December 14, he erred from over-caution, and as Chesney says: "Missed an opportunity of further advantage, such as even a great victory has rarely offered; it must be borne in mind that his troops were not on this occasion suffering from over-marching, want of food and ammunition."[124] The reason may have been, as Henderson supposes, that it was out of consideration of the inhabitants of Fredericksburg that *Lee* did not attack;[125] but personally I think it was that once battle was joined, he handed his command over to God. At Gettysburg, Colonel *Taylor* says: "The whole affair was disjointed. There was an utter absence of accord in the movements of the several commands, and no decisive result attended the operations of the second day."[126] In the Seven Days' Battle it had been the same; days of chaos and slaughter, and as *Taylor* writes, "a record of lost opportunities."[127]

More often than not this reliance in Providence deprived him of all possible chance of gaining a decisive victory; besides the Army of Northern Virginia was so lacking in military equipment and supplies, that it was far easier for its commander to win victories than to reap their fruits; often the fruits were—boots and ammunition.[128] Of Fredericksburg, Rhodes, the historian, exclaims: "The feeling in regard to *Lee* might have found expression in the words of Barcas, a Carthaginian, after the battle of Cannae. 'You know how to gain victory, but not how to use it.'" And "Chancellorsville," Hamlin writes, "seems to have been a tragedy of errors. . . . It may be said, with some truth, that the campaign was *Lee's* masterpiece in audacity and celerity, but his victory was like that won in ancient times by Pyrrhus, for it was indeed a mortal blow to the vitality of the Army of Northern Virginia."[129] A mortal blow, above all, because of the loss of *Stonewall Jackson,* who could above all other men render tangible the inspirations of his chief; he was as *Lee* himself said, "his right arm."

Taylor says: "If *Lee* was the Jove of the war, *Stonewall Jackson* was his thunderbolt."[130] *Jackson*, though he believed in the omnipotence of God as fervently as *Lee* did, could demand the impossible. "Did you order me to advance over that field, sir?" said an officer to him. "Yes," answered *Jackson*. "Impossible, sir! My men will be annihilated! Nothing can live there. They will be annihilated!" "General," replied *Jackson*, "I always endeavour to take care of my wounded and to bury my dead. You have heard my order—obey it."[131]

Without *Jackson*, *Lee* was left a one-armed pugilist. *Jackson* possessed that brutality essential in war; *Lee* did not. He could clasp the hand of a wounded enemy, whilst *Jackson* ground his teeth and murmured: "No quarter to the violators of our homes and firesides,"[132] and when someone deplored the necessity of destroying so many brave men, he exclaimed: "No, shoot them all, I do not wish them to be brave."[133] With all his ability there was something repellent about *Jackson*; in spite of his many faults there was always something ennobling about *Lee*. *Jackson* was the Old Testament of War, *Lee*—the New.

Lee, as *Stonewall Jackson* said, was "a phenomenon . . . the only man whom I would follow blindfold."[134] Can we wish that he had been otherwise? I do not think so; for his spirit as a man was so exalted that it obliterated his failures as a general, and a cause which in the long run was bound to fail could not have failed more heroically than in the hands of one who, if he could not compel success, could sanctify failure. In his farewell order to his army he said: "You will take with you the satisfaction that proceeds from the consciousness of duty faithfully performed."[135] But did this satisfaction bring consolation to his own heart? I do not think so, for I feel that his surrender, on April 9, 1865, was his crucifixion; to him it was the judgment of God, consequently it was God's will that the Northern cause should prove victorious. What this revelation meant to him in terms of spiritual anguish none will ever discover, for it is the secret which *Lee* took with him to his grave.

From the boom of the last cannon he entered a silence which he never broke, and except for its sorrows the war vanished from his life. To Mrs. Jefferson Davis he wrote on February 23, 1866: "*I have thought from the time of the cessation of hostilities, that silence and patience on the part of the South was the true course,* and I think so still. *Controversy of all kinds* will, in my opinion, only serve to continue excitement and passion, and will prevent the public mind from the acknowledgment and acceptance of the truth. These considerations have kept me from replying to accusations made against myself, and induced me to recommend the same to others."[136] On another occasion he wrote: "The statement is not true, but I have not thought proper to publish a contradiction."[137] To a lady he said, "I know of nothing good I could tell you of myself, and I fear I should not like to say any evil,"[138] and to an editor: "I must acknowledge that I have not read the article on Chancellorsville . . . nor have I read any of the books published on either side since the termination of hostilities."[139] The war was past and dead, let it be buried and forgotten; why should his head agonize his poor broken heart?

He had never been hostile to the Union; it was a union maintained by the sword which had antagonized his conscience. Once the war was ended, seeing God's will in this final act, to General *Beauregard* he wrote: "I need not tell you that true patriotism sometimes requires of men to act exactly contrary at one period to that which it does at another, and the motive which impels them, the desire to do right, is precisely the same. The circumstances which govern their actions change, and their conduct must conform to the new order of things."[140] It was for this reason that, in October, 1865, he accepted the presidency of Washington College. "We must look to the rising generation for the restoration of the country,"[141] he said, and though a prematurely old and weary man, he felt that it was his duty to accept this appointment in order to smooth out a few of the many wrinkles the war had caused, and so spend the remaining years of his life in assisting to establish in his own humble way, now that the sword was sheathed, a more perfect union based on brotherly love.

On September 28, 1870, he returned from his work to find his family waiting tea for him. He rose to say grace, but his lips could not utter the words that were in his heart. Unable to speak, he sat down quietly and without agitation. He was resigned to the end, and at nine o'clock on the morning of October 12 he closed his eyes on this troubled world. *Lee* is dead, yet the national hero lives on, an all inspiring example to his fellow countrymen of duty accomplished.

CHAPTER IV

THE GENERALSHIP OF GRANT AND LEE, 1861-62

First Bull Run and West Virginia

THE histories of Grant's and *Lee's* generalships are very different: the one is as it were a continuous story, the other a series of brilliant essays based on one theme—the defence of Virginia. The first is woven round a definite plot—the Union, the maintenance of the Union, and the re-establishment of the Union through a unifying strategy; the second meanders through the freedom of individual States, revealing a deep-founded weakness for the want of unity, disclosing cross purposes and ending in disruption through lack of strategy. It is important to bear this in mind, for just as the war itself, like a storm cloud, was influenced by the great geographical features of the area in which it was fought, so were the personalities of these two generals consciously and unconsciously influenced by the political features.

For long, as I have shown in Chapter I, the clouds of war had been gathering and darkening the social horizon. Charged with human electricity as they now were, a pretext alone was awaited to detonate the storm. And as is so often the case in war, particularly so in wars of the first magnitude, the pretext found was an insignificant one—a small fort so weakly garrisoned as to be of no real tactical value.

South Carolina had throughout her history been a

truculent State. She was so before the Revolution, after the Declaration of Independence, and for years before the outbreak of the Civil War. The capital of this State was Charleston, the harbour of which was protected by several small forts, the most important being Fort Sumter, built on an island. On December 20, 1860, having passed an Ordinance of Secession, South Carolina became in her own eyes a sovereign State and forthwith claims were laid to these forts. Sumter was garrisoned by about a hundred United States troops under Major Anderson, and the South Carolina Convention demanded that this fort should be evacuated. This being refused, on January 9, 1861, fire was opened on U.S.S. *Star of the West*, which had been sent to revictual the fort. Tension grew intense; then on March 3 General *Beauregard* took over command at Charleston and on April 11 he sent Major Anderson a formal demand to surrender. This being promptly rejected fire was opened on the fort at 4.30 a.m. on the 12th. At noon on the 14th the Stars and Stripes was hauled down and Sumter passed into Confederate hands.

This insult to the United States flag detonated the war. Emotions had been running high, now they burst into fury and frenzy. On April 15 Lincoln signed a proclamation calling out 75,000 militiamen; on the 17th, though he could not enforce it, he declared the entire coasts of the South to be under blockade. This same day Virginia seceded and the navy-yard at Norfolk was occupied as well as the arsenal at Harper's Ferry. On May 3 Lincoln, beginning to realize the seriousness of the situation, issued a second proclamation calling for 42,000 three-year volunteers.

In the West, *Jackson*, the Governor of Missouri, attempted to occupy St. Louis and hold this city for the South, but on June 17 his forces were routed by

General Lyon at Boonville. Between Missouri and Virginia stretched Kentucky, which had passed a resolution of neutrality, nevertheless, as neither side troubled to recognize it, the war swept into this State. East of Kentucky lay West Virginia, an area of great strategic importance because the Baltimore and Ohio Railway which traversed it was the main line of communications connecting Washington with the West. To this area General George B. McClellan, who had been placed in command of the Military Department of Ohio, proceeded, and driving out the Confederate detachments not only gained the northern half of West Virginia for the Federal cause but also much popular glory for himself.

When *Beauregard's* guns opened fire on Fort Sumter Colonel *Robert E. Lee* was still in the United States Army. On April 20 he resigned his commission and wrote to his brother, Sidney Smith Lee, saying: "Save in the defence of my native State, I have no desire ever again to draw my sword";[1] and when three days later he was entrusted with the command of the forces of Virginia, it was only in her defence that he was asked to act.[2] His first order was a defensive one: on April 27 he sent[3] Colonel *Thomas J. Jackson*, soon to become famous as *Stonewall Jackson*, to seize Harper's Ferry, which he did, reporting that he would defend it "with the spirit which actuated the defenders of Thermopylae."[4] Thus at the opening of this war defence and not defiance resounded through the South.

On May 10, in order to establish a defensive policy, *Lee* was appointed Commander-in-Chief of the forces of the Confederacy and held this appointment until June 8, when Jefferson Davis assumed direct control, *Lee* becoming his nominal Chief of Staff. His first problem was to secure Northern Virginia from immediate attack, and this was accomplished by blocking the main Federal lines of approach at Harper's Ferry, Manassas Junction and Aquia Creek.

Harper's Ferry was held by General *Joseph E. Johnston* and some 11,000 men, and Manassas Junction by *Beauregard* with 22,000. Opposed to them were Patterson, an old general who had served in the 1812-15 War, and General McDowell, both of whom came

FIG. I

under the command of General Winfield Scott, the Federal Commander-in-Chief, then in his seventy-fifth year. Scott's plan was to contain *Beauregard* and drive back *Johnston*; he was cautious and rightly so, for he feared the ill-discipline of his raw militiamen far more than the prowess of his enemy.

As is common in this democratic age, the people, knowing nothing of war, demanded an immediate advance, and the Press, eager to lead popular opinion, made such good use of the slogan "On to Richmond" that the hands of Lincoln and his ministers were forced and it was decided to hold *Johnston* and strike at *Beauregard.*

On July 18, having concentrated some 36,000 men at Centerville, McDowell, wishing to avoid a frontal attack on *Beauregard,* whose army lined the southern bank of the Bull Run, determined to turn the Confederate left flank, the safety of his outflanking attack depending upon Patterson being able to hold *Johnston* at Harper's Ferry. This Patterson failed to do and *Johnston* slipped back to Winchester. *Beauregard* wanted to attack, but both Jefferson Davis and *Lee* were opposed to this idea; they wanted McDowell to clinch with *Beauregard* and then to bring *Johnston* down onto McDowell's right flank and rear. This is what happened, for when, on July 21, the battle was fought, McDowell, who at first succeeded in driving back his enemy, found himself deficient of reserves when the pressure of *Johnston's* troops became felt. Not able to stay the Confederates, McDowell's men broke in panic and no effort could rally them until the defences of Washington were reached. As it happened, the Confederates being utterly disordered by the fighting were in no fit condition to carry out a pursuit.

Though this battle led to no strategical results, its influence on the grand strategy of the war was profound. First, it imbued the Southern politicians with an exaggerated idea of the prowess of their soldiers and so led them to under-estimate the fighting capacity of their enemy; secondly, it so terrified Lincoln and his Government, that from now onwards until 1864, east of the Alleghanies, the defence of Washington became the pivot of Northern strategy.

Except for having originally selected[5] the position

south of the Bull Run from a defensive rather than an offensive point of view, *Lee* in no way influenced this the first important battle of the war; neither would he allow himself to be drawn into the acrimonious discussions which followed it[6] and which were altogether antipathetic to his high sense of discipline.

Soon after this battle he was sent[7] to West Virginia to take over command of the forces in that area. There, though freed from the President's immediate influence and though his subordinates were at loggerheads, his personality at once crippled his generalship, for he refused to take command, that is to say—he refused to impose his will upon them and so establish unity of direction.

The more acrimonious of these quarrels was between Generals *Floyd* and *Wise*. On August 7 *Wise* asked *Lee* to assign to himself and *Floyd* "respective fields of operation;"[8] to which *Lee* answered that he hoped that *Wise* "will join General *Floyd*."[9] *Floyd* then sent *Wise* peremptory orders, which *Wise* referred to *Lee*, pointing out that they should be issued by him. *Lee* answered that he thought this was so apparent that no orders on the subject were necessary. On August 24 *Wise* wrote to *Lee*: "We are now brought into a critical position by the vacillation of orders and confusion of command;" to which *Lee* answered: "I beg, therefore, for the sake of the cause . . . you will permit no division of sentiment to disturb its harmony. . . . In accordance with your request I will refer your application to be detached from General *Floyd's* command to the Secretary of War. At present I do not see how it can be done without injury to the service, and hope, therefore, you will not urge it." On September 21 *Lee* pointed out to *Wise* the danger of his force being divided from *Floyd's*, and the same day *Wise* replied: "But, sir, I am ready to join General *Floyd* wherever

137

you command, and you do not say where. . . . I will delight to obey you, sir."[10] So the quarrel continued, *Wise* having already written to *Lee*, on September 11, "Disasters have come, and disasters are coming which you alone, I fear, can repair and prevent."[11] This was very true, for the campaign in the Kanawha Valley and around Cheat Mountain ended in a complete fiasco, leaving the western slopes of Virginia in Federal hands.

Public opinion condemned *Lee*, and for once it was right; for in this his first command in the field he completely failed as a commander, with the result that in November he was removed from his command and placed in charge of the coast defences of South Carolina, Georgia and Florida—not, however, a back-water, as the ports of these States were essential to the maintenance of the Confederacy. There he remained until March 13, 1862, when he was "assigned to duty at the seat of government . . . under the direction of the President . . . charged with the conduct of military operations in the armies of the Confederacy."[12] This step was taken because storm clouds were rapidly gathering north of Richmond.

Paducah, Donelson and Shiloh

In the East *Lee's* personality ruined his first campaign. In the West the personality of one man set in motion a strategy which was destined to win the war. This man was Captain Ulysses S. Grant.

"It cannot be denied," once wrote Lord Bacon, "but outward accidents conduce much to fortune; favour, opportunities, death of others, occasion fitting virtue. But chiefly, the mould of a man's fortune is in his own hand." Applied to Grant this observation fits like a glove. It was fortunate that he had served in the army during the Mexican war; it was fortunate that he had been a regimental quartermaster and had learned to equate energy in terms of rations; it was fortunate that he had left the army several years before the Civil War broke out, for had he remained in it, he might easily have become petrified by its dull routine; and above all, when this war did blaze forth, it was exceedingly fortunate that his first command found him at Cairo, the strategical pivot of the war and the pivot of his own success; for from the first, from September 4, 1861, when as a brigadier-general he established his brigade headquarters there, he recognized it, if not as such, at least as a point of extreme importance.

Failing a rapid decision in the East—in that small area embraced by the James river, the Alleghany mountains, the Susquehanna and Chesapeake Bay— an unlike contingency, for even a great victory there could scarcely have done more than have driven the political centres further apart, the hub of the war lay at Cairo, and why? A glance at Map No. 2 will at once answer this question: The area Memphis-St. Louis-Louisville-Chattanooga may be looked upon as the sally-port of the South. For unless the Confederacy was to stand on a passive defensive, which in the end was likely to spell ruin, it was in this area that the chances of a successful offensive predominated. As I have pointed out in Chapter I, it was here that Virginia could be protected, and the strategical centre of this offensive area was Cairo, from which town river communications ran to St. Louis, Louisville, Nashville and Chattanooga; and the railroad connection between Union City (thirty miles south of Columbus) and Nashville was the waist of all railroad communications between the Northern and Southern States west of the Alleghany range. This waist was about 120 miles wide, and to protect it the Confederates established strong works at New Madrid and Island No. 10 in the Mississippi, Fort Henry on the Tennessee and Fort Donelson on the Cumberland river, east of which forces were pushed out into southern Kentucky.

From Cairo Grant saw the importance of Paducah which lay on the Ohio river some twenty-five miles east of Cairo, and which blocked the exits of the Tennessee and Cumberland rivers. On September 5 he asked General Frémont, then in command of the Department of Missouri, for authority to occupy it, and receiving no reply he set out that evening and seized this town.[13] Thus did the struggle for the sally-port begin. On November 7 he fought a small battle with General *Pillow* at Belmont, on the west bank of the Mississippi, immediately opposite Columbus, in which he proved himself to be a novice in tactics, as inexpert as his men were ill-disciplined. Two days later Frémont was replaced by General Henry Wagner Halleck, a bookish type of man, stupid and jealous by nature, nicknamed "Old Brains," and rightly called by W. E. Woodward "a large emptiness surrounded by an education."[14] A new campaign now began, a campaign between the opacity of Halleck and the rising genius of Grant, which endured until March 3, 1864, when Grant was called to Washington.

Lincoln, who was a strategical visionary, that is to say he could often see what should be done without possessing an idea of how to do it, had long hankered after carrying the war into East Tennessee, not only because this would bring relief to the loyal population in this area, but because such an advance would threaten Chattanooga, a vital strategic point. General McClellan who, on November 1, succeeded Scott as Commander-in-Chief of the Federal Armies, though soon to become absorbed in his projected campaign against Richmond, placed General Don Carlos Buell in command of the Department of Ohio, and favoured an advance into East Tennessee because it was likely to draw the Confederates westwards and so away from Virginia. Buell and Halleck could not agree,[15] and Buell ordering General Thomas to attack *Zollicoffer*, the Confederates were defeated at Mill Springs on January 19, 1862.

Strategically this battle was an important Federal victory as it drove the Confederate forces in Kentucky away from the main line of communications leading to Cumberland Gap and thence into East Tennessee, this Gap being the connecting link between the sources of the Cumberland and Tennessee rivers. It was a blow at the right flank of the Confederate forces under General *Albert Sidney Johnston* in command of the Department of the West, forces which were holding Kentucky and which were strung out on an enormous arc extending from the Mississippi to the foot-hills of the Cumberland mountains. (See Map No. 2.) Opposed by Halleck on the left with his headquarters at St. Louis, and by Buell in the centre with his at Louisville, *Johnston's* distribution was a precarious one, and doubly so because his main lateral line of communications ran immediately in rear of it, namely, the railway from Hickman *via* Clarksville to Bowling Green where he established his headquarters.

Buell, realizing the weakness of *Johnston's* distribution, had suggested to McClellan a move on Nashville, but Halleck occupied with minor difficulties in Missouri, would not agree. Meanwhile Grant, at Cairo, became so fully convinced that to strike at the centre of the railroad waist, that is at Forts Henry and Donelson, with the object of separating the Confederate forces in Missouri from those in Kentucky, was the first step toward forcing the sally-port, that on January 6 he asked Halleck for permission to do so.[16] On the 23rd he again asked him, but with no further success; yet Halleck, whose jealousy had been roused by Buell's victory at Mill Springs, had already on the 20th telegraphed McClellan for authority to move against the forts, in order to "turn Columbus, and force the abandonment of Bowling Green."[17] On February 1 he ordered Grant to take and hold Fort Henry,[18] which he did, thanks to Foote's gunboats, the fort surrendering to him on the 6th. "The effect of the capture of Fort Henry," writes Ropes, "on the people of the whole country . . . was electrical. . . . It was accomplished, too, so suddenly and so unexpectedly that the spirits of the Northern people were elated beyond measure, while those of the people of the South were correspondingly depressed."[19] Further still, *Johnston*, assuming that the gunboats were invincible, decided to abandon Bowling Green and retire to Nashville with 14,000 men whilst 12,000 were sent to Donelson; what for it is difficult to say, unless he considered that they would enable this fort to hold out until he had slipped back, and that after this operation had been completed they would in turn be able to slip back and rejoin him. Whatever his object was, this division of force was a fatal mistake, for had the whole of his 26,000 men reinforced Donelson it is more than probable that Grant would have been defeated.

Grant was also elated, for he expected to find Fort Donelson as easy a nut to crack as Fort Henry. This was not to be, for it was far better sited, and its batteries being well above the water-line were practically invulnerable to gunboat fire. On the 11th he moved forward, his plan being to surround the fort on its landward side and attack it from the river. On the 14th the investment was completed, C. F. Smith's division being on the left, McClernand's on the right and Lewis Wallace's in the centre. At 3 p.m. Foote steamed up-stream, opened fire, steamed in unnecessarily close, was driven back and he himself wounded. The attack had failed.

Within the Fort, General *Floyd*, the Confederate Commander, seeing that he was surrounded, determined to cut his way out, and launching his attack early on the 15th, he drove back McClernand's and Wallace's divisions in much confusion. Grant at the

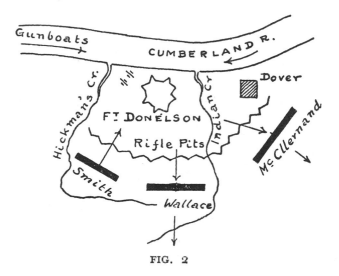

FIG. 2

time was some miles away in consultation with Foote. Foolishly he had appointed no representative, consequently, when his army was half-routed, it was left without a directing head. Returning, he at once realised that both sides were in a state of confusion, and that the one which struck first would win. Withdrawing McClernand's and Wallace's divisions to refit, he ordered Smith, who had not been attacked, to assault the works in front of him; then returning to McClernand and Wallace he moved them forward to re-occupy their former lines.[20] What is remarkable about his action is the coolness with which it was carried out, and this coolness which resulted in quickness of action led to Smith carrying the key point of the fort.

Floyd thereupon handed his command over to *Pillow*, and *Pillow* handed it over to *Buckner*, the junior general in the fort; the first two accompanied by some 3,000 of the garrison escaping under cover of night. On the 16th *Buckner* surrendered unconditionally with 11,500 men and 40 guns; [21] Grant's losses were 3,000 men killed, wounded and missing.[22]

Such was Grant's first real success, and though there has been much discussion as to who originated the move, Colonel *William P. Johnston,* son of *Albert Sidney Johnston,* is undoubtedly right when he says, "Grant made it, as it made Grant."[23] According to Colonel Bruce, the fall of Donelson was "The most damaging" blow "inflicted upon the South, up to the time *Lee* surrendered."[24] This may seem an exaggeration, but it is not so, for it forced the Confederates back into their sally-port, and so not only broke their western front, but began to drive them out of that offensive area in which the true defence of Virginia lay. It opened not only the road to the capture of New Orleans by drawing the enemy's troops northwards, but also to the Vicksburg campaign, as it led to the evacuation of Columbus and Nashville. It won Kentucky and laid Tennessee open to invasion, and it deprived the Confederacy of 175,000 potential recruits.[25] No other battle during the war effected such results or opened out such possibilities.

On Halleck these were entirely lost. Grant saw quite clearly that "the way was open to the National forces all over the south-west";[26] but Halleck confessed to McClellan that he had no plan.[27] Meanwhile

Albert Sidney Johnston fell back on Corinth, and there drew in his scattered forces, Nashville being occupied by Buell on February 24. From there Buell suggested that a blow should be struck against the Memphis-Charleston railroad (see Map No. 2), and Halleck agreeing, accused Grant of insubordination,[28] and placed General C. F. Smith in command of the expedition. Why did Halleck do this? There can be but one answer, namely, that he was jealous of Grant. He was afraid that his subordinate might gain fresh laurels and supersede him.

Two events now took place, both of which had an important influence on the trend of affairs in the West. The first was that in the beginning of March McClellan was relieved of his responsibilities as Commander-in-Chief in order that he might concentrate all his time on the Army of the Potomac, which was to operate against Richmond. This change in command was followed on March 11 by Halleck being placed in command of all the Federal forces in the West, which brought Buell under his orders, whereupon, two days later, he reinstated Grant and lied to him in order to excuse his behaviour.[29] The second was, that, on March 7-8, General Curtis secured the State of Missouri by decisively defeating General *Van Dorn* at Pea Ridge, which victory relieved Halleck of all anxiety as regards the security of the western side of the Mississippi river, whereupon he decided to move his combined armies on Corinth.

Meanwhile Smith carried out several minor raids, and eventually established himself at Savannah, with two divisions, Sherman's and Hurlbut's, at Pittsburg Landing, whilst Lewis Wallace's division occupied Crump's Landing some four miles further down stream. Grant arrived at Savannah on the 17th, under instructions from Halleck to act on the defensive, and

145

not to bring about a general engagement until Buell arrived.[30] Buell was then at Columbia, 40 miles south of Nashville. Realizing the faulty distribution of Smith's forces, Grant concentrated the whole army at Pittsburg and Crump's Landings, and there began to organize and drill his raw troops.

Grant expected Buell on the 24th or 25th, but owing to delays *en route*, he telegraphed Grant that he could not arrive at Savannah before April 5.[31] In spite of this delay, which enabled *Johnston* to collect and re-organize his forces at Corinth, only a little more than 20 miles from the Landings, Grant failed to realize the necessity of entrenching his position; in fact he committed the very common military blunder of conjecturing what his enemy would do and acting upon his conjecture. As he himself says: "I regarded the campaign we were engaged in as an offensive one and had no idea that the enemy would leave strong entrenchments to take the initiative when he knew he would be attacked where he was if he remained."[32] Also: "Up to that time the pick and spade had been little resorted to at the West."[33] Worse still, Grant established his headquarters at Savannah, and Sherman, who was in nominal command of the three forward divisions at Pittsburg Landing, failed to secure or adequately to patrol his front.[34]

On April 4 Grant was thrown from his horse and severely bruised his leg. Late on the 5th he returned to Savannah to meet Buell, Sherman sending him the following message: "I have no doubt nothing will occur to-day more than the usual picket firing. The enemy is saucy, but got the worst of it yesterday, and will not press our pickets far. I will not be drawn out far unless with certainty of advantage, and I do not apprehend anything like an attack on our position."[35]

When he wrote this message, 45,000 Confederates

were but two miles from his encampment; what had happened?

After the fall of Fort Donelson *Johnston* retired to Nashville, then to Murfreesborough and finally to Corinth. There he drew in his scattered forces, and on the evacuation of Columbus on March 2 was joined by a considerable force under General *Beauregard*, who had been sent out West some time after the battle of Bull Run. Further still, on the 29th, being reinforced by General *Bragg* with some 10,000 men, he found himself at the head of about 45,000 troops; thereupon he determined to strike at Grant before Buell could support him.

On April 4 he moved out of Corinth hoping to fall upon Grant the following morning and drive him into the Tennessee; but the straggling of his troops was such that he was unable to deliver his attack until the 6th. The astonishing thing is, so close were the Confederate pickets to the Federal that in certain cases they could look right into their enemy's encampments without being seen.

Early on the 6th the attack was launched, and it came as a complete surprise, the forward Federal divisions after putting up a good fight being driven back towards the Landing to where thousands of non-combatants, sick and stragglers had fled in panic.[36] There a scene of pandemonium greeted Grant when he arrived from Savannah at 6 a.m.

It was a spectacle of complete defeat, and any ordinary general would have at once planned a retreat, hoping to save some small fraction of his shattered army. But Grant was no ordinary general; for he was one of those rare and strange men who are fortified by disaster in place of being depressed. He at once sent forward ammunition, organized reserves and then rode to the front. Between 6 a.m. and nightfall he carried out eighteen important operations,[37] stabilizing his shattered divisions, and holding the enemy back until Buell could come to his assistance. *Johnston* was killed at 2.30 p.m., and by that hour the Confederate reserves were practically exhausted.

On the 7th the attack was renewed, and *Beauregard*, now in command of the Confederates, decided on a withdrawal. Grant did not pursue, and this was his

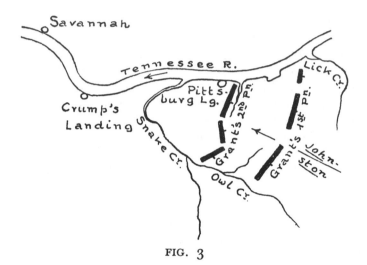

FIG. 3

cardinal error; for had he done so he might well have destroyed his enemy. He did not do so because he was not prepared to do so; he himself says: "I wanted to pursue, but had not the heart to order the men who had fought desperately for two days . . . to pursue;" and again: "I did not meet Buell in person until too late to get troops ready and pursue with effect. . . ."[38] Sherman, asked by John Fiske why there was no pursuit, answered: "I assure you, my dear fellow, that we had quite enough of their society for two whole days, and were only too glad to be rid of them on any terms."[39] This, I suspect, is the true reason.

Thus far fortune and misfortune had smiled on Grant as they smile on most of us, that is in a haphazard way. When things went well he was like any other man, but when they went awry, as they did at Belmont, Donelson and Shiloh, we have seen, as Bacon said, that "chiefly the mould of a man's fortune is in his own hand." Because of his dauntless spirit of resolution, far more so than through his genius, he had pulled his army out of the bogs into which he had led it. Now he found himself in what appeared to be a bottomless morass. After Donelson Halleck had treated him in a shameful way, and again he did so after Shiloh. On April 11 he arrived at Pittsburg Landing; collected there an army of over 100,000 men;[40] began, on the 30th, to move on Corinth, and arrived there on May 30 to find the town evacuated. He had taken 31 days to march 21 miles!

He made Grant his second in command, deprived him of all power over his men, and treated him in so intolerable a manner that he asked to be relieved of his duties in the field. This was agreed to, and he established his headquarters at Memphis. There he was, when, on July 11, came that crowning mercy for the North, McClellan's campaign against Richmond having failed: Lincoln called Halleck to Washington and appointed him General-in-Chief of the entire land forces of the United States. Meanwhile, on June 10, Buell had set out on his march to Chattanooga.

Grant was still in command of the Department of West Tennessee; his forces numbered about 46,000 men, and were nominally in reserve should Buell require them. He had learned much whilst in disgrace. He had had two months to think things over, and there can be little doubt that during this dismal period he analysed his own mistakes, learnt many lessons from them, and began to elaborate in his mind that strategy which was to win the war.

The Peninsula Campaign and the Seven Days' Battle

To return now to the East. The Battle of Bull Run, as I have already pointed out, imbued the Confederacy with a confidence in itself for which there was no real justification, so much so that after this victory little was done to take advantage of the pause in operations and set the Southern military house in order. With the Federal Government it was otherwise, for McClellan, the popular favourite, was at once called to Washington and, on November 1, Lincoln appointed him General-in-Chief in place of Scott. From the date of his arrival at the capital until the spring of 1862 he raised and organized the Army of the Potomac and was loath to embark on any offensive operation until he had completed its equipment and training.

As months passed by and nothing happened, public opinion began to demand action and became so clamorous that, on January 27, Lincoln issued an order that the Army of the Potomac would on February 22, the anniversaty of Washington's birthday, move south against the Confederate forces, still at Manassas Junction. To this McClellan strongly objected and placed before the President his own plan which was as follows: To transport the bulk of his army by sea to Urbana on the lower Rappahannock, which was but one day's march from West Point and three from Richmond. Once at Urbana he was of opinion that he would be able to bottle up *Magruder's* forces which were holding the Yorktown Peninsula and capture Richmond before *Joseph E. Johnston* could fall back from Manassas and intervene. Failing Urbana, he suggested Mob Jack Bay, north of the mouth of the York river, or as a last resort Fortress Monroe as possible places of disembarkation.

Lincoln did not like this plan, for the terrors of the First Bull Run still obsessed him. In his opinion it would uncover the capital, leaving it open to direct

FIG. 4

attack by *Johnston* supported by *Jackson,* who was at this time occupying the Shenandoah Valley. In spite of this, on February 27 the Government accepted the plan as long as sufficient troops were left behind to defend Washington. And on March 8 McClellan was instructed to open his campaign on the 18th.

Meanwhile at Richmond the fall of Forts Henry and Donelson had so disconcerted the Confederate Government that Jefferson Davis ordered *Johnston* to fall back on Fredericksburg on March 9. Simultaneously a most unlooked for event took place: The *Merrimac*, an ironclad vessel built by the Confederates at Norfolk, steamed out on March 8, attacked the Federal squadron at Hampton Roads, and on the following day fought her epoch-making duel with the *Monitor*. The result of these two events was that McClellan was ordered to change his place of disembarkation to Fortress Monroe and to leave 40,000 men to garrison Washington.

On March 17 the disembarkation of McClellan's army began, but it was not until April 4 that it moved northwards, and even then, though McClellan had under his immediate command over 100,000 men, and was opposed by less than 13,000 under *Magruder*, his progress was slow and cautious. *Johnston's* idea was to concentrate all available forces, including those in the Carolinas and Georgia, and accept battle with the invader under the fortifications of Richmond. *Lee*, who as we have seen was recalled to Richmond on March 13, opposed this suggestion, because it would expose the seaports of Charleston and Savannah to capture, and Jefferson Davis agreeing with him, *Johnston* was ordered to take command against McClellan.[41] This he did, delaying him before Yorktown until May 3, when he retired towards Richmond, and, on the 20th, took up a position south of the capital, his right resting on Drury's Bluff and his left on the Chickahominy in the vicinity of New Bridge.

When McClellan left Washington it was found that in place of leaving 40,000 men to garrison it he had left less than half this number, and the upshot was that the Government detained there one of his Corps, namely, that under General McDowell. McClellan, having now established his headquarters at White House on the Pamunkey, urged Lincoln to send this Corps, then assembled in the neighbourhood of

Fredericksburg, back to him. This the President agreed to do, whereupon McClellan decided to advance on Richmond on May 20, three Corps to operate north of the Chickahominy and two to the south of this river; obviously a dangerous distribution of force were it not for the fact that McDowell now at the head of 40,000 men would be advancing south-

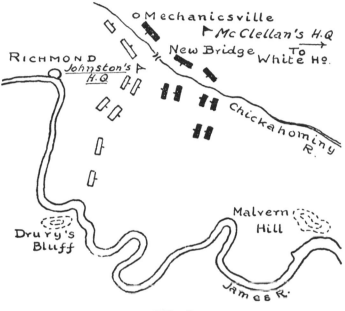

FIG. 5

wards from Fredericksburg on the 26th. Then, on the 24th, he received information from Washington that as Banks had been defeated in the Valley McDowell had sent 20,000 to support him and so could no longer move south. What had actually happened?

Though *Lee* had taken no direct part in the Peninsula campaign, indirectly his influence had been considerable. On April 5 *Jackson*, from the Valley, had written to him: "If Banks is defeated, it may greatly retard McClellan's movements."[42] Whether this set *Lee* thinking northwards it is impossible to say. From his subsequent strategy it would appear that all along he had realized that an indirect attack on the nerves of the Washington Government would be a more profitable operation than any direct attack in the field. On April 21 he had written to *Jackson*: "I have no doubt that an attempt will be made to occupy Fredericksburg and use it as a base of operations against Richmond. Our present force there is very small. If you can use General *Ewell's* division in an attack on Banks and to drive him back, it will prove a great relief to the pressure on Fredericksburg."[43] On the 29th *Jackson*, in reply, outlined his projected campaign against Milroy, McDowell and Banks, which resulted in his defeating Milroy at the village of McDowell on May 8, and Banks at Winchester on May 23. It was this electric campaign which had struck such terror into the Federal Government and which resulted in the withdrawal of McDowell from McClellan's command.

Jackson's activity, which ever since November 1861, when he took command of the Confederate troops in the Shenandoah Valley, had perturbed the Federal Government by offering a standing threat to the capital, now wrecked McClellan's campaign, for had McDowell joined him he would have been able to concentrate 150,000 men against *Johnston*, and with so numerically superior a force almost certainly would the Confederates have been defeated and Richmond occupied.

Before this shattering news was received McClellan had set in movement an operation against a Confederate force under General *Branch* which was located at Hanover Court House, his object being to clear

McDowell's line of advance and to destroy the bridges on the Virginia Central Railroad. Hearing of McDowell's withdrawal he nevertheless decided to continue with this operation, as he was afraid that *Branch* might attempt to fall upon his base depots at White House. Though this operation was successful it would have been wiser for McClellan to have

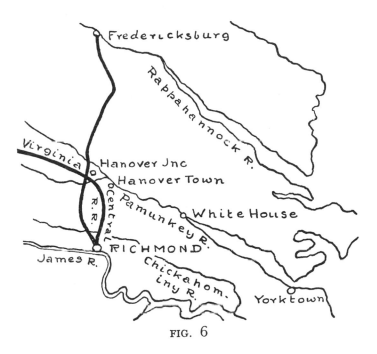

FIG. 6

changed his base to the James river, for White House was not entirely protected by his right wing.

Johnston, realizing the dangerous situation McClellan was in, decided to concentrate against and attack his right wing before McDowell could come to his support, but directly he heard that this general had been despatched to the Valley he changed his plan and decided to attack the Federal left flank. On

May 31 the attack was launched and in the battle which ensued, called Seven Pines, or Fair Oaks, McClellan's left wing was driven back and *Johnston* was severely wounded, and his place was taken by *Lee*, who, on June 1, assumed command of the "Armies in Eastern Virginia and North Carolina."[44]

Lee's position, though an exceeding anxious one, would have been far more perplexing had he not already formulated a plan. On May 16, from the following communication to *Jackson*, it can clearly be seen what this plan was. He wrote: ". . . you will not, in any demonstration you may make," against Banks, "lose sight of the fact it may become necessary for you to come to the support of General *Johnston*, and hold yourself in readiness to do so if required. . . . Whatever movement you make against Banks, do it speedily, and if successful drive him back toward the Potomac, and create the impression as far as possible that you design threatening that line."[45]

From June 1, 1862, until his surrender to Grant at Appotomax Court House, *Lee* was the central military figure in the South, and never did this great soldier show his worth more than at this moment. Though the defences of Richmond had been greatly improved by him, McClellan and his army had approached so close to them that the abandonment of the capital was seriously considered.[46] The army was in a state of despondency, and the principal officers unanimously urged a retirement to the Richmond works. *Lee* rightly objected to this, and in place strengthened the front of the army and carefully reconnoitred the whole line from flank to flank; his presence amongst his troops doing more than anything else to re-establish confidence.

His first action was to construct a strong defensive base from which he could manoeuvre; for, his army being numerically inferior to McClellan's, he realized that to stand still and adopt a passive defence meant annihilation. From his reconnaissances he learned that not only was McClellan's right flank open, but that on this flank no more than a fraction of his force was north of the Chickahominy. At once he decided to destroy this fraction. To do so he determined to entrench his right flank so strongly that he would be able to reduce its garrison to a minimum; this would enable him to concentrate the strongest possible mobile force on his left. Thus his right became the base of action for his left—the hinge of his attack. This base he decided to hold with 30,000 men under Generals *Magruder* and *Huger* facing McClellan's left, 75,000 strong, and to concentrate some 50,000 against McClellan's right — 25,000 strong under General Porter. To effect this concentration of force meant recalling *Jackson* from the Valley.

In order to verify this plan, on June 11 he ordered General *Stuart* with 1,000 cavalry "to make a secret movement to the rear of the enemy,"[47] the object being to locate the exact position of McClellan's right.[48] On the same day he notified *Jackson* that he was sending him 6 regiments under General *Lawton* and 8 under General *Whiting* to assist him in crushing the forces opposed to him; then *Lee* adds: "move rapidly to Ashland by rail or otherwise . . . and sweep down between the Chickahominy and Pamunkey, cutting up the enemy's communications . . . while the army attacks General McClellan in front."[49]

Stuart's reconnaissance was as successful as it was bold; he made the entire circuit of the Federal army at the cost of one officer killed. Not only did he destroy $7,000,000 worth of stores, but what was much more important, he discovered that McClellan's entrenchments did not extend beyond Beaver Dam, that there was no indication that McClellan intended to change his base at White House, and that he had "neglected to fortify the ridge between the head waters of the Beaver Dam Creek . . . and an affluent of the Pamunkey,"[50] and it was by the road running along this ridge that *Lee* hoped to gain the Federal communications.

On the 8th *Jackson* defeated Frémont at Cross Keys and the next day Shields suffered a similar fate at Port Republic. The news from *Stuart* being received on the 14th, on the 16th *Lee* realizing that the favourable moment had arrived, asked *Jackson* to meet him.[51] At this meeting *Jackson* expressed his belief that his men could arrive at Ashland's Station on the 23rd, but *Lee* doubting this gave him an extra day, and decided to attack on the 26th. He, therefore, based his plans on *Jackson* being able to move forward from Ashland on the 25th,[52] which necessitated his arriving there on the 24th. In brief, the final plan was this: *Magruder* and *Huger* to hold McClellan's left south of the Chickahominy, whilst *Longstreet*, *A. P. Hill*, *D. H. Hill* and *Jackson* were to attack McClellan's right wing. *Lee's* idea was to draw McClellan out of his works and compel him to defend his line of communications with White House, *Jackson* and *D. H. Hill* were to threaten this line, and when they had drawn McClellan in, *Longstreet* and *A. P. Hill* were to fall upon the left flank of whatever forces McClellan engaged.[53]

This entire plan pivoted upon *Jackson* advancing at 3 a.m. on the 26th and turning Beaver Dam.[54] In place, from Merry Oaks, he reported at 9 a.m., on the 26th, that the head of this column had only crossed the Virginia Central Railroad,[55] and at 10 p.m. he reported: "The head of my column is nearly two miles from where it crossed the Central Railroad, and is marching on the Hanover Court House and Mechanicsville turnpike."[56] Consequently it had taken him eleven hours to advance two miles! What had happened? Apparently he had lost his way, for Thomas Nelson Page informs us that *Lincoln Sydnor*, who was *Jackson's* guide on this occasion, told him that his column lost its way "on account of the new

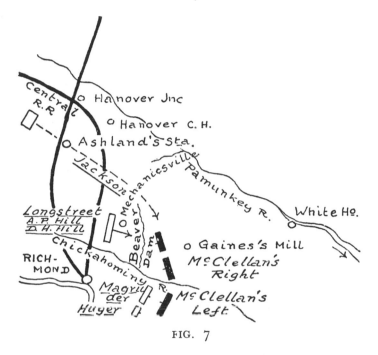

FIG. 7

roads cut by the Federals."[57] Personally, I think, straggling must be added to this error; for a wrong road alone would scarcely account for a delay of eleven hours.

Meanwhile nothing being heard of *Jackson*, on the afternoon of the 26th the van of *Lee's* army crossed to the northern bank of the Chickahominy, and at Mechanicsville *A. P. Hill* became heavily engaged and was repulsed with great slaughter.[58] Had McClellan possessed a spark of true generalship *Lee's* plan would have been wrecked; for on the night of the 26th/27th, he could have either strongly reinforced his right flank—Porter—or else on the morning of the 27th have broken through *Lee's* right and advanced on Richmond. That evening *Lee* must have felt a little nervous, for he telegraphed *Huger*: "Hold your trenches to-night at the point of the bayonet if necessary";[59] nevertheless he knew his man, and rightly gambled on McClellan's cautious nature. This general believing that *Lee's* army numbered 180,000 men,[60] decided to abandon the attack and transfer his base from White House to the James river, and from there recommence offensive operations as occasion offered.[61]

At dawn on the 27th Porter fell back to a prepared position at Gaines's Mill, and was followed up by *Longstreet* and *A. P. Hill*, who were once again compelled to delay their attack on account of the non-arrival of *Jackson*.[62] At about 1 p.m. *Lee*, unable to wait any longer, ordered *Longstreet* and *A. P. Hill* forward, and a disjointed series of furious assaults took place. *A. P. Hill* was first repulsed, then *Longstreet* struck Porter's right, later *D. H. Hill* struck at his left, and at length *Jackson* appeared. Porter, all but unsupported by McClellan, was then driven from his position, and during the night withdrew to the south bank of the Chickahominy.

From the night of June 27 until July 1 *Lee* lost all grip of the battle, because his staff organization was defective in the extreme; this may be seen from many of the battle reports, and especially *Magruder's*,[63] in which everyone seems to have been issuing orders to everyone else; also the country was enclosed, the troops scattered and his subordinate commanders

160

far too independent. On the 28th touch was lost with McClellan, and *Lee* himself says: "We were . . . compelled to wait until his purpose should be developed."[64] To clear up the situation he pushed *Ewell* out to Bottom Bridge, and, considering that he was now in pursuit, committed the egregious error of sending the whole of his cavalry under *Stuart* to break up the York River railroad and so prevent McClellan reopening connection with his base on the Pamunkey.[65] Thus *Stuart* was lost to him, and did not rejoin him until after his defeat at Malvern Hill.[66]

McClellan's army being discovered moving towards the James, the pursuit was taken up on the 29th, *Huger* and *Magruder* being ordered to strike the retiring Federals in flank whilst *Longstreet*, the two *Hills* and *Jackson* were to attack them in rear (see Map No. 3). In this combined movement *Jackson* played a sorry part. Finding Grape Vine Bridge over an affluent of the Chickahominy destroyed, he lost the whole day in repairing it,[67] and *Magruder* left single-handed, was repulsed at Savage Station. The next day *Lee* hoped that *Longstreet* and *A. P. Hill* would be able to hold the enemy at Fraiser's Farm, *Huger* coming in on their right whilst *Jackson* and *D. H. Hill* came in on their left, attacking the enemy on their flank and in rear. *Huger* never appeared, and *Jackson* and *D. H. Hill* remained the whole of the day north of White Oak Swamp Creek.

Jackson's behaviour this day was either due to utter exhaustion[68] or to a fit of religious mania; as Colonel Munford says, this day *Jackson* "was in a peculiar mood."[69] Whatever was the reason, this delay not only wrecked *Longstreet* and *A. P. Hill's* attack, but enabled McClellan to withdraw in safety to Malvern Hill. There he took up an extremely strong position, which he protected with tier after tier of guns. In spite of the fact that *A. P. Hill* reported that the position was too formidable to warrant attack,[70] *Lee* ordered one to be made, believing the enemy to be demoralized.[71] Once again the assaults were piecemeal. The signal was to be a shout from one of *Huger's* brigades, and late in the afternoon of July 1 *D. H. Hill* hearing a shout, which was not, however, the right one, pushed forward unsupported by *Jackson*, who again was late in rendering assistance.[72] Then *Huger* and *Magruder* attacked, only to be thrown back with great slaughter. These disjointed assaults cost *Lee* over 5,000 men killed and wounded,[73] McClellan losing about a third of this number. Thus ended the Seven Days' Battle, in which McClellan lost 15,849 and *Lee* 20,614 men.[74]

Lee deserved well of his countrymen, for it was he and he alone who saved Richmond. His conceptions were brilliant, his executions faulty and unnecessarily costly. This was due to the lack of co-operation between his subordinate commanders. General *Taylor* says: "Indeed it may be confidently asserted that from Cold Harbor to Malvern Hill inclusive, there was nothing but a series of blunders, one after another, and all huge. The Confederate commanders knew no more about the topography of the country than they did about Central Africa. . . . We had much praying at various headquarters, and large reliance on special providence; but none were vouchsafed, by pillar of cloud or fire; so we blundered on, like people trying to read without knowledge of their letters."[75] This lack of co-operation was due to two cardinal defects in *Lee's* system of command, and this we shall see again and again, namely, his dislike to interfere with his subordinates once battle was engaged, and his reliance on verbal orders.

Second Bull Run, Antietam and Fredericksburg

On the day upon which *Lee* first attacked, namely, June 26, the forces of Frémont, Banks and McDowell were placed under the command of Major-General John Pope,[76] who was ordered to cover Washington, secure the Valley, and by operating against Charlottesville draw Confederate forces away from McClellan.[77] On July 11, as we have seen, Halleck was called to Washington and became General-in-Chief;[78] he arrived at Washington on July 22; meanwhile on the 12th Pope moved part of his force on Gordonsville.[79]

Though McClellan at Harrison's Landing appealed to Halleck: "Here directly in front of this army, is the heart of the Rebellion. . . . It is here on the banks of the James, that the fate of the Union should be decided,"[80] he so exaggerated *Lee's* numbers, reporting that he had 200,000 men,[81] that it was found impossible sufficiently to reinforce him, and on August 3 he was ordered to withdraw his army north.

Meanwhile *Lee* foreseeing that McClellan would not move, and learning of Pope's advance on Charlottesville, on July 13 he sent *Jackson* to Gordonsville, north of which place, at Cedar Mountain, he fought a successful action against Banks on August 9, and then retired across the Rapidan (see Map No. 4). Four days later, hearing rumours of McClellan's embarkation, *Lee* at once made up his mind to move north, and, leaving only two brigades for the defence of Richmond, he ordered his army on Gordonsville.[82] There, on the 15th, he decided to turn Pope's right flank, by interposing his army between the Rapidan and Washington. Fortunately for Pope, *Lee's* order fell into his hands,[83] and at once realizing the danger of his position Pope withdrew to the Rappahannock.[84]

Lee followed him up, and after spending five days in endeavouring to turn his right he decided on a move of extraordinary audacity, but one which in the circumstances was entirely justified, namely, before McClellan could complete his withdrawal and support Pope in full, to hold Pope and his 70,000 men with 25,000 to 30,000, and to send *Jackson* with part of *Stuart's* cavalry, some 24,000 in all, by a circuitous route through Thoroughfare Gap and strike at his base—Manassas Junction. Though the danger of so widely separating his forces was great, it was not unwarranted; for his idea was to compel Pope to fall back and not to risk a battle with him, and after he had fallen back to advance *Longstreet* and threaten Washington by carrying his entire army into the Valley.[85]

From now onwards the key to *Lee's* strategy is to be sought in the name of the army he commanded: "Northern Virginia" was his strategical goal, and at this moment it was undoubtedly towards this goal that he was aiming.

On the 25th *Jackson* set out from Jefferson and marched to Salem via Amissville; on the 26th he marched through Thoroughfare Gap and arrived at Bristoe Station; from there he sent forward *Stuart*, who captured Manassas Junction.[86] Meanwhile Pope, on the 25th, had learned of *Jackson's* movement, but thought he was bound for the Valley.[87] Hearing of his raid he abandoned the line of the Rappahannock and ordered a concentration on Manassas Junction.[88]

By the retirement of Pope's army the first of *Lee's* two objects was gained, and to carry out the second, namely, an advance into the Valley, all that was necessary was an order to *Jackson* to move with all possible rapidity via Aldie and Snicker's Gap on

Berryville, whilst he with the rest of the army marched via Ashby's Gap to the same place. Holding Front Royal and the Gaps north of it, he could have advanced on Harper's Ferry, and from there by threatening Washington could have compelled the withdrawal of the Federal forces for the defence of this city.

Considering that the policy of the South was defensive, and that it demanded an offensive strategy and defensive tactics, and further considering that *Lee* was a past-master in offensive strategical movements, it is astonishing to find him committing the same error he committed during the Seven Days' Battle, of abandoning the strategical offensive and assuming a tactical offensive. In place of moving on Ashby's Gap he moved through Thoroughfare Gap, which had it not been for an error on the part of Pope's subordinates would have been held. By moving through this Gap it is obvious he intended to unite with *Jackson* west of the Bull Run Mountains, and fight a battle with Pope before McClellan could join him. This he did on the 29th and 30th, handsomely defeating Pope in the Second Battle of Bull Run, or Manassas, but not decisively, for on the 31st Pope fell back on Centerville, and was there left in peace—there was no pursuit. Further it must not be overlooked that on the 29th *Jackson* stood unsupported, or practically so, and had Thoroughfare Gap been held he would have found himself in a similar predicament on the 30th. *Jackson's* brilliant manoeuvre with all its risks was sound strategy and redounds to *Lee's* generalship. *Lee's* manoeuvre was unsound; further, it was not strategically remunerative, for out of an effective total of 48,527 men he lost between August 27 and September 2 9,197.[89]

On the 31st, not considering it a profitable operation to attack Pope in position, *Lee* decided to turn his right flank, and to effect this envelopment he ordered his army to move north of Centerville and advance on Fairfax Court House.[90] An assault on the fortifications of Washington was out of the question, for *Lee's* army was so badly supplied that it was impossible for him to remain more than a few days in the same place;[91] further, McClellan was arriving, and *Lee* would soon be so vastly outnumbered that he would be compelled to retreat.

Where move to? He was loath to fall back on the Rappahannock until winter prevented a Federal move south; further his army was so badly found that he was compelled to look for a well-stocked area to feed his troops. He could do so in the Shenandoah Valley, or by crossing the Potomac and advancing into Maryland and Pennsylvania. The second course, though the more risky, was nevertheless strategically sound as long as a battle was avoided. Maryland was enemy country, and not only was it well stocked, but many of its inhabitants were sympathetic to the Southern cause. *Lee* could supply himself here, possibly gather in recruits, and certainly draw the Federal forces further and further away from Richmond.[92]

On September 3 he wrote to Jefferson Davis pointing out, that "The present seems to be the most propitious time since the commencement of the war for the Confederate Army to enter Maryland," but that the army "is not properly equipped for an invasion . . . is feeble in transportation . . . the men . . . in thousands of instances are destitute of shoes. . . ."[93] On the 4th, without waiting for a reply, he issued his orders for an advance,[94] and the next day, in a letter to Davis, he asked for a bridge to be built over the Rappahannock so that in the event of falling back he could take up a position about

Warrenton, and threaten any advance on Richmond.[95] Between the 4th and the 7th his army crossed the Potomac in the vicinity of Leesburg,[96] and much straggling occurred.[97] On the next day, the 8th, he wrote to Davis as follows: "The present position of affairs, in my opinion, places it in the power of the Government of the Confederate States to propose with propriety to that of the United States the recognition of our independence."[98] His recent startling successes appear to have upset his balance; to him the Union was virtually down and out, and as for the Northern soldiers, "those people" as he called them, they were beneath contempt. He appears to have overlooked two obvious and important points: that the invasion of Maryland would rouse the North, and that his past successes were due not to lack of courage on the part of the Federal soldiers, but to lack of leadership in the Federal generals.

He crossed the Potomac east of the Blue Ridge, because he considered this would threaten Washington and Baltimore.[99] At Frederick City he was surprised to learn that the Federal garrisons at Harper's Ferry and Martinsburg had not been withdrawn.[100] On the 9th he detached *Jackson* and *McLaws* to round them up. This was an astonishing move, for though his eventual line of retirement would almost certainly be the Valley, and these places lay on this line, he had no intention of holding them once they were captured, consequently there was nothing to prevent their re-occupation after he had proceeded north. The truth would appear to be that though McClellan had now replaced Pope in command of the Army of the Potomac, *Lee* held his enemy in such utter contempt that he saw no danger in sending half his army in one direction whilst he proceeded with the remaining half in the other; and this in face of an army which outnumbered his own by nearly two to one! Of this suicidal dispersion of force General *Longstreet* writes: "The great mistake of the campaign was the division of *Lee's* army. If General *Lee* had kept his forces together, he would not have suffered defeat. . . . The next year on our way to Gettysburg, there was the same situation of affairs at Harper's Ferry, but we let it alone."[101]

To make matters worse, on the 13th a copy of *Lee's* order (No. 191) was found in an abandoned Confederate camp and sent to McClellan. Thus, through a stroke of unexpected good fortune, finding himself in possession of his enemy's order of battle, this general should have made a night march on the Gaps in the South Mountain, have stormed them, and have dealt with the halves of his enemy's army in detail. In place he delayed to advance until the 14th. *Lee* learning[102] that his plans had been disclosed, hurriedly turned about his column at Hagerstown and marched towards the Gaps to support their weak garrisons. On the afternoon of the 14th Turner's Gap being stormed by the Federals, *Lee* was forced to retire. He decided to recross the Potomac by the ford at Shepherdstown;[103] then a few hours later he determined to concentrate[104] his divided army at Sharpsburg and there accept battle.

What persuaded him to change his mind is difficult to say. Harper's Ferry had not yet fallen, it fell on the 15th; this cannot have been the reason, for he could have crossed the river on the 16th. General Sir Frederick Maurice suggests that it was to gain time for the rebuilding of the bridges over the Rapidan and Rappahannock for purposes of supply.[105] This seems a little far-fetched; in any case it would not have prevented him crossing the river in place of fighting with his back to it. The reason was, I think, *Lee's* excessive contempt for his enemy; further, his personal pride could not stomach the idea that such an enemy could drive him out of Maryland, and this in spite of the fact that there was nothing to prevent him being attacked on the 16th, and before *Jackson's* force would rejoin him.

The battle of Sharpsburg, or Antietam, was fought on the 17th, a totally unnecessary battle, and a very costly one; for though the Federal assaults were repulsed *Lee* lost 13,724 men.[106]

That this battle was fought to indicate personal pride its sequel shows: When, on the evening of the 17th, *Longstreet, D. H. Hill, Hood* and *S. D. Lee* recounted their losses, and urged *Lee* to retire, his reply was the one I have already quoted, namely: "Gentlemen, we will not cross the Potomac to-night. . . . If McClellan wants to fight in the morning I will give him battle again. Go!"[107] Again, on September 25, writing to Davis he said: "In a military point of view, the best move, in my opinion, the army could make would be to advance upon Hagerstown and endeavour to defeat the enemy at that point. I would not hesitate to make it even with our diminished numbers, did the army exhibit its former temper."[108] That it did not do so is not surprising, seeing that it lost 25 per cent. of its total strength at Sharpsburg.

Having assuaged his pride, the torn and shattered Army of Northern Virginia, amidst scenes of awful grandeur,[109] crossed the Potomac on the night of the 18th, and withdrew to Winchester, where *Lee* collected his stragglers and recruited his forces.

Obviously McClellan should have followed him up hot-footed, but still obsessed by the idea of *Lee's* numerical superiority,[110] he did not cross the Potomac until October 26, and then at the head of 110,000 men. On November 7 he moved to the neighbourhood of Warrenton, at which place he was relieved of his command by General Burnside.

Leaving *Jackson's* corps at Winchester,[111] on November 2 *Lee* with *Longstreet's* corps moved to Front Royal, and thence to Culpeper Court House. On the 10th he pointed out[112] to the Secretary of War that as he was too weak to attack he would be compelled to rely on manoeuvre. In truth his army was not sufficiently well equipped to do either, for a little later on he deplores that he has between 2,000 and 3,000 barefooted men, and then adds: "I am informed that there is a large number of shoes now in Richmond in the hands of extortioners, who hold them at an extravagant price."[113]

Burnside's plan was to give up the Orange and Alexandria railroad, base himself on Aquia Creek, and from Fredericksburg march directly upon Richmond. Lincoln when giving this plan his blessing, ominously added that he thought it might succeed if Burnside moved rapidly, "otherwise not." This decision was made on November 14, yet on the 24th Burnside was still waiting for pontoons, and it was not until December 11 that his army began to cross the Rappahannock.

Such a delay was more than enough for *Lee* to fathom his adversary's plan, and, on November 18, he ordered *Longstreet* from Culpeper Court House to Fredericksburg. The next day he wrote to *Jackson* stating that he did not anticipate "making a determined stand north of the North Anna,"[114] to which *Jackson* agreed, but the Richmond Government objected. In spite of this objection it was not until the 26th that he ordered[115] *Jackson* to join him, which he did on the 30th, five days after Burnside's

pontoons had arrived, and four days after the Aquia
Creek-Falmouth railroad was completed.[116]   To
delay so long in concentrating his army was to accept
a risk scarcely justifiable in the circumstances. Thus
by the end of November the two armies faced each
other on the Rappahannock, Burnside's numbering
122,000 and *Lee's* 78,500.[117]

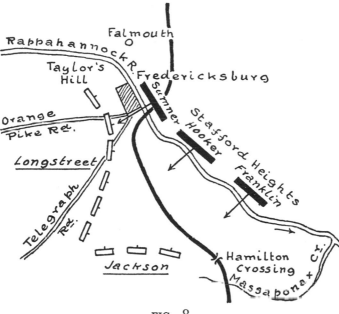

FIG. 8

Under cover of a powerful artillery assembled on
Stafford Heights, Burnside's plan was to cross the river
a little below Fredericksburg, with Sumner's corps on
his right, Hooker's in the centre, and Franklin's on
his left, and advance on *Lee*, whose position, a most
formidable one, ran from Hamilton Crossing a little
north of Massaponax Creek on the right to Taylor's
Hill immediately opposite Falmouth on the left.

171

This position was to all intents and purposes un-attackable, and to make matters worse Burnside selected *Lee's* left flank, his strongest, as the objective of his decisive attack.

On the 12th the Federal deployment on the right bank of the Rappahannock was completed, and, according to *Heros von Borcke, Jackson* and *Stuart* were of opinion that the best plan was "to make a sudden general attack upon the enemy under cover of the fog," but *Lee* wisely had decided against an offensive, "preferring to fight behind his entrenchments and to inflict a severe blow upon the enemy without the risk of fearful loss of life."[118]

The following morning, the 13th, the attack was launched, "A military panorama," writes *von Borcke*, "the grandeur of which I have never seen equalled. On they came in beautiful order, as if on parade, a moving forest of steel, their bayonets glistening in the bright sunlight."[119] At the sight of it *Jackson* turned to *von Borcke* and exclaimed: "Major, my men have sometimes failed *to take* a position, but *to defend* one never! I am glad the Yankees are coming."[120] Every assault was shattered, Burnside losing 12,653 men to *Lee's* 5,309.[121]

Burnside's repulse was complete, and *Lee* still had in hand two-thirds of his force intact.[122] *Taylor* says: "It was certainly the most easily won of all the great battles of the war."[123] "It was very cold and very clear," writes *Robert Stiles*, "and the aurora borealis of the night of December 13th, 1862, surpassed in splendour any like exhibition I ever saw."[124] For *Lee* to have attacked that night was probably impossible, but when on the following morning Burnside's army remained inactive and still on the right bank of the Rappahannock with its back to the river, an opportunity was offered to the Confederate commander which seldom occurs in war. It is true that the guns on Stafford Heights covered the Federal forces; nevertheless in the early morning mist of the 14th it would have been possible for *Lee* to have advanced so close to his enemy as to have rendered their protective fire as dangerous to friend as to foe. "Had *Lee*, on the morning of the 14th," writes Chesney, "thrown his whole force frankly against the Northern Army, reduced as the latter was in numbers, and much more in morale by its severe repulse, it is scarcely to be doubted that a mighty advantage would have been obtained. . . . It is possible, indeed, that the scenes of Leipsic or the Beresina might have been repeated on the Rappahannock, and the greater part of the Federal corps have been captured or destroyed. . . ."[125] But no, on the evening of the 13th no preparations for a counter-offensive were made, "Our commander-in-chief," says Major *von Borcke*, "adhering to his earliest idea, still objected to a forward movement, for which, in my judgment, the golden moment had now passed, had he inclined to favour it."[126] Further, he writes: "Not one of our Generals was aware of the magnitude of the victory we had gained, of the injury we had inflicted upon the enemy, and of the degree of demoralization in the hostile army; everybody regarded the work as but half done, and expected a renewal of the attack the following morning."[127]

When morning dawned, and no renewal of the battle was attempted, *Jackson* proposed a night attack, and, in order to avoid the confusion and mistakes so common in these operations, he recommended, says Colonel Fremantle, "that we should all strip ourselves perfectly naked."[128] (N.B. Time of year, mid-winter!)

When, on the 15th, Burnside recrossed the river and returned to his encampments at Falmouth, *Lee* was "extremely chagrined that the Federals should have succeeded in so cleverly making their escape."[129] Clever Burnside certainly was not, and *Lee* in this campaign missed his one and only opportunity of ending the war, just as McClellan missed his, on the morning of September 18 at Antietam.

Bragg and Grant in the West

Whilst *Lee* was establishing a reputation in the East which petrified the Union Government and in consequence addled its strategic brain, in the West, because there was no directing organ, a series of campaigns took place which was doomed to end in failure.

Corinth having been occupied by Halleck the West was open to him; yet he did nothing, worse, for in place of following up his enemy, compelling him to battle or driving him into Vicksburg, he suggested to Washington that the road was now clear for Buell and the Army of the Ohio to advance on Chattanooga and so drive the Confederates out of East Tennessee. This was agreed upon; his other two armies, the Army of the Tennessee under Grant and the Army of the Mississippi under Pope (soon to be relieved by Rosecrans), did nothing except repair the Memphis-Charleston railroad. Then came the crowning mercy, for, as we have seen, on July 11 Halleck was called to Washington to become General-in-Chief.

Grant, who had been in disgrace ever since the battle of Shiloh, now assumed command of the Armies of the Tennessee and Mississippi, which according to Halleck's orders were to constitute a reserve for Buell to draw on should he require more men. Watching the summer slip by Grant grew fretful, and, on July 30, he asked Halleck for permission to move against *Van Dorn*, then at Holly Springs and Grand Junction. This eventually was allowed, and on September 18 and October 2-6 he won two brilliant engagements over the Confederate forces at Iuka and Corinth. Of the second of these battles he himself says that it "was a crushing blow to the enemy, and felt by him much more than it was appreciated in the North."[130]

The battle of Memphis won by Admiral Davis on June 6, 1862, had gained for the Federal cause the command of the upper Mississippi, and the occupation of New Orleans by General Butler's troops, on May 1, had opened the mouth of this same river. And now Grant's victory at Corinth, compelling the Confederates to retire southwards, opened the way to Vicksburg, the strongest point left on the Mississippi and the main link between the Confederate States west and east of this river. Halleck should have advanced on Vicksburg in June. Grant recognised this, and three weeks after the battle of Corinth he wrote to Halleck: "You never have suggested to me any plan of operation in this department. . . . With small reinforcements at Memphis I think I would be able to move down the Mississippi Central road and cause the evacuation of Vicksburg."[131] On November 6 Halleck approved of this advance, and promised to send Grant 20,000 reinforcements.[132]

When this encouraging news was received, the position which confronted him was as follows: *Bragg*, who had replaced *Beauregard* in June, now opposed Buell in East Tennessee. Buell's danger lay in the exposure of his right flank, for even if he gained Chattanooga, a turning movement from the West, that is from Northern Alabama, might easily drive him out of it. Grant saw that his projected campaign depended on the possibility of Buell's advance, and that this advance depended for its security on his own army moving south on Vicksburg, which would draw Confederate reinforcements away from Buell. This is proved by the fact that, on November 6,[133] he informed Sherman that it was not possible for him to make a plan until he was certain what the other Union armies, not only Buell's but Burnside's, were going to do. He saw that all must co-operate, so he asked Halleck to inform him what the exact situation was. The only answer he received was: "Fight the enemy when you please."[134]

I will now turn to Buell and see what he was doing, for the failure of his campaign was destined to raise Grant to the pinnacle of his generalship.

Bragg, having succeeded *Beauregard* on June 27, found the bulk of his army at Tupelo, Buell's van having reached Decherd, some thirty miles north of Bridgeport, where, on July 13, *Forrest* raided his communications at Murfreesborough and forced him to halt. *Bragg* thereupon determined to regain East Tennessee by invading Middle Tennessee and Southern Kentucky. His plan was a bold one, namely, to reinforce *Kirby Smith* at Cumberland Gap and direct him on to Louisville, Buell's base of operations, whilst he advanced from Chattanooga. (See Map No. 2.)

Once again a raid, this time at Gallatin on the railway between Nashville and Bowling Green, forced Buell to halt; whereupon *Kirby Smith* advancing from Cumberland Gap pushed back the weak enemy force confronting him, and, on September 2, established his headquarters at Lexington, from where he threatened Louisville and Cincinnati. Meanwhile *Bragg* moved to Sparta, whereupon Buell concentrated his forces at Murfreesborough. A race north now took place,

Buell falling back on Bowling Green and *Bragg* advancing to Glasgow. Then, in place of forcing Buell further back and bringing *Kirby Smith* down on his rear, *Bragg* cast all strategy aside, and decided to join up with *Kirby Smith*, not to fight a battle but to inaugurate a Secessionist State capital at Frankfort! Thus Buell was saved and he fell back on Louisville.

On October 1 Buell moved out of Louisville. Sending a small force towards Frankfort to protect his left flank, he advanced on Bardstown which compelled *Bragg* to fall back, and on September 8, an encounter took place at Perryville. Not wishing to risk a battle against numerically superior forces, *Bragg* then fell back into East Tennessee, and, on October 30, Buell, who had fallen foul of Halleck, was replaced by General Rosecrans, the Army of the Ohio being renamed the Army of the Cumberland.

The winter having now set in Rosecrans decided not to advance south until he had repaired the railways and re-established his depots. This done, on December 26 he advanced from Nashville, and was confronted by *Bragg* at Murfreesborough, where, on the last day of the year, a sanguinary battle was fought. Though the results were indecisive *Bragg's* losses were so heavy that he decided on a withdrawal to Chattanooga, where he went into winter quarters.

Whilst Rosecrans was reorganizing his army, a shabby intrigue against Grant, in which Lincoln was involved, was taking place. The victories of Iuka and Corinth, which were entirely due to Grant's strategy, were attributed to Rosecrans, and it was because of this that Buell, a far abler soldier, had been relieved of his command. Now General McClernand, one of Grant's subordinates and a political general, had brought pressure to bear on Washington to place him in command of a force[135] to be collected at Memphis from where it was to move down the Mississippi and attack Vicksburg. Accidentally hearing of this proposal and realizing that McClernand was unfit for an independent command, Grant decided to hasten forward an operation he was then preparing. On November 13 he had informed Halleck that his cavalry had entered Holly Springs,[136] but that he

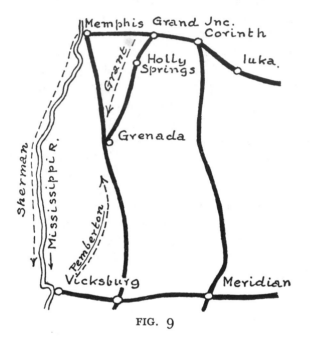

FIG. 9

did not intend to move further south until his line of communications was in full working order. Now he decided to move as soon as possible; to send Sherman by river from Memphis to Vicksburg whilst he advanced from Grand Junction. In short, his plan was to draw *Pemberton*, then in command at Jackson, towards Grenada, and by thus weakening the Confederate forces at Vicksburg facilitate Sherman's attack.

178

By December 12, when Grant was 60 miles south of Grand Junction, Sherman set out at the head of 32,000 men, landing at Milliken's Bend on Christmas Day. On December 29 he fought the battle of Chicaksaw Bluff and was repulsed. On January 2 McClernand, who was senior to him, arrived at Milliken's Bend and took over command of the expedition.

As Grant moved southwards his supply difficulties increased, and being a general who realized the importance of supplies, he established a depot at Holly Springs, informing[137] Halleck that on account of his long line of communications he would not, without further reinforcements, be able to advance beyond Grenada. Meanwhile Jefferson Davis, becoming thoroughly alarmed, appointed[138] General *Joseph E. Johnston* to command the whole of the Confederate forces distributed between the Blue Ridge and the Mississippi river. Arriving at Chattanooga *Johnston* ordered[139] *Bragg* to send out a force of cavalry and fall upon Grant's communications, with the result that, on December 20, *Van Dorn* made a dash for Holly Springs, surprised its garrison and destroyed the depot.

This raid completely upset Grant's plans, and fearing McClernand's incompetence, he asked[140] Halleck for authority to retire on Memphis and take command of the river expedition. Being now compelled to forage, he soon found that the country was so well stocked that he could have "pushed on to the rear of Vicksburg, and probably have succeeded in capturing the place."[141] On January 10 he returned to Memphis, and, on the 30th, arrived at Young's Point, at the mouth of the Yazoo river, and there took over command from McClernand.

CHAPTER V

THE GENERALSHIP OF GRANT AND LEE,
1863

The Vicksburg Campaign

ESTABLISHED at Young's Point, Grant's problem was a perplexing one, for having decided on the river approach there was no question of turning back, as such a move would have at once caused his many political enemies to pronounce him to be a vacillating general and to demand his removal. He could not attack the fortress frontally, that was out of the question, and he could not establish a base south of it until the winter rains had ceased. "From the moment of taking command in person," he says in his report, "I became satisfied that Vicksburg could only be turned from the south side."[1] But what was he to do? He could not sit still for four or five months, so he decided to carry out a series of operations amongst the bayous mainly to the north of Vicksburg, not only to keep his army employed but to keep *Pemberton* perplexed. His apparent slowness gave rise to an outcry that he was incompetent. Badeau tells us that "he was pronounced utterly destitute of genius or energy; his repeatedly baffled schemes declared to emanate from a brain utterly unfitted for such trials; his persistency was dogged obstinacy, his patience was sluggish dullness."[2]

At length, towards the end of March, the waters on the Louisiana bank of the Mississippi began to recede, and Grant determined to move south (see Map. No. 5). Sherman, McPherson, Logan and Wilson offered strong opposition to such an advance, Sherman asserting that the only way to take Vicksburg was to return to Memphis, and from there move down the Mississippi Central railroad. Grant saw that politically if not strategically, this was impossible, consequently he adhered to his plan, and in order to mystify his enemy he moved Sherman's corps 150 miles north of Vicksburg and sent Colonel Grierson on a raid of 600 miles through Mississippi—from La Grange to Baton Rouge. This force killed 100 and captured 500 Confederates at a cost to itself of three men killed and seven wounded.

On the night of April 16 Admiral Porter successfully ran a convoy past the Vicksburg batteries, and, on the 30th, at last, after four months' wrestling with rain, river and mud, Grant landed his army on the eastern bank of the Mississippi at Bruinsburg. "I felt a degree of relief scarcely ever equalled since," he writes, ". . . I was on dry ground on the same side of the river with the enemy. All the campaigns, labors, hardships and exposures from the month of December previous to this time that had been made and endured, were for the accomplishment of this one object." [3]

At 2 a.m., on May 1, McClernand's corps advanced on Port Gibson, and at that place defeated a Confederate force which, on the 3rd, was driven over the Big Black river; whereupon Grant established his base at Grand Gulf.

The problem which now faced him was one of exceptional difficulty. Vicksburg was immensely strong, and it commanded though it did not entirely block his sole line of supply—the Mississippi. His army numbered about 51,000 all told, *Pemberton's* [4] some* ten thousand less; but as Vicksburg was connected by railroad to the interior this number might rapidly be increased. To attack Vicksburg from the south was out of the question, for the risk of being taken in rear by forces assembled at Jackson was too great. Grant decided, therefore, to strike at the decisive point, the rear of Vicksburg; that is to advance on Jackson, and cut the fortress's line of supply. To do so and simultaneously maintain his own line of supply with Grand Gulf would have absorbed so large a force, that Grant (having learned his lesson at Holly Springs) decided on one of the boldest steps ever taken in war, namely, to "cut loose from" his "base, destroy the rebel forces in rear of Vicksburg and invest or capture the city."[5]   The audacity of this strategy completely bewildered *Pemberton*, and it may well bewilder the reader; for on May 2 the disastrous battle of Chancellorsville was begun, and any inkling in Washington of this audacious move would almost certainly have led to its cancellation. As it was, when Halleck learned of the movement he at once ordered Grant to return; but fortunately there was no telegraph line in operation south of Cairo, and Grant was well on his way before this order reached him.

Once he had made up his mind Grant moved like lightning. He called in Sherman, loaded five days' rations in his trains and keeping the Big Black river picketed, on the 7th he moved forward on Raymond, where he defeated a small force under General *Gregg*. On the 14th Jackson was in his hands, *Joseph Johnston* withdrawing to Canton whilst *Pemberton* was manoeuvring against Grant's none-existent line of communications in order to force him to fall back and protect it. Then turning westwards from Jackson, on May 16 he met *Pemberton* at Champion's Hill and defeated him, but owing to McClernand delaying his assault *Pemberton* escaped annihilation. The next day he was driven across the Big Black river and into Vicksburg. On the 18th Grant reached Walnut Hills immediately north of the fortress, and there, looking down upon the Mississippi, Sherman said to him: "Until this moment I never thought your expedition a success. I never could see the end clearly, until now. But this is a campaign; this is a success, if we never take the town."[7]

"Relying," as he says, "upon the demoralization of the enemy,"[8] on the 19th Grant ordered a general assault on the fortification; this failed. Foolishly, so I think, he ordered another on the 22nd, and this failing also he resorted to a regular siege, lines of circumvallation being dug from Haines's Bluff to Warrenton, and of countervallation from the Yazoo to the Big Black river. At 10 a.m., on July 4, *Pemberton* surrendered the fortress and 31,000 men. So ended one of the most remarkable campaigns in history.

The losses of this campaign are instructive. Between April 30 and July 4 Grant lost 1,243 killed, 7,095 wounded and 535 missing, a total of 8,873;[9] he killed and wounded about 10,000 Confederates and captured 37,000;[10] among these were 2,153 officers, of whom 15 were generals; also 172 cannon fell into his hands.

The lightness of the Federal casualties is remarkable, and it was entirely due to Grant's superb strategy, a strategy based on surprise and which surprise alone justified. In the first eighteen days after crossing the Mississippi, he established his base at Grand Gulf, fought five battles—Port Gibson, Raymond, Jackson, Champion's Hill and Big Black river, and marched 200 miles carrying only five days' rations, and for the rest living on the country. Well may Greene say:

"We must go back to the campaigns of Napoleon to find equally brilliant results accomplished in the same space of time with such small loss."[11]

The fall of Vicksburg was a staggering blow to the South, and when, on July 9, Port Hudson surrendered to General Banks the Mississippi became a Federal river, and the Confederacy was split in two; with the result that not only were the cotton growing eastern States cut off from the stock raising western, but what was far more disastrous, the sally-port was now definitely turned, and could at any moment be threatened from the east.

To take advantage of this situation, on July 18 Grant suggested[12] that an expedition should set out from New Orleans with the object of capturing Mobile, whence by operating northwards towards Montgomery, *Bragg*, at Chattanooga, would be compelled to detach troops to protect his rear. Again he repeated this vital suggestion in August and September, but the only result was that for purely political reasons his army was broken up and scattered to the winds as it had been after the occupation of Corinth. Then suddenly, on September 29, when he was lying in bed at New Orleans suffering from an injured leg, an order was dispatched to him by Halleck calling for all available reserves to be hurried north to the relief of Chattanooga.

Battle of Chancellorsville

Before I enquire into the reasons for this urgent appeal I must turn back to the eastern theatre of the war and outline what had taken place there after Burnside's decisive repulse at Fredericksburg. On January 26 this general had been relieved by General Joseph Hooker, a bold but insubordinate officer, who

184

had actively intrigued against Burnside. Once in command Hooker set to work with a thoroughness unrivalled since the dismissal of McClellan to discipline his army and so prepare it for yet another advance on Richmond.

We now come to *Lee's* masterpiece in audacity—the battle of Chancellorsville, a battle in which the combination of *Lee* and *Jackson* was seen at its best, and yet a battle which Hamlin says "seems to have been a tragedy of errors,"[13] not only on the part of Hooker but of *Lee*. The main reason for this was, that the complexity of the two plans, combined with the complexity of this particular theatre of war, placed far too great a strain on the staffs of the contending armies. Both plans, as we shall see, were of a high order; but it is one thing to devise a brilliant operation of war and quite another thing to carry it out, especially if the machinery of control is defective. Both generals divided their forces in an enclosed and thickly wooded country, a country in which the control of separated forces would even to-day with wireless telegraphy be a most difficult operation.

This battle from the grand-strategical point of view was also strongly influenced by a change in Northern politics. Hitherto the hopes of the South had firmly rested upon European intervention; but, on January 1, 1863, these hopes were undermined by Lincoln signing the Proclamation of Emancipation, which not only abolished slavery but won over British public opinion.[14] Though its immediate influence in the North and on the Northern armies[15] was to create dissension, it covered the South with a pall of gloom, and was in fact a decisive moral victory. It was in the midst of this excitement that General Hooker took over command of the Army of the Potomac.

Meanwhile *Lee's* army clung to the Rappahannock

185

(see Map No. 6), not that it was threatened, or had lost courage and confidence, but that its defective administration reduced it almost to ruin. *Fitzhugh Lee* says: ". . . the troops were scantily clothed, rations for men and animals meager. The shelters were poor, and through them broke the sun, rains and winds."[16] Here in the forest land and the ravines 63,000 men were bivouacked, and opposite them lay encamped Hooker's army, 130,000 strong, stretching from Falmouth to Fletcher's Chapel.

Hooker's plan was a bold one, too bold for his subordinates, his staff and himself. It would seem that it was based on *Lee's* strategy at the Second Battle of Manassas; for he decided to divide his army into two separated wings, the left under General Sedgwick was to cross the Rappahannock below Fredericksburg, threaten, and so hold, the bulk of *Lee's* army, whilst he himself with the remaining half cross above this town. This he considered would compel *Lee* to retire, when both halves would unite and pursue.

On April 28 and 29 Hooker's army crossed the Rappahannock and, on the 30th, the right wing was concentrated about Chancellorsville. Then he committed his first blunder; he sent his cavalry, 10,000 strong under General Stoneman,[17] on a raid towards Richmond. His next blunder was a mental one; his move thus far had proved so successful that he considered *Lee* "must either ingloriously fly, or come out from behind his defences and give us battle on our own ground, where certain destruction awaits him."[18]

He little knew his enemy, and this mental picture of him proved his ruin. *Lee*, on the 28th, when Sedgwick crossed, took up the defensive position he had occupied at the battle of Fredericksburg.[19] Then, on the 29th, he began to close in on his left, and early on the 30th he made up his mind. He says: "The enemy in our front near Fredericksburg continued inactive, and it was now apparent that the main attack would be made upon our flank and rear. It was, therefore, determined to leave sufficient troops to hold our lines, and with the main body of our army to give battle to the approaching column."[20]

On May 1 both sides advanced, when, about 1 p.m., Hooker, hearing of *Lee's* approach, cancelled the advance and withdrew closer in towards Chancellorsville; meanwhile Sedgwick carried out a mild demonstration in the vicinity of Fredericksburg.

About sunset *Jackson*, who had followed up Hooker's withdrawal, sent word to *Lee* that he was checked by the enemy at Chancellorsville. *Lee* at once rode to the front, meeting *Jackson* "in the south-east angle of Chancellorsville and Catherine Forge road." There, at about 10 p.m., a report having been received that Hooker's front was too strong to be attacked, *Lee* with a map in his hand, turned to *Jackson* and said: " 'How can we get at these people?' To which *Jackson* replied, in effect, 'You know best. Show me what to do, and we will try to do it.' General *Lee* looked thoughtfully at the map; then indicated on it and explained the movement he desired General *Jackson* to make, and closed by saying, 'General *Stuart* will cover your movement with his cavalry.' General *Jackson* listened attentively, and his face lighted up with a smile while General *Lee* was speaking. Then rising and touching his cap, he said, 'My troops will move at four o'clock.' "[21]

What was the movement indicated? About 13,000 men under *Early* had been left to hold Sedgwick at Fredericksburg; of the remaining 46,000, *Lee* decided to hold Hooker's 72,000 with 14,000 and march *Jackson* with 32,000 men ten or more miles round Hooker's front and right flank and fall upon his right

187

rear. This plan was similar to that attempted by the Russians and Austrians at Austerlitz, but *Lee* realized that Hooker was no Napoleon; nevertheless this division of force was without exception one of the most audacious in the history of war. His army was now divided into three fragments: his right safe enough for the time being, for it was strongly entrenched and could, if necessary, fall back on

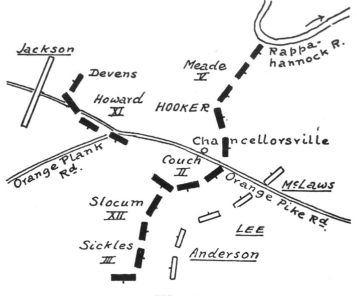

FIG. 10

Richmond; his left strong enough to look after itself; but his centre was so weak that had Hooker been even only moderately well served by cavalry he must have discovered its weakness, when he could scarcely have failed to destroy it. Nevertheless *Lee* was right, he took a risk and he took it wisely; he knew that Stoneman was away, and he realized that the forest covered and shielded his audacity. This was not an Austerlitz campaign, this was a scalp hunt. At about 7 a.m.,[22] on May 2, *three hours late, Jackson* set out on his march westwards, and at 12.30 p.m., striking the Orange Pike road, came into contact with enemy pickets. Already at 9 a.m. his long column had been sighted through the woods,[23] and Hooker warned Howard who commanded the Eleventh Corps on the right of the Federal line to protect his exposed flank.[24] This was a wise precaution, but by 3 p.m., when he knew that more than half of *Lee's* army had moved westwards, he should have launched a bold attack on the weak Confederate centre, held by *Anderson* and *McLaws,* and simultaneously have ordered Sedgwick forward at top speed. He seems to have been hallucinated by the idea that *Lee* was retiring towards Culpeper Court House, and that once his enemy was out of the way all he himself would have to do was to advance on Richmond.

Jackson took ten hours to march twelve miles and deploy at right-angles to Howard's right, and it was not until 5.15 p.m. that he gave the order to attack.[25] "A more ridiculous and stupid surprise did not occur in the history of the Civil War,"[26] says Hamlin, and I think that this is no over-statement, for General Devens on Howard's right knew the attack was coming. The pickets of the Eleventh Corps were not surprised, but no proper distribution of defence in depth had been made, consequently when the picket line broke it was hurled back like an explosive bomb on to the unprepared troops in rear. By 8.30 p.m. *Jackson's* troops had advanced about two miles, and were in considerable confusion when he rode forward to reconnoitre and fell mortally wounded by the fire of his own men. For *Lee* this was a calamity of the first order; the fate of Hooker's army was in the balance; but when *Jackson* fell no one knew what his

object was—presumably to cut Hooker off from the
United States ford. About midnight *Stuart* took over
command, but as Major McClellan says: he "had
no information . . . concerning his [*Jackson's*] plans
. . . and he was of course ignorant of the position of
the troops . . . the fall of *Jackson* developed the fact
that no one of his subordinates had received from him
the least intimation of his plans and intentions. . . ."²⁷

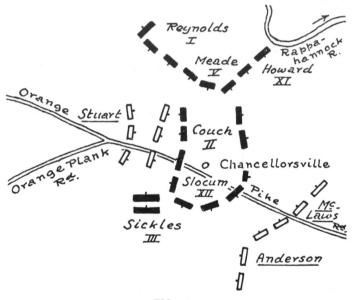

FIG. II

At 3.30 a.m., on the 3rd, *Lee* ordered *Stuart* to turn
the enemy's right and simultaneously "drive him from
Chancellorsville,"²⁸ as this would enable the left
wing and the centre of the Confederate forces to
re-unite. This was not a feasible operation, for Hooker
had 43,000 men at Chancellorsville and 42,000
covering the United States ford. In fact *Lee* should
have at once withdrawn *Stuart*, for his position was

perilous in the extreme.[29] Hooker was, however, morally beaten, and though at 8.45 a.m., when *Stuart's* attack had failed, this general was in a more desperate position than Howard had been the day before, Hooker did nothing. Half an hour later he was stunned by some falling masonry. Regaining consciousness he handed his command over to General Couch, instructing him to withdraw the army. At 10 a.m. *Lee's* attention was suddenly directed towards Fredericksburg.

On May 2 Hooker had ordered Sedgwick to advance, which he did, coming into contact with *Early* who, with 9,000 infantry, occupied an entrenched line six miles in length. On the next day he attacked, and at 11 a.m. carried Marye's Heights and Lee's Hill, whereupon *Early* fell back part of his force along the Orange Pike road and part along the Telegraph road, for his little army had been cut in half.

Hearing of Sedgwick's advance, *Lee* ordered *McLaws* to reinforce that part of *Early's* force on the Orange Pike road, which resulted in an engagement at Salem Heights. This was sound strategy, but it weakened *Lee* at Chancellorsville, and so should have roused Hooker to the importance of pressing *Lee*. Hooker, however, did nothing outside instructing Sedgwick to look after himself. Finding that Hooker was inanimate, on the 4th *Lee* sent *Anderson* to reinforce *McLaws* and *Early*, and took personal charge of his right wing. *Early*, who had re-occupied Marye's Heights, was repulsed, and *Anderson* and *McLaws* were held up. This action ended the battle, for that night Hooker decided to withdraw to the left bank of the Rappahannock, which he did on the following day, having lost 16,845 men to *Lee's* 12,764.[30]

Thus ended *Lee's* greatest battle, a battle which it is difficult to assess, as it was for the most part fought in densely wooded country where numbers were of less account than audacity and celerity of movement. True, there was no pursuit, no rout, no decisive tactical victory; but to have attempted a pursuit would have been madness, for *Lee's* losses had been in proportion greater than his enemy's, and so indifferent was the administration of his army that at

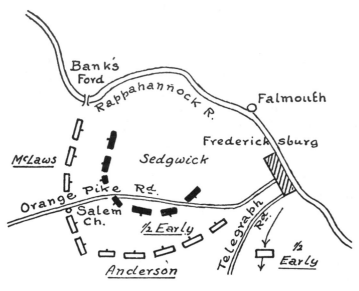

FIG. 12

no time in the war was it in a fit state to carry out a pursuit. To *Lee* the Wilderness had been his staunchest ally. It was not only a natural fortress protecting Richmond, but a spider's web to any army advancing on Richmond from the north. *Lee* never fully realized this, for had he done so his strategy would have been based upon manoeuvring his enemy again and again into this entanglement and there defeating him.

The Gettysburg Campaign

It will be remembered that the policy of the Confederate Government had from the opening of the war been a defensive one; *Lee*, however, had never held this opinion, and though circumstances had compelled him again and again, like a spider, to retire into the web of the Wilderness, it was towards Northern Virginia that his eyes were fixed. On April 9 he had written to Seddon: "Should General Hooker's army assume the defensive, the readiest method of relieving the pressure upon General *Johnston* and General *Beauregard* would be for this army to cross into Maryland."[31] And now that Hooker had been defeated he returned to this idea though circumstances had vastly changed, for Grant was on his way to Vicksburg and more than ever did *Johnston* require assistance.

In this change in the strategical situation what was the best course to adopt? There were two only: Either to co-operate with *Johnston*, or make a diversion which would compel the Federal Government to recall Grant. The first was suggested by *Beauregard*, who was probably the ablest of the Confederate generals, the second was proposed by *Lee*—the most noted.

Beauregard saw clearly that the decisive point lay in the West and not in the East, and he advised a campaign in Tennessee and Kentucky to relieve the Mississippi Valley and Vicksburg, strong reinforcements being temporarily drawn from the Army of Northern Virginia for this purpose.[32] *Lee* thought otherwise, for he was so obsessed by the idea of threatening Washington in order to relieve Northern Virginia, that throughout his generalship he never saw the war as a whole. On June 8 he wrote to Seddon, the Southern War Minister, explaining that it was no good remaining on the defensive,[33] and two days later he points out to Jefferson Davis that every encouragement should be given to the peace party in the North.[34] How he expected to accomplish this end by invasion, which would at once rouse the North, as it eventually did, can only be explained by the fact that he and the President were still gazing at Europe. Davis certainly, if not *Lee* also, was unaware that Lincoln's Emancipation Proclamation had once and for all settled the possibility of intervention. On the 10th Seddon answered *Lee's* letter of the 8th, saying: "I concur entirely in your views of the importance of aggressive movements by your army";[35] yet it is strange that Stephens, the Vice-President, knew nothing of this decision until *Lee* crossed the Potomac on the 23rd.

Stephens wanted to negotiate for peace, and he foresaw rightly that *Lee's* offensive would strengthen and not weaken the war party in the North; but Seddon thought that Lincoln would more likely listen to terms of peace if *Lee's* army was actually threatening Washington than if it was lying quietly on the Rappahannock.[36] Stephens was strongly of opinion that *Lee* should have remained on the defensive and have detached a strong force to assist *Johnston* against Grant at Vicksburg.[37]

In brief, the reasons for the forthcoming campaign were confused. Something had to be done to save Vicksburg; something had to be done to prevent Hooker recrossing the Rappahannock; something had to be done to win European recognition, or compel the North to consider terms of peace; and added to all these, as Colonel *Taylor* says, was *Lee's* design to free the State of Virginia from the presence of the enemy.[38]

Lee's plan was to move down the Shenandoah Valley, penetrate into Pennsylvania in the direction of Chambersburg, York or Gettysburg (see Map No. 4);

if opportunity should arise, defeat the Federal army in a pitched battle, drive it across the Susquehanna, and thus cause the evacuation of Washington.[39] In all he had 57,000 infantry, 9,000 cavalry and 250 guns.

Picketing the Rappahannock with his cavalry, and leaving *Hill's* corps at Fredericksburg, on June 2 and 4 he moved *Ewell's* and *Longstreet's* corps to Culpeper Court House, and when Hooker, on the 13th, was ordered to fall back and defend the approaches to Washington, *Hill* was called up and the whole army began to cross the Potomac at Shepherdstown and Williamsport on the 23rd, completing its crossing two days later.

On the 23rd *Lee* seems to have first realized that the North was not so demoralized as he had supposed. He wrote to Davis suggesting that an army should be raised under General *Beauregard*, and pushed forward to threaten Washington from the south.[40] Again he made the same suggestion on the 25th; for he discovered that his advance "has aroused the Federal Government and people to great exertions and it is incumbent upon us to call forth all our energies."[41] In spite of the fact that he now began to realize that he had stirred up a hornet's nest, he committed the same blunder Hooker committed at the opening of the battle of Chancellorsville—he sent the bulk of his cavalry under *Stuart* on a raid.

Lee's orders[42] were as usual vague. Leaving the decision to *Stuart*, he instructed him to carry out a variety of operations: To hold the mountain passes south of the Potomac, raid round the rear of Hooker's forces then about Leesburg, damage his communications and eventually place himself on the right of General *Ewell* about York in Pennsylvania.

Stuart moved off on the 24th, bumped into Hancock's corps, swung round him, capturing a Federal wagon train near Rockville, which so greatly delayed his march that his invaluable services were lost to *Lee* until July 2.

Hearing that Confederate troops had crossed the Potomac, Hooker followed suit on the 26th and 27th, moving on Frederick City where, on the morning of the 28th, he was ordered[43] to hand over his command to General Meade, who decided to move on Harrisburg and deliver battle with the enemy wherever met.[44] Meanwhile *Lee*, hearing of Hooker's crossing, but for lack of cavalry not being able to ascertain the enemy's intentions, ordered a concentration of his army about Cashtown; *Ewell* in the van was instructed to move directly on Cashtown, or by the Gettysburg turnpike; as *Lee* says himself: "The advance of the enemy to the latter place was unknown,"[45] consequently, the weather having broken, the march of the columns was not hurried.

On the 30th Meade ordered two of his seven corps, namely, Reynold's and Howard's, to move on Gettysburg where, early the next day, July 1, the Federal cavalry came into contact with part of *Hill's* corps. This led to a battle between *Hill's* and *Ewell's* corps on the one side and Howard's and Reynold's supported by part of Slocum's on the other. The result of this engagement was that the Federal forces were driven through Gettysburg, and took up a strong position on Seminary Ridge immediately south of the town (see Map No. 7).

It had not been *Lee's* intention to fight a battle so far from his base; this he tells us in his report, in which he says: ". . . but, finding ourselves unexpectedly confronted by the Federal Army, it became a matter of difficulty to withdraw through the mountains with our large trains. At the same time the country was unfavourable for collecting supplies while in the presence of the enemy's main body, as he was enabled to restrain our foraging parties by occupying the passes of the mountains with regular and local troops. A battle thus became, in a measure, unavoidable."[46] In short, his defective supply arrangements and the absence of his cavalry (to disengage himself) compelled him to fight, and to fight an offensive action in place of a defensive one; for, as he had to live on the country, it was impossible for him to stand still for any length of time.

By the morning of the 2nd Meade had four corps in line, his left resting on Round Top hill and his right on Cemetery hill and Culp's hill. The position was an exceedingly strong one, and one which could not be attacked frontally with an assurance of success. *Longstreet* suggested moving round Meade's left and so compelling him to attack; but *Lee* could not move and forage simultaneously, his defective supply system *compelled him* to attack. At 7 p.m., on the 1st, he had formed no plans outside attacking Culp's Hill;[47] then, according to *Fitzhugh Lee*, he decided to turn Meade's left with *Longstreet's* corps, demonstrate against his centre and right with *Hill's* and *Ewell's* corps, and convert this demonstration into a real attack directly *Longstreet's* attack succeeded.[48]

This was a thoroughly bad plan, because for success it depended on the earliest possible attack and the most careful timing to effect co-operation; further, *Lee's* troops were by no means concentrated, and to make things worse he issued no written operation orders.[49] As was his custom, he relied on verbal instructions, and left all detail to his subordinates. General *Pendleton* says[50] *Lee* instructed *Longstreet* to attack at sunrise; Colonel *Taylor* says that he never heard of such an attack,[51] and he is the more likely to be correct, for at 5 a.m. Colonel Fremantle tells

us that seated quite close to him were Generals *Lee,
Hill, Longstreet* and *Hood* in consultation.[52] *Lee* then
visited Seminary Ridge, and according to Colonel
Marshall, "at about 11 o'clock issued orders to General
Longstreet to begin his attack upon the enemy's left as
soon as possible."[53] *Longstreet* was not ready, three of
his brigades were still on the line of march, further
reconnaissances had to be made and a covered line of
approach discovered, and it was not until 4 p.m. that
the attack was launched. Though it drove in the
advanced troops on Meade's left, it did not affect its
object, namely, to take his left in reverse. The truth
is that *Longstreet's* force was not strong enough for
this operation. Meanwhile on *Lee's* left *Ewell* attacked
the Federal right, but accomplished little outside a
lodgment.

Thus the second day of the battle led to no decision,
not only because *Lee's* army was too weak, but because
he maintained no grip over the operations. Colonel
Fremantle writes: "What I remarked especially was,
that during the whole time the firing continued, he
only sent one message, and only received one report.
It is evidently his system to arrange the plan thoroughly
with the three corps commanders, and then leave
to them the duty of modifying and carrying it out
to the best of their abilities."[54] But when things go
wrong, how can subordinates modify a plan? They
can only muddle it. This is what happened during
this day's fighting; but such an "overweening
confidence" in the superiority of his soldiers over his
enemy possessed him, that he decided to continue the
battle, and in spite of the fact that Meade had now
assembled his entire army on the heights of Gettysburg.

The partial success of *Longstreet* on the 2nd, in spite
of the muddle that had taken place, persuaded *Lee*
that with proper concerted action and the support of

artillery, it was still possible to assault and break through Meade's front.[55] *Longstreet*, who was detailed to carry out this attack supported by *Ewell* on his left, was opposed to this operation, because his assaulting columns, 15,000 strong, would have to march "a mile under concentrated battery fire, and a thousand yards under long range musketry."[56]

The assault was to be made against Meade's left centre, the column consisting of two brigades of *Pickett's* division in front and one in second line with *Wilcox's* brigade in rear of its right, and *Heth's* division in echelon on *Pickett's* left. The field was open, and hitherto *Lee's* army had fought in wooded and broken country "which," Colonel *Taylor* writes: "in some respects unfavourable for the manoeuvres of large armies, was of decided advantage to us; for, in moving upon the enemy through bodies of woods, or in a broken, rolling country, not only was the enemy at a loss how to estimate our strength, but our own men were not impressed with that sense of insecurity which must have resulted from a thorough knowledge of their own weakness."[57] According to *Taylor*, *Hood* and *McLaws* should have moved forward in support of the assault, "as they were ordered to do by General *Lee*." He states that Colonel *C. S. Venable*, one of *Lee's* staff officers, heard *Lee* give this order;[58] but *Longstreet* states that *Lee* decided that these divisions "could remain on the defensive line."[59] As *Lee* issued no written orders it is impossible to say who is right.

Between 10 and 11 a.m. the cannonade opened; practically the whole of the Confederate artillery, 138 guns, having been brought into position on the Emmitsburg road and Seminary Ridge to crush Meade's centre. General Hunt, Meade's chief of artillery, realizing what this bombardment meant, namely, the preparation of an assault, ordered the

199

Federal guns to cease fire and save their ammunition for the inevitable infantry attack.[60]   At 1.40 p.m.[61] General *Alexander, Lee's* chief of artillery, finding that his ammunition was running short, at 2.30 p.m.[62] *Pickett* was ordered to advance.

"The infantry," says *Alexander,* "had no sooner debouched on the plain than all the [Federal] line, which had been nearly silent, broke out again with all its batteries."[63]   In spite of this terrific fire *Pickett* continued his forward movement, and though a small party of men, under General *Armistead,* actually penetrated the Federal position, his assault rolled back shattered.   The great attack had failed, as *Longstreet* had predicted; the battle of Gettysburg was lost. *Lee* had expected the impossible.   In the three days of this tremendous fighting he lost 22,638 men to Meade's 17,684.[64]

When *Pickett* failed Meade should have counter-attacked, and he should have made his preparations to do so directly the Confederate cannonade opened. "About this time," writes Colonel Fremantle, "it is difficult to exaggerate the critical state of affairs as they appeared" to the shattered Confederates.   "If the enemy or their general had shown any enterprise, there is no saying what might have happened. General *Lee* and his officers were evidently fully impressed with a sense of the situation. . . ."[65]   Meade, however, sat tight, though it was not until the night of the 4th that *Lee* began to withdraw, and even then Meade did nothing to molest him.   Not until the 13th was *Lee* able to begin fording the Potomac, which had been in flood; yet Meade did nothing, thus it happened that the Army of Northern Virginia once again found itself on the banks of the Rapidan.

The campaign had been a grotesque and costly failure, and I agree with Captain Battine when he says: "Gettysburg was the worst battle *Lee* ever fought, not excepting Malvern Hill."[66] It began as a political move and it ended in a political fiasco. On July 1 Jefferson Davis resolved to make an overture of peace, and he hoped that a great victory would compel Lincoln to consent to an immediate truce. On the 4th Vice-President Stephens asked to see Lincoln; Lincoln refused, for *Lee's* army lay shattered and Vicksburg had fallen. Had *Beauregard's* plan been accepted, there would have been no Gettysburg and Vicksburg might have still been holding out when these proposals were made.

Ever increasing desertions followed Gettysburg, and so numerous were they that success in the field was endangered.[67] Then, in November, followed a desultory campaign between Meade and *Lee* on the Rappahannock, known as the Mine Run Campaign, in which *Lee* did not attempt his former outflanking movements because the improved staff and cavalry of the Federal army did not warrant their risk. Then came winter with its physical and moral gloom.

Battles of Chickamauga and Chattanooga

Whilst Vicksburg was besieged in the west and Gettysburg was being fought in the east a third campaign was in progress in Tennessee. There, after his repulse of *Bragg* at Murfreesborough, Rosecrans halted for several months, for his line of communications was constantly raided and each raid meant time expended in repairs. Being short of cavalry and *Bragg* having been reinforced by *Pemberton's* cavalry under *Van Dorn*, Rosecrans asked Halleck for cavalry reinforcements, and these being refused, Rosecrans was in no great hurry to speed up his advance south, and this in spite of the fact that Grant was anxious that he should do so in order to prevent *Bragg* detaching troops to reinforce *Pemberton*. At length, on June 23, Rosecrans moved forward, drove *Bragg's* detachments back and occupied Stevenson.

In the original plan of operations it was the intention that whilst Rosecrans moved on Chattanooga Burnside was to protect his left flank by moving on Knoxville; but as he was ordered to send reinforcements to Grant this move was postponed, and without his co-operation Rosecrans, considering it too hazardous to push farther south, discontinued his advance until after the fall of Vicksburg, when Burnside's troops were returned to him.

On August 16 the advance began again, Rosecrans from Winchester and Burnside from Lexington (see Map No. 2). On September 7 *Bragg*, having been out-generalled by Rosecrans, was compelled to evacuate Chattanooga, cross the Tennessee and move to Lafayette. Two days later Chattanooga was occupied by Federal forces, and Rosecrans believing his enemy to be in full retreat pressed on after him, when, on the 12th, with his army strung out on a frontage of nearly sixty miles he found *Bragg* concentrated to meet him. Drawing in his scattered detachments but unable to fall back on Chattanooga he was compelled to accept battle, and on September 19-20 was severely defeated at Chickamauga and was driven back into Chattanooga where he was besieged and his line of communications cut. Meanwhile Burnside occupied Knoxville, and though by holding this town he prevented *Bragg* receiving reinforcements by the Virginia and East Tennessee railroad, he was in imminent danger of being invested.

The news of Rosecrans's defeat threw the Union Government into a panic, and the result was that, on

October 9, Grant was urgently called north, the Departments of Tennessee, Cumberland and Ohio being fused into the Military Division of the Mississippi and placed under his command. From Nashville he telegraphed General Thomas to take command of the Army of the Cumberland, and after making hasty arrangements for supplies and reinforcements, on the 19th he set out for Chattanooga where he arrived on the evening of the 23rd.

The sight which greeted him was a depressing one; the army was surrounded, overlooked and starving, its only line of supply being a cart track leading over sixty to seventy miles of mountainous country. Ten thousand horses and mules had died, and "not enough left to draw a single piece of artillery or even the ambulances to convey the sick."[68]

The situation could scarcely have been worse, consequently Grant was at his best. His first problem was to establish a line of supply, and this he did by re-opening the road to Bridgeport on the 27th, at the cost of 4 men killed and 17 wounded. The next was to hurry forward reinforcements: Hooker, then at Bridgeport, and Sherman at Corinth, were forthwith ordered on Chattanooga. Meanwhile Burnside getting into difficulties at Knoxville, *Bragg* seeing an opportunity of destroying him before Grant could concentrate his forces, on November 4 despatched *Longstreet* to Knoxville to round him up. This caused such alarm in Washington that Grant was plied with dispatch after dispatch to do something to relieve him.

The only thing Grant could do was to attack, but Thomas very rightly persuaded him to delay a forward movement.[69] Grant then decided on his plan, which was as follows (see Map No. 8): To effect a double envelopment with the forces of Sherman and Hooker pivoted on Thomas's army in the centre. Sherman to attack *Bragg's* right, threaten his rear and cut him off from the Knoxville road, whilst Hooker advanced from Lookout Valley against the left of *Bragg's* main position on Missionary Ridge, whilst Thomas threatened it frontally.

On November 22, hearing that Burnside had been attacked, Grant ordered[70] Thomas to make a reconnaissance in force next day. This was unfortunate, for it awoke *Bragg* to the danger threatening his right flank, which he at once strengthened.[71]

Sherman, whose advance had been delayed on account of the rains, was in position by the night of the 23rd, consequently the attack was ordered for the 24th. Moving forward at 2 a.m. he effected a lodgment on the left bank of the Tennessee river near the mouth of the South Chickamauga river, threw a bridge 1,350 feet in length over the Tennessee, crossed, attacked, and was held up a little north of Tunnel Hill. Meanwhile Hooker, after a running fight, occupied the point of Lookout Mountain.

Reinforcing his right, *Bragg* was able to hold up Sherman on the 25th; but as this weakened his left, Hooker was able to push on towards Rossville, but was delayed several hours in crossing Chattanooga river. Not reporting this delay, and Grant becoming anxious as to Sherman's safety, at 3.30 p.m. he ordered Thomas to advance and carry the rifle pits at the foot of Missionary Ridge. This was done, but the men were so elated that they did not stop there, and to Grant's consternation they swarmed up the four hundred feet slope and carried the main position. What had happened was this: Hooker's attack having made itself felt on *Bragg's* left, the Confederate centre had become demoralized, and broke back before Thomas's double assault.

The battle was decisive, *Bragg* losing 2,521 men

killed and wounded, 4,146 prisoners and 40 guns to Grant's 5,824 killed, wounded and missing. The pursuit was discontinued on the 27th in order to relieve Knoxville, to which place Sherman was despatched. Arriving there on December 6 he found that *Longstreet* had raised the siege on the 4th and was in full retreat up the Holston Valley.

The importance of this battle was, that it not only closed the enemy's sally-port, but it opened the back-door of the Confederacy.

CHAPTER VI

THE GENERALSHIP OF GRANT AND LEE,
1864-65

Plans for the 1864 Campaign

ONCE established at Chattanooga, the situation became clear; clear to Grant, if not to his Government, and, on December 7, 1863, he wrote as follows to Halleck:

". . . I take the liberty of suggesting a plan of campaign that I think will go far towards breaking down the rebellion before spring. . . . I propose . . . to move by way of New Orleans and Pascagoula on Mobile. I would hope to secure that place or its investment by the last of January. Should the enemy make an obstinate resistance at Mobile, I would fortify outside and leave a garrison sufficient to hold the garrison of the town, and with the balance of the army make a campaign into the interior of Alabama and possibly Georgia. . . . It seems to me that the move would secure the entire States of Alabama and Mississippi and part of Georgia, or force *Lee* to abandon Virginia and North Carolina. Without his force the enemy have not got army enough to resist the army I can take. . . ."[1]

This plan was not, however, adopted, and after a brief campaign in the Meridian area, in which Sherman did great damage to the railroads, Grant was called to Washington on March 3, and on the 9th was promoted to the rank of lieutenant-general and placed in command of the entire military forces of the United States.

In all Grant had eight weeks to prepare in; that is from March 10 to May 4, when his great combined campaign began. Not only was he unknown in the

East, but was acquainted with few of the officers of the Army of the Potomac, only once before had he visited Washington, and Lincoln he had never as yet met. The situation which confronted him is described by Badeau as follows: "A score of discordant armies; half a score of contrary campaigns; confusion and uncertainty in the field, doubt and dejection, and sometimes despondency at home; battles whose object none could perceive; a war whose issue none could foretell—it was chaos itself before light had appeared, or order was evolved,"[2]—and only eight weeks to evolve it in!

Lack of grand strategy had not only prolonged the war, but had encouraged the peace party in the North, and the next presidential elections were to take place in the autumn. Lincoln's position was not secure, and Grant realized this; he also realized that Washington must be rendered safe against any sudden thrust, and that by making it safe strategically he would disarm *Lee*.

Considering the possibilities of a coastal move, such as McClellan had carried out in 1862, he soon discarded this idea in favour of an overland advance, for such a movement would cover Washington. To effect this operation he decided to move direct upon *Lee*, whilst from Chattanooga Sherman manoeuvred against *Lee's* rear; the object of the Army of the Potomac, the immediate command of which he left to General Meade, being to hold *Lee* by constant attack. On April 9 he wrote to Meade: "*Lee's* army will be your objective point. Wherever *Lee's* army goes you will go also."[3] The Army of the Potomac, supported by the Ninth Corps under Burnside, was to constitute the fulcrum of his strategy; on it Sherman's lever at Chattanooga was to work.

Soon after assuming supreme command he sent

Sherman a letter and a map (see Map No. 9), which were received by that general on April 2. Unfortunately the letter has been lost, but the map clearly explains its contents, for on it are drawn a series of blue lines showing the proposed operations. Sherman answered this letter on April 5 saying: "From that map I see all, and glad am I that there are minds now at Washington able to devise; and for my part, if we can keep our counsels I believe I have the men and ability to march square up to the position assigned to me and to hold it. . . ."[4] Again, on April 10, he wrote: "Your two letters of April 4th are now before me and afford me infinite satisfaction. That we are now all to act in a common plan on a common center, looks like enlightened war."[5]

According to this map Sherman was to advance from Chattanooga on Atlanta, his first objective being the Confederate army under *Joseph E. Johnston*, who had replaced *Bragg*, and his second Atlanta.[6] From there the map shows that he was to move via Milledgeville on Savannah. To assist Sherman, General Banks, then engaged in a useless political campaign on the Red River, Louisiana, which Grant could not stop, was to hasten on his operations, occupy Shreveport, and then despatch a force of 25,000 men to Mobile.[7] Once this city was captured this force was to move on Montgomery, and threaten *Johnston* in rear, whilst Sherman attacked him in front. This part of Grant's plan, however, broke down, for, on April 8, Banks was decisively defeated.

Whilst Sherman was advancing, Meade's army was to be supported by two flanking armies—Sigel's operating in the Shenandoah Valley, and Butler's based on Fortress Monroe. Sigel was to move on Staunton and threaten the Virginia and Tennessee and the Virginia Central railroads (see Map No. 4),

208

whilst Butler was to move on Petersburg and Richmond. Realizing that the command of the sea was the backbone of his strategy, and well aware that efficient strategy is based upon adequate supply, Grant decided to move Meade's army as close to the coast as possible, for though on account of the nature of the country this was tactically a disadvantage, strategically it was essential, as the sea coast would enable him to change his base of supply at will; further, no troops would be required to protect this line of supply.

On April 29 he sent the following dispatch to Halleck, now Chief of Staff at Washington:

"The army will start with fifteen days' supplies; all the country affords will be gathered as we go along. This will no doubt enable us to go twenty-five days without further supplics, unless we should be forced to keep in the country between the Rapidan and the Chickahominy, in which case supplies might be required by way of the York or the Rappahannock Rivers. . . . When we get once established on the James River, there will be no further necessity of occupying the road south of Bull Run."[8]

This dispatch is interesting, for it is often asserted that in the forthcoming campaign Grant was out-generalled, and that *Lee* compelled him to abandon his overland campaign, base himself on the James and operate south of this river. Though Grant naturally hoped that he would be able to crush *Lee* north of Richmond, it must not be overlooked, as most historians have overlooked it, that this was not his central idea, which was *to hold Lee*, as it were in a vice, by constant attack, until Sherman could swing round from Chattanooga and not only attack *Lee's* source of supply—his rear—but telescope the Confederacy, now virtually reduced to Georgia, the Carolinas and Virginia, and crush it out of existence. In this dispatch Grant definitely expects that he will have to establish himself on the James river; already on April 9, when writing to Meade, he hinted[9] that this might be necessary, and shortly before the Wilderness campaign opened he informed Meade and Butler that it was his intention "to put both their armies south of the James River in case of failure to destroy *Lee* without it."[10] Further he informed Meade: "Should a siege of Richmond become necessary, siege guns, ammunition, and equipment can be got from the arsenals at Washington and Fort Monroe."[11]

Having elaborated his strategic plan, Grant turned to tactics: What was to be his method of fighting? He knew full well *Lee's* liking for manoeuvre, he also knew that the Confederate cause was on the wane, and what *Lee* dreaded most of all was a heavy casualty list. He decided, therefore, that his tactics must be offensive; that *Lee's* army must be reduced in strength by constant attack; that it must be thrown on the defensive, and that once it was reduced to defend itself freedom of movement would be denied to it.

Whilst this plan was being thought out and prepared for, what was happening in the Confederate camp? In September, 1862, *Longstreet* had pointed out to *Lee* that the next campaign should be fought in Tennessee, and that a defensive attitude should be assumed in Virginia.[12] *Lee* regarded such a campaign with doubt,[13] and all that came of this suggestion was that *Longstreet* was sent to reinforce *Bragg* at Chattanooga.

In December *Beauregard* once again sketched out a comprehensive plan of campaign which was forwarded to Richmond. He pointed out that the total available forces were 210,000, and that unless the Government ordered the army to concentrate against one decisive point, the war would end by it being beaten in detail. He suggested withdrawing 40,000 men from the East and creating an army of 100,000 strong in the West to operate against Grant by moving against his communications from about Knoxville.[14] Nothing came of this plan though *Lee* also saw the danger in the West. On December 3 he pointed out to Davis, "that the enemy may penetrate Georgia," and "I think that every effort should be made to concentrate as large a force as possible under the best commander to ensure the discomfiture of Grant's army."[15] To which Davis answered: "Could you consistently go to Dalton?"[16] to which *Lee* replied: "I can if desired, but of the expediency of the measure you can judge better than I. Unless it is intended that I should take permanent command, I can see no good that will result, even if in that event any could be accomplished."[17] Then, on January 10, 1864, *Longstreet* suggested transferring the whole of his infantry to the East and operating against Washington.[18] To which *Lee* answered: "I believe, however, that if Grant could be driven back and Mississippi and Tennessee recovered, it would do more to relieve the country and inspirit our people than the mere capture of Washington."[19] Then *Longstreet* wrote on February 2: "It seems to me that we should concentrate and recover Tennessee and Kentucky,"[20] and on March 4 he made similar and more detailed proposals.[21] To which *Lee* replied four days later: "I think the enemy's great effort will be in the West and we must concentrate our strength there to meet them."[22]

These extracts are sufficient to show two things: The total incapacity of the Confederate Government to control the war, and the total incapacity of *Lee* to control the Government. "The expediency of the measure you can judge better than I can" is not the voice of a great general but of a submissive clerk.

The winter of 1864 was one of great anxiety to *Lee*.

The army was in rags, half-starved and lacking in supplies, in clothing, shoes and equipment. Desertions were frequent, for life in the bivouacs on the Rapidan was all but unbearable; yet as Chesney says,[23] at this period the Confederacy was not so short of men as of discipline, not because the men were indifferent soldiers, they were superb soldiers, but because the administration of the army was so utterly rotten that even the staunchest soldiers succumbed to it. Added to these anxieties, as we have seen, was the doubt in *Lee's* mind as to what Grant would do. At length this uncertainty ended, for on April 5, 1864, *Lee* wrote to Davis that it is apparent that Richmond is Grant's object,[24] and the same day he issued a general order— "The army will be immediately placed in condition to march."[25] His opinion was that "a great battle would take place on the Rapidan,"[26] and his thoughts were at once attracted towards their old centre—a distracting raid down the Valley.[27]

His staunch ally was, however, no longer the Valley of Virginia, but the Wilderness; it covered his numerical weakness and his administrative deficiencies; his army had so long inhabited it that every cow-path, fastness and ravine was known to his men. *Lee's* whole strategy now depended upon holding this natural stronghold, of entrapping Grant in it, of preventing his army penetrating it, and so exhaust the patience and resources of the North. His idea was to bring his enemy to battle as soon as possible,[28] and his plan was an able one, namely, to let Grant cross the Rapidan and get throughly entangled in the forest, where numbers, cavalry and artillery were of little account, and there attack him in flank and force him to retire as he had forced away Hooker. For such an operation his distribution was, however, a faulty one (see Map No. 10); Army headquarters and *Hill's* corps were at Orange Court House, *Ewell's* along the Mine Run and *Stuart's* cavalry covered the front and right flank; but *Longstreet's* corps, at Gordonsville, was too far in rear to be able rapidly to support the other two. The result of this was that when, on May 5, the battle opened, *Lee* was unable to strike in full force, and had he been in a position to do so it is possible that his plan might have succeeded.

From the Wilderness to Cold Harbor

Grant's army, that is the Army of the Potomac and Burnside's corps, numbered about 115,000 officers and men of all arms "equipped for duty." Sheridan's Cavalry Corps (13,287) covered the front from northwest of Culpeper Court House on the right to near Richardsville on the left (see Maps No. 4 and No. 10); Army headquarters and the Fifth Corps, under Warren (25,663), were at and around Culpeper Court House; the Second Corps, under Hancock (28,333), south of Brandy Station; the Sixth Corps, Sedgwick (24,213) north of this place, and the Ninth Corps, Burnside (22,762), stretched from a little north of Rappahannock Station to within a few miles of Manassas Junction. South of the Rapidan stood *Lee*, as already described.

On May 4 and 5 all the Federal armies moved forward, on a common plan and towards a common centre: Grant on *Lee*, Sherman on *Johnston*, Sigel up the Valley, and Butler towards Richmond. It was a wonderful object lesson in co-operative effort when compared to the individual and unconnected operations which had hitherto characterized Federal strategy.

Strategically Grant's immediate problem, namely, the movement of the Army of the Potomac, was not difficult once the Rapidan was crossed, but tactically it was a plunge into a jungle in which numbers were of little account, and local knowledge of the highest value, where cavalry were virtually dismounted and artillery spiked, and where every extra wagon was an encumbrance. In the Wilderness of Virginia Hooker had met his fate, and Meade who, in 1863, had penetrated its fringes, had rapidly withdrawn from them and sought safety in more open ground. Here the

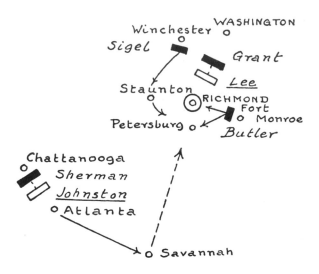

FIG. 13

clash took place on the 5th, and of the fighting Badeau says: it was "a wrestle as blind as midnight, a gloom that made manoeuvres impracticable, a jungle where regiments stumbled on each other and on the enemy by turns, firing sometimes into their own ranks, and guided often only by the crackling of the bushes or the cheers and cries that rose from the depths around."[29]

Tactically, Grant was not prepared for this type of

214

fighting—Indian warfare. His formations were far too heavy, his lines of attack too cumbersome, and his tactics too rigid. He had hoped, yet scarcely expected, to traverse the Wilderness without a battle; he should, therefore, on the 4th have pushed on as far as he could; but he did not do so, apparently because he was afraid of uncovering his trains. Had he, in place of attacking *Lee*, or rather counter-attacking *Lee* when *Lee* attacked, entrenched his position, let *Lee* attack it, and under its protection had he continued his movement forward, throwing up entrenchments on his right flank as he advanced, it is possible that he might have got through the Wilderness at considerably less loss, and yet have inflicted an equal loss on the Army of Northern Virginia, the tactics and very deficiencies in the organization of which made it more adaptable for forest warfare.

On the 5th, as Swinton says: "The action . . . was not so much a battle as the fierce grapple of two mighty wrestlers suddenly meeting."[30] On the 6th it was the same, both sides were fought to a standstill, and under cover of night *Lee* withdrew his army behind its entrenchments.

Tactically this battle was indecisive; the losses were heavy, Grant's numbering 17,666, and *Lee's*, though unknown, cannot have been less than 7,750.[31] Strategically it was the greatest Federal victory yet won in the East, for *Lee* was now thrown on the defensive—he was held. Thus, within forty-eight hours of crossing the Rapidan, did Grant gain his object—the fixing of *Lee*.

In this the first battle of the campaign, Grant's will to succeed, cost what it might, soon revealed to *Lee* that, in spite of the forest and the shelter it afforded, numbers in the end would count. Again and again throughout this campaign he writes: "Thanks to a merciful Providence our casualties have been small."[32] It was remarkable also in that, as Colonel Lyman says: "The great feature of this campaign is the extraordinary use made of earthworks. . . . When our line advances, there is the line of the enemy, nothing showing but the bayonets, and the battle-flags stuck on the top of the works. It is a rule that when the Rebels halt, the first day gives them a good rifle pit; the second a regular infantry parapet with artillery in position; and the third a parapet with an abattis in front and entrenched batteries behind. Sometimes they put this three days' work into the first twenty-four hours. Our men can, and do, do the same; but remember, our object is offense—to advance. You would be amazed to see how this country is intersected with field works, extending for miles and miles in different directions and marking the different strategic lines taken up by the two armies, as they warily move about each other."[33]

In this type of war *Lee* excelled. A field engineer by upbringing, and possessed of a wonderful tactical eye for defensive positions, after May 7 he fought with entrenchments in a manner which elicits our highest admiration. At 5 a.m. on the 7th he appears to have been under the illusion that Grant was retiring "in the direction of Chancellorsville."[34] To the Secretary of War he telegraphed on the 8th: "The enemy has abandoned his position and is moving towards Fredericksburg";[35] and to *Ewell* he wrote, "We must try and attack his rear."[36] Yet, on the 7th, Colonel *Taylor*, his Assistant Adjutant-General, sent the following message to *Stuart*: "The enemy now and then advance and feel our lines, and the general thinks there is nothing to indicate an intention on his part to retire, but rather that appearances would indicate an intention to move towards Spottsylvania Court

House,"[37] which contention is supported by General *Gordon*.[38]

As was so often the case, *Lee's* staff duties were muddled; nevertheless, on the morning of the 7th he ordered[39] *Anderson*, now in command of *Longstreet's* corps, for, like *Jackson*, this general had been wounded by his own men, to move to Spottsylvania on the morning of the 8th; but as *Anderson* could find no

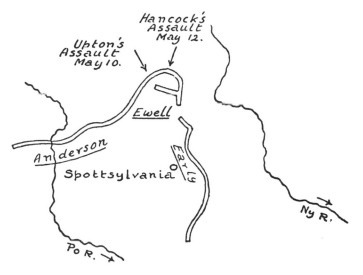

FIG. 14

place to bivouac, he did so that night, and as it happened short-headed Grant by a few hours.

In spite of his losses and the confusion which such a battle rendered inevitable, Grant was in no way dismayed. A lesser man would have halted and reorganized, but Grant determined to push on. To a staff officer he said: "To-night *Lee* will be retreating South,"[40] and within twenty-four hours of the battle being drawn, the Army of the Potomac was heading for Spottsylvania. There he found *Anderson* blocking his way, and there he learned that Sherman's and Sigel's advances were progressing, but that Butler was in difficulties. In order to relieve the pressure on Butler's army[41] he ordered Sheridan and the whole of the Cavalry Corps to "cut loose" and to proceed on a raid against the north of Richmond.

At Spottsylvania *Lee* ably entrenched himself between the rivers Po and Ny, his entrenchments taking the form of an inverted V. This enabled him to place the bulk of his men in line, and to use the garrison of one face of the V to reinforce the other as occasion demanded. The weak point was the apex, and this was not unnoticed by Grant, who, on the 10th, launched an attack under Colonel Upton against its western face and captured some 1,200 prisoners. This attack was so successful that he decided to employ the whole of Hancock's corps in an assault upon the apex of the salient. At 4.35 a.m. on the 12th Hancock moved forward through the mud and mist, marching on a compass bearing, and in massed formation struck the Confederate entrenchments and surged over them;[42] but his assault formations were so dense that the mass of his men at once melted into an uncontrollable mob. "You could see," says General Barlow, "men of all commands intermingled and lying, in some places forty deep, on the other side of the captured works, and on the slope which ran down from them."[43] At 5.45 a.m. came the first Confederate counter-attack; then the struggle for the "Bloody Angle" began, in which *Lee* lost between 9,000 and 10,000 officers and men, and Grant 6,820.[44]

Grant has been blamed for these persistent attacks, and mainly because it is not realized that had he attempted to manoeuvre *Lee* out of his position, which he might have done, he would have forced *Lee* back

towards Butler. This was the very thing he did not
want to do, for by holding him as far away from
Butler as he could, he facilitated his advance along
the James River, which was causing as great a consternation[45] in Richmond as *Jackson's* in the Valley
had to Washington two years before, which shows
the wisdom of this distracting movement.

Beauregard, then in command of the Petersburg
area, realizing that *Lee* must inevitably be forced out
of the Spottsylvania position, on May 12 put up the
following plan[46] to *Bragg*, then Chief of Staff to
Davis: *Lee* to fall back behind the Chickahominy
and send 10,000 men to *Beauregard*, who was also to
be reinforced by 5,000 from Richmond, bringing his
force up to 25,000. Butler to be attacked in flank and
destroyed, after which, whilst *Lee* held Grant's front,
Beauregard was to fall upon his left flank. Like all
Beauregard's plans, this was an admirable one; but
Jefferson Davis would not agree to it; nevertheless,
on the 15th, *Beauregard* attacked Butler at Drury's
Bluff and drove him back to Bermuda Hundred. On
the 18th *Beauregard* outlined a somewhat similar plan
in which he said: "Without such concentration
nothing decisive can be effected, and the picture
presented is one of ultimate starvation";[47] which was
only too true. Nothing, however, would move *Lee*,
and when, on the 19th, Davis informed him of
Beauregard's suggestion, *Lee* refused to make a decision,
leaving this to Davis.[48]

Thus far Grant's central idea had been that
wherever *Lee* went Meade should follow; for this he
now substituted a bolder one, namely, wherever
Meade went *Lee* should be compelled to follow. On
the 20th Hancock's corps was moved south to Guinea's
Station, and the next day *Lee* discovering this move
began to withdraw from his entrenchments; but he

was too wary a general to get involved with Hancock; instead he placed himself between Richmond and his enemy by falling back on a position in the neighbourhood of Hanover Junction immediately south of the North Anna River.

Once again Grant's manoeuvre had succeeded strategically, but tactically it had failed. It had moved *Lee* out of his entrenchments, but it had not brought him to battle in the open; far from it, for the works *Lee* now occupied had been constructed during the previous winter and were formidable in the extreme, and there can be little doubt that from them *Lee* should have assumed an offensive. Grant's situation was an anxious one, and realizing the difficulty and cost of an assault, and no longer having to consider Butler, who was bottled up at Bermuda Hundred, he determined on another flanking movement.

On the afternoon of the 25th he withdrew his forces across the North Anna, and directed[49] Meade to move on Hanover Town. This movement, which was a complex one on account of the proximity of the two armies, was carried out successfully, and a new battle front was established on Totopotomoy Creek. *Lee* followed suit, both armies drifting southwards, *Lee* covering Richmond and Grant hoping against hope to compel *Lee* to come out of his trenches. By June 1 both armies confronted each other in the vicinity of Old and New Cold Harbor; *Lee*'s right flank resting on the Chickahominy and his left extending north of Gaines's Mill, the locality in which McClellan was repulsed in 1862.

On this ground was fought the battle of Cold Harbor, a battle which in the history of the Civil War has been given a prominence it does not deserve. it was not a great battle or a decisive one, *Lee's* losses were slight and Grant's not excessive, for they amounted to 5,617, of which 1,100 were killed and 4,517 wounded;[50] by most historians these losses have been grossly exaggerated. Its notoriety may be traced to political reason. The North was growing weary; intrigue was rife; the presidential election was approaching, and Lincoln's position was by no means secure. All hoped for speedy victory, and as battle followed battle Grant's stock fell in terms of public opinion.

Grant was not blind to this situation. He realized the urgency of an early success; but he also realized that if he now refrained from attacking *Lee*, politically this would be construed as the failure of the entire campaign. The alternative was a frontal assault, and rightly, so I think, he decided on one, but his method was faulty in the extreme.

First he postponed his attack twenty-four hours, timing the assault for 4.30 a.m. on June 3, which gave *Lee* ample time to strengthen his position. Secondly, he ordered an attack *all along the line* in place of massing his guns opposite a fraction of *Lee's* front, and then after a heavy bombardment assaulting this fraction. As it happened, each of his divisions was taken in enfilade[51] as well as decimated by frontal fire, and all were so severely handled that the attack was decided in less than an hour.[52] General McMahon says,[53] that the time taken in the actual advance was not more than eight minutes; Swinton says[54] ten.

Grant's military excuse for fighting this battle was that as *Lee* refused to assume the offensive he considered him "whipped,"[55] and though afterwards he regretted ever having fought it, he undoubtedly believed that the morale of *Lee's* army was spent, and remembering the successful assaults at Missionary Ridge and Spottsylvania, he considered that one tremendous blow would overthrow his antagonist. Of Grant's offensive tactics Badeau says: "I have often heard him declare that there comes a time in every hard-fought battle when both armies are nearly or quite exhausted, and it seems impossible for either to do more; this he believed the turning-point; whichever after first renews the fight, is sure to win."[56] Unfortunately for Grant, though he expected the highest heroism from his own men, he failed to realize that his enemy was of the same stock.

The Petersburg Campaign

Grant was checked but not checkmated; to a lesser man Cold Harbor would have been a death blow, but to Grant it was to prove the stepping-stone of one of the most audacious and difficult operations of war ever attempted. Halleck suggested that Grant should invest Richmond from the north bank of the James; but as its most important lines of supply lay on its southern side, Grant saw that this suggestion was worthless. As *Lee's* front could no longer be attacked, he decided to attack *Lee's* rear—"to move the army to the south side of the James River by the enemy's right flank," in order to "cut off all his sources of supply except by the [James River] canal."[57]

Meanwhile, as *Beauregard* had foreseen, *Lee* had been forced back to the defences of Richmond, and even now in place of concentrating, as *Beauregard* suggested, he dispersed his forces. Not only did he send *Breckinridge's* division back to the Valley, but, on June 11, *Early* was ordered to proceed to this same locality and threaten Washington. It was his old game, now a little worn by constant application. This time there was no panic; at Fort Stevens outside the

Northern capital General Wright, in command of the reinforcing Sixth Corps which Grant had sent back from the James, met General McCook, who pointing out *Early's* pickets a few rods from the work said: "Well, Wright, there they are; I've nothing here but quartermaster's men and hospital bummers; the enemy can walk right in if he only tries; let's go down below and get some lager beer."[58] *Early* could have walked in, but had he done so he would never have walked out again; so wisely, he retired.

The detachment of *Early* seems to have had a curious psychological influence upon *Lee*. On June 7 *Beauregard* had telegraphed *Bragg*: "Should Grant have left *Lee's* front, he doubtless intends operations against Richmond along James River, probably on south side."[59] He pointed out the extreme danger Petersburg was in.[60] Two days later he writes: "The present movements of Grant's army have a significance which cannot have escaped your observation. He clearly seeks to move around *Lee's* forces, by an advance upon his left flank, in the direction of the James River, with a view to operate between that river and the Chickahominy, and in case of his meeting with no adequate resistance to plant himself on both sides of the former, throwing across it a pontoon bridge, as close to Chaffin's Bluff as circumstances may permit, and failing in this scheme, he may continue his rotary motion around Richmond, and attack by concentrating the whole of his army on the south side of the James River, using the fortified position at Bermuda Hundred Neck as a base for his operations."[61] (See Map No. 11.)

This was an exact picture of what was about to take place, for, on June 7, Grant, in order to rid himself of *Lee's* cavalry, ordered Sheridan to move on Charlottesville. It is an interesting picture this:

Lee weakening his already over weak forces at a time when he wanted every man, and Grant forcing *Lee* to weaken himself still more by sending out Sheridan to strike at the Confederate communications. Thus we see that whilst *Lee* looked northwards Grant thought southwards. His plan was to withdraw his army, cross the Chickahominy swamps, bridge the James, a tidal river 700 yards wide, shift his base of supplies from White House to City Point, and advance on Petersburg. To accomplish this move, which, as Badeau says: "transcended in difficulty and danger any that he had attempted during the campaign," he first strongly entrenched his front, and under cover of these entrenchments began to withdraw his army at nightfall on the 12th. This astonishing manoeuvre was effected within close range of *Lee's* army, and in a hostile country swarming with spies. Not until the 18th, as we shall see, did *Lee* become fully aware of what was happening.

Grant's plan entailed the seizing of Petersburg before *Lee* could come to the support of *Beauregard*, who held the city with a small garrison. General Smith and the Eighteenth Corps were detailed for this operation.[62] This corps was withdrawn from the Chickahominy on the 12th, and on the 14th Smith reported to General Butler, who strongly reinforced him. On the morning of the 15th he set out, and at about 10 a.m. came under range of the guns of Petersburg. From this hour until 5 p.m. he reconnoitred the position, and at length ordering his artillery up, discovered that the horses had been sent to water; this delayed the attack until 7 p.m. By 9 p.m., hearing that the first position was carried, he deemed "it wiser to hold what we had than . . . to lose what we had gained . . ."; these are his own words.[63]

Smith must have known that *Beauregard's* force was a weak one, actually it consisted of 2,200 artillery and infantry, and Smith had 18,000 troops. His delay and caution were inexcusable, he "feared to run any risk" and "preferred to sleep on his arms that night."[64]

The importance of Petersburg to Richmond and the Confederate forces was so great, and its occupation so vital to the fulfilment of Grant's strategy that General

FIG. 15

Smith's lack of energy may well be considered one of the most serious errors of the entire campaign. Though a highly educated soldier, this failure proved him to be totally unfitted for command. Muddle now followed muddle; Hancock, who should have followed Smith's corps at short interval, lost hours of invaluable time in awaiting an issue of rations,[65] and when he caught up with Smith, this general made no proper use of his corps.[66]

Meanwhile, on the 13th, *Lee* discovered that Grant had left his front[67] and simultaneously *Early* began his northern movement.[68] In place of recalling *Early*, the next day he wrote to Davis: "I think the enemy must be preparing to move south of the James," and further: "I apprehend that he may be sending troops up the James River with the view of getting possession of Petersburg before we can reinforce it."[69] He repeated this apprehension on the following day, and also wrote to Davis saying that "*Early* was in motion this morning at 3 o'clock and by daylight was clear of our camp. . . . *If you think it better to recall him,* please send a trusty messenger to overtake him to-night. I do not know that the necessity for his presence to-day is greater than it was yesterday. His troops would make us more secure here, but success in the Valley would relieve our difficulties that at present press heavily upon us."[70]

The italics in the above quotation are mine; not only do these words, as usual, throw the onus of decision on Davis, but they suggest that *Lee* considered that *Early* should not be recalled, and further, that even should Grant move south of the James and seize Petersburg, *Early's* attack on Northern nerves would force his recall from the James as it forced McClellan's in 1862. No other assumption can explain his lethargy between the 15th and 18th.

Fortunately for *Lee, Beauregard* played his part with consummate skill. He was in fact so weak that he was compelled to call in the garrison of the works at Bermuda Hundred. This unbottled Butler, and enabled him to advance and place his army between Petersburg and Richmond, which must inevitably have resulted in the fall of the capital. Once again he blundered, and lost the opportunity of a life's time. Meade, meanwhile, persisted in attacking Petersburg at its strongest point,[71] and in consequence wrecked Grant's strategy.

On the 15th *Beauregard* reported his position at Petersburg to be critical,[72] and *Lee* answered that he did "not know the position of Grant's army."[73] *Beauregard* was attacked on the 15th, 16th and 17th, and sent message after message asking for support; *Lee*, however, did nothing until the 17th, when he ordered *A. P. Hill* to move to Chaffin's Bluff.[74] Not until the 18th would he believe *Beauregard's* reports, when he telegraphed *Early*, "Grant is in front of Petersburg. Will be opposed there. Strike as quickly as you can, and if circumstances authorize, carry out the original plan, or move upon Petersburg without delay."[75]

Between June 13 and 18 no impartial critic can doubt that *Lee's* generalship was of a low order. General *Alexander* writes: "Thus the last, and perhaps the best, chances of Confederate success were not lost in the repulse at Gettysburg, nor in any combat of arms. They were lost during three days of lying in camp, believing that Grant was hemmed in by the broad part of the James below City Point, and had nowhere to go but to come and attack us."[76] Grant's constant attacks had hypnotized *Lee* into believing that his adversary had no other cards to play. He sees that Grant may cross the James, then he doubts that he will do so, and stakes all on his old bluff— a Valley raid. When he arrived at Petersburg at 11.30 a.m. on the 18th, *Beauregard* urged him to order *Hill's* and *Anderson's* corps to attack Grant's left flank and rear. "*Lee* refused his assent, on the ground that his troops needed rest, and that the defensive having been thus far so advantageous to him against Grant's offensive north of the James, and to *Beauregard*, at Petersburg, he preferred continuing the same mode of

warfare."[77] This meant the assumption of a passive
defensive, and *Lee* knew it, for, on June 21, he wrote to
Davis: "I hope your Excy will put no reliance in what
I can do individually, for I feel that will be very little.
The enemy has a strong position, and is able to deal us
more injury than from any other point he has ever
taken. Still we must try and defeat them. I fear he
will not attack us but advance by regular approaches.
He is so situated that I cannot attack him."[78]

From the date of this dispatch, that is from the
date Grant began to lay siege to Petersburg, the end
of the Confederacy, like a gathering storm cloud,
loomed over the horizon of the war, daily growing
greater and more leaden. Some reckoned on a
Northern political collapse, a refusal to re-nominate
Lincoln, and the consequent abandonment of the
war; but *Lee* knew that as long as Grant held him
at Richmond and Petersburg this was an event so
unlikely as to be beyond practical politics. Grant's
tactics of attrition were telling, and during the siege
of Petersburg they continued to tell for his shuttle-
cock operations of feinting here and striking there,
says *Lee*, "fatigue and exhaust our men, greatly
impairing their efficiency in battle."[79] The only
hope was to break this strangle-hold, to cut loose
from Richmond and transfer the struggle to some
other area. *Lee* looked furtively at *Early*. On June 29
he wrote to Davis: "I still think it is our policy to
draw the attention of the enemy to his own territory.
It may force Grant to attack me";[80] and then, on
July 11: "I fear I shall not be able to attack him to
advantage, and if I cannot I think it would be well to
reinforce General *Early*";[81] but where from?

Turning to Grant, we find no recrimination, no
excuses, no blame. His plan had been wrecked by
the incompetence of his subordinates. He once again

had failed, but he refused to accept failure, and instead modified his strategy without changing its central idea, which was to hold on to *Lee*. As he could not destroy *Lee* he would invest Petersburg, and then work round to the south of the city against *Lee's* lines of supply, the chief of which were the Weldon, the South Side and the Danville railroads. (See Map No. 11.) Though means vary, his idea remains constant, to hold fast to *Lee* so that Sherman's manoeuvre may continue.

Between June 18 and the end of October Grant waged incessant war on these railways, ever threatening Petersburg and so compelling the Confederate Government and *Lee* to concentrate on its protection. He realized that as long as Petersburg was in danger Richmond was threatened; not only would *Lee* be compelled to maintain a powerful force in its neighbourhood, but by doing so it would be most difficult for him to detach troops to oppose Sheridan now operating in the Valley, or to reinforce *Johnston*.

The Campaigns of Sheridan and Sherman

Whilst Grant was moving southwards through the Wilderness, attacking at Spottsylvania and on the Chickahominy, crossing the James and besieging Petersburg, it must be remembered that two other campaigns were in progress, namely, one in the Valley of Virginia and the other in Georgia, and that these two campaigns were as closely linked to his own as his was to them. These three were in fact essential parts of one grand campaign, and can only be correctly appreciated when related to each other.

In the Valley, on May 15, General Sigel had been badly defeated at Newmarket, and was replaced by

General Hunter who, on June 17, advanced to within five miles of Lynchburg. (See Map No. 4.) The next day meeting with *Early's* corps, sent north by *Lee* as already related, he retired into the Kanawha Valley, leaving the Shenandoah Valley open to *Early*, who forthwith advanced down it, and on July 11 threatened Washington. Foreseeing what was likely to happen, on the 5th Grant had already sent the Sixth Corps to Washington;[82] in consequence, on the 14th *Early* recrossed the Potomac and retired towards Strasburg. In order to close the Valley Grant determined systematically to devastate it, and to carry out this work General Sheridan was given the command of the troops in that area on August 7.

At first Sheridan got into difficulties with the politicians at Washington, which necessitated Grant visiting him. Then he got into his stride, and decisively defeated *Early* at Opequon Creek on September 19. Following him up he again defeated him at Fisher's Hill on the 22nd, and again at Cedar Creek on October 19. These victories had a most encouraging influence on the political situation.

Meanwhile Sherman's lever was moving forward on Grant's fulcrum—the Army of the Potomac; it consisted of 100,000 men and 254 guns, and was opposed by *Johnston* at the head of 43,000 men[83] at Dalton. Imaginative and fertile in resources, Sherman saw clearly that in spite of his numerical superiority every mile he advanced would lengthen his communications and so reduce his strength. He determined, therefore, not to do what *Johnston* wished him to do, namely, attack him in strongly fortified positions; but instead, by constant manoeuvre, to keep a grip on him whilst Grant was hammering *Lee* in the East. On May 4 he advanced his united forces, the Army of the Cumberland, under Thomas, in the centre, the Army of the Tennessee, under McPherson, on the right, and the Army of the Ohio, under Schofield, on the left; his tactical idea being: to advance on his enemy, gain contact with him, pin him down and then, by outflanking him, compel him to abandon his position and fall back. This he successfully did at Dalton, again on the Oostanaula

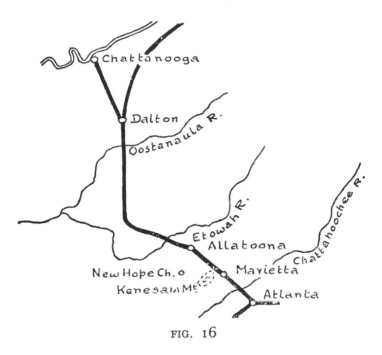

FIG. 16

river, at Etowah, Allatoona, New Hope Church and Marietta. At Kenesaw Mountain, on June 18, he attacked his enemy but with no great success;[84] nevertheless *Johnston*, on July 2, withdrew to the Chattahoochee River, where, on the 17th, the Confederate Government, not understanding his able tactics and disapproving of his constant retreats, replaced him by General *Hood*.

Hood, who was of an impetuous nature, attacked Sherman three times, and on each occasion was repulsed with heavy losses. Being compelled to fall back on Atlanta, Sherman followed him up; there *Hood's* position became untenable, and on September 1 "the gate city of the South" was in Sherman's hands.

Once Atlanta was occupied, according to Grant's strategical map, the next operation was to advance to the Atlantic coast; but this presupposed that *Hood's* army had first been annihilated, which was not the case, for, on September 20, this general withdrew to Palmetto Station, south-west of Atlanta and there entrenched himself. Further still, though Mobile Bay was now in Federal hands, Mobile itself had not been captured, and continued to hold out until March 11, 1865. On September 10 Grant wrote to Sherman suggesting that General Canby, who was operating against Mobile, should "act upon Savannah" whilst he (Sherman) moved on Augusta;[85] but this was most difficult to do, seeing that Sherman's base of supply was still at Louisville, 474 miles away, that he had nearly 1,000 miles of railway to protect, and that *Hood* now flanked an advance on Augusta, and was himself comparatively secure as long as Mobile held out. On the 20th Sherman replied that if Grant could secure Wilmington and the City of Savannah, he could keep *Hood* employed and put his own army "in fine order for a march on Augusta, Columbia and Charleston."[86] Meanwhile, as *Hood* threatened his line of supply, he sent Thomas back to Chattanooga.

Hood, seeing that he could no longer impede Sherman by direct opposition, decided in place to strike at his communications and so compel him to fall back in order to protect them. On the 29th he crossed the Chattahoochee and advanced on Marietta.

The effect of this move was that Sherman decided to leave a corps to hold Atlanta and set out in pursuit of him; but by October 11 he realized that it was a hopeless task, and so he suggested[87] to Grant that he should abandon this operation, and in place carry out the original plan of moving on Savannah or Charleston. Again, on the 20th, he wrote: "To pursue *Hood* is folly, for he can twist and turn like a fox, and wear out any army in pursuit."[88]

At first Grant hesitated,[89] then, hearing from Sherman that Thomas could hold the line of the Tennessee, on November 2 he agreed to the advance.[90] On the 15th Sherman set out from Atlanta at the head of 60,000 men, and arrived at Savannah on December 21. Though on the way he was but weakly opposed, beyond all question his march had a decisive strategical and political influence on the war, for the destruction he wrought in Georgia, which was estimated at $100,000,000, had a most demoralizing effect on the whole of the Confederacy, and particularly on *Lee's* army, thousands of his men deserting to their homes in order to succour their families.

Meanwhile *Hood* pushed on northwards, and Thomas failing to concentrate his army was compelled to fall back on Nashville. From there he sent out General Schofield to cover his concentration; this led to a battle at Franklin, in which, though Schofield was pushed back on Nashville, he crippled *Hood's* army by inflicting on it a loss of 6,300 casualties.[91] Thomas, who now outnumbered *Hood* by nearly two to one, should have attacked him forthwith, in place he delayed to do so for fifteen days, causing the greatest perturbation to the Federal Government. When he did, on December 15, he easily defeated his antagonist.

Thus the defeat of *Hood* at Nashville and the

occupation of Savannah by Sherman ended the stupendous Federal campaign of 1864.

On May 5 Grant had opened the throttle of this great combined operation. He had hoped to end the war that summer, and though this hope was not realized, his strategy was so sound that in spite of many changes and modifications, his central idea remained unchanged. *Lee* was held as in a vice, and because he was thus held Sherman's grand manoeuvre prospered.

The end of the year brought the end of the war in sight. Lincoln had been re-elected President, thanks mainly to the enthusiasm aroused by the victories of Sherman and Sheridan; *Lee* was still held fast in Richmond, the Valley of Virginia was clear of Confederate troops, and beyond the silence of winter "there came," as Swinton says, "rolling across the plains of the Carolinas, beating nearer and nearer, the drums of Champion's Hill and Shiloh." Come what might, unless Sherman could be stopped, the Confederacy was doomed. Thus ended the memorable year of 1864.

Five Forks and Appomattox Court House

On January 11, 1865, *Lee* wrote to Seddon: "We have but two days' supplies";[92] on the 19th: "There is great suffering in the Army for want of soap";[93] on the 27th he mentions the "alarming frequency of desertions";[94] on February 4 he acknowledged his "confirmation by the Senate as General-in-Chief of the Armies of the Confederate States";[95] and then, on the 22nd, he hinted to *Breckinridge*, the new Secretary of War, that he can do nothing until he abandons the James River.[96] The date of this announcement coincides with that of the fall of

234

Wilmington, and without Wilmington Richmond was throttled. *Lee* seems to have realized this, for again on this same day, February 22, he wrote to *Longstreet*: If forced to withdraw, "I propose to concentrate at or near Burkeville. . . . We might also seize the opportunity of striking at Grant, should he pursue us rapidly, or at Sherman, before they could unite."[97]

On this same day, in spite of the fact that he was now Commander-in-Chief, he suggested to *Breckinridge* that General *Johnston* should be sent south to command against Sherman, adding "if he was ordered to report to me I would place him there on duty."[98] This wise move appears to have originated out of two suggestions[99] made to Davis by General *Beauregard*, one on February 3, and the other on February 21, that the only policy to adopt was to stop Sherman. On February 22 *Johnston* was detailed to do so, but it is *Lee* who should have gone South, for a General-in-Chief should always face the position of greatest danger and importance. With Sherman in North Carolina, Richmond had become a theatre of secondary value. *Lee* should have realized this directly Fort Fisher, the key to Wilmington, fell on January 15. Perhaps he did, but his subservience to Davis was so complete that he refused to move; he was paralyzed by his theory that duty demanded that he should suggest and must obey but should never decide.

General *Gordon* informs us, that during the first week in March he saw *Lee*, and placed before him three suggestions, which in order of precedence were:

(1) To make the best possible terms with the enemy;
(2) To abandon Richmond, join *Johnston*, and strike at Sherman;
(3) To strike at Grant.

Lee's answers were typical of the man: As regards the first he said: "that he scarcely felt authorized to suggest to the civil authorities the advisability of making terms." As regards the second, "he doubted whether the authorities in Richmond would consent to the movement," besides his men were in a starving condition, and he could not move half his artillery or trains. Whereupon *Gordon* urged him to assume his powers as Commander-in-Chief, and to point out to the Government the absolute necessity of securing favourable terms of peace while the army was still organized and resisting. Then *Gordon* says: "His long training as a soldier and his extreme delicacy were still in his way—a barrier against even apparent interference in any department not his own and against any step not in accord with the strictest military and official ethics. He said as much, but then added: 'I will go, and will send for you again on my return from Richmond' . . ." On his return "he said nothing could be done at Richmond. The Congress did not seem to appreciate the situation. Of President Davis he spoke in terms of strong eulogy: of the strength of his convictions, of his devotedness, of his remarkable faith in the possibility of still winning our independence, and of his unconquerable will power. The nearest approach to complaint or criticism were the words which I can never forget: 'You know that the President is very pertinacious in opinion and purpose' . . . 'What then is to be done, General?' He replied that there seemed to be but one thing that we could do—fight. To stand still was death. It could only be death if we fought and failed."[100]

Grant's plan for 1865 was to draw the net closer and closer round his antagonist. His first problem was to occupy the remaining sea ports—Charleston,

Mobile and Wilmington, of which the last was by far
the most important. Its entrance was protected by
Fort Fisher which, as I have already noted, fell on
January 15. The capture of this fort was, says Vice-
President Stephens, a blow equal to the loss of
Vicksburg.[101]

FIG. 17

Hood disposed of and Fort Fisher in Federal hands,
Grant fearing that *Lee* might attempt to break away
and unite with *Johnston*, decided to watch him rather
than attack him, holding his army in readiness to
spring upon *Lee* should he abandon Richmond. Next
he decided to close four columns in on *Lee*: Sherman
to advance on Branchville, Columbia, and eventually

237

on Raleigh;[102] Schofield to be transferred from Tennessee to North Carolina, secure Wilmington and then occupy Goldsboro, in order to open a base of supplies for Sherman;[103] Sheridan to move on Lynchburg; Thomas to move on Selma, sending a strong force of cavalry under General Stoneman towards Columbia, and Canby to take and occupy Mobile.

Thomas's movement, on account of his extreme slowness, failed; Schofield, however, occupied Wilmington on February 22, and Sherman advancing north on February 1, after a march of 425 miles joined hands with Schofield at Goldsboro on March 23. Meanwhile Sheridan set out towards Staunton, annihilated the remnants of *Early's* army, occupied Charlottesville, and then turning south rejoined the Army of the Potomac on March 19.

Lee's situation was now a desperate one. On February 19 he warned[104] his Government that Richmond might have to be abandoned, and on March 23 hearing[105] from *Johnston* that Sherman had joined hands with Schofield, two days later, apparently to disengage himself, he assumed the offensive, attacked Fort Steadman and failed hopelessly on account of faulty staff arrangements.[106] The initiative was now Grant's absolutely, and not waiting for Sherman, who was unable to advance on the Roanoke River until April 10, Grant decided to strike, and on the 24th issued his orders.

His plan was to hold the trenches north of the James with one corps—the Twenty-fifth; mass two, the Ninth and the Sixth in the Petersburg area ready to break the enemy's front should *Lee* strip it; the remainder, in all 66,000 men, preceded by Sheridan and 14,000 cavalry, to move west and turn *Lee's* right flank.[107]

Hearing that *Lee* was concentrating on his right, in spite of the rain which in many places had rendered the ground impassable for wheeled traffic, Grant, on the 30th, ordered Sheridan to seize the road junction at Five Forks. (See Map No. 11.) This he did on April 1, decisively beating General *Pickett*. The result of this battle was that the South Side railroad was now at Grant's mercy, consequently the fate of Petersburg was sealed.

Learning of this success, in order to prevent a concentration against Sheridan, and to enable him to advance on the South Side railroad, Grant ordered an assault along the whole of the Petersburg front. This took place at 4 a.m. on April 2, the Confederate works west of Petersburg[108] being penetrated and *Lee's* army cut in two. All west of *Lee's* centre was now being driven by Sheridan beyond the Appomattox, and all east of it was forced into Petersburg by Grant wheeling his left flank inwards. Early on the 3rd Petersburg was occupied, and Richmond was at last in Federal hands.

Correctly surmising that *Lee* would follow the Danville railroad in order to gain the Roanoke, Grant decided not to follow him and become involved with his rear guards, but instead to get ahead of him and intercept his line of retreat.[109] On the 3rd, before leaving Petersburg, Grant had written to Sheridan saying: "The first object of present movement will be to intercept *Lee's* army and the second to secure Burkesville";[110] consequently Sheridan continued his movement westwards, intercepting *Lee's* retreat on Danville; whereupon *Lee* decided to march upon Farmville. He was now to all intents and purposes hemmed in; on his left was Sheridan and the Sixth Corps, on his right the Fifth Corps, and in rear of him the Second; nevertheless he pushed on,

239

deciding to cross to the left bank of the Appomattox at Farmville and gain Danville by the road leading through Appomattox Court House.

On April 2 *Lee* had turned the head of his army towards Amelia Court House, his one idea now being to join up with *Johnston*. Not only was this move weeks, if not months, too late, but as he advanced his half-starved army began to dissolve, men deserting by hundreds and thousands. Yet, on the 1st, at Richmond, or within easy call of this city, were stored up 4,000,000 rations of meat and 2,500,000 of bread, without counting considerable supplies of tea, coffee and sugar. *Lee* could have drawn on these immense supplies not only before the evacuation of Richmond but during it; this is made abundantly clear by Jefferson Davis; but he issued no orders concerning them, and when asked at what point on the railroad he would like supplies sent, he replied "that the military situation made it impossible to answer."[111] The final dictum of history must be that whatever excellence *Lee* possessed as a strategist or as a tactician, he was the worst Quartermaster-General in history, and that, consequently, his strategy had no foundations, with the result that his tactics never once resulted in an overwhelming and decisive victory.

As the Army of Northern Virginia straggled onwards to its doom, Grant ordered the Second and Sixth Corps to move north of the Appomattox and press the enemy's rear, while Sheridan, the Fifth and Ord's[112] Corps, were directed on to Appomattox Station,[113] as information had been received that *Lee* intended to resupply his army at that place. On the evening of the 8th Sheridan reached Appomattox Station, from where he pushed *Lee's* advanced troops back towards the Court House. On the morning of the 9th *Lee* advanced to attack him, when Sheridan's cavalry "parting to the right and left," disclosed the Fifth and Ord's Corps in line behind them. Simultaneously the Second and Sixth Corps arrived in rear of *Lee's* men. The white flag was then raised,[114] and a little later, at McLean's house, in "a naked little parlour containing a table and two or three chairs," *Robert E. Lee* at the head of 7,892 infantry with arms, 2,100 cavalry, 63 guns and not a single ration, surrendered to Ulysses S. Grant.

CHAPTER VII

THE TWO GENERALS

Grant and Lee

COMPARISONS are often waste of time, and more especially so when they are made out of place and out of date. Thus, to compare Alexander the Great with Napoleon would not be a profitable task, in spite of the fact that both were great generals, great conquerors and great autocrats; because the conditions in which they lived, thought and worked were so different. To compare Cromwell with George Washington would be still less profitable, though both were revolutionary leaders, and to compare Wellington with Edward III would border on the ridiculous, yet their tactical predilections were very similar.

Grant we can, however, compare with *Lee*, and *Lee* with Grant; for though in so many ways these two men were different, they were of the same nation, they fought at the same date and in the same war; yet, in spite of these common links, they nevertheless were representatives of two diverging epochs, *Lee* belonging to the old agricultural age and Grant to the new industrial. The one was the expression of spiritual energy, the other of physical; and it is because of this difference in the intellectual and moral spheres in which they were called upon to work, that a comparison between them is so interesting and instructive.

Outwardly it would be impossible to discover men

so different as Grant and *Lee*, yet inwardly they were very similar in type, endowed as they were with the same high principle of duty. Further, both possessed an indomitable resolution, high moral and physical courage and remarkable self-control in the face of danger. Both may be called fatalists. Grant did not believe in chance, *Lee* with all his heart and soul believed in God; and it is here, I think, in their moral and spiritual outlooks upon men, the affairs of men, and upon the world generally, that we can discover the one great difference which toned their sense of duty. To the one the good in mankind must ultimately triumph over the evil; to the other all triumph was of God, through God and by God. Both discovered that calmness of spirit which was the soul of their respective generalships, the pivot upon which they worked. To *Lee*, a rigid pivot which was beyond all rational control; to Grant, a rational one under ethical direction. To the first virtue was reflected from without, to the second it was generated from within. The one may be compared to a mirror which must be kept spotlessly clean, the other to a dynamo which must be well cared for.

As is ever the case, the inner man, that personal factor which makes one man one thing and another man another thing, controlled all their actions, and was in consequence the mainspring of their differences, the workings of which were further set apart by their respective ages, for on the outbreak of the war *Lee* was 53 and Grant 39, and, as is normally the case, the older man was far less resilient to change and, consequently, far more fixed in his opinions. Both in a way started as amateurs, for though both had served in the Mexican War, the Civil War was something quite different. At Belmont, at Donelson and at Shiloh Grant's mistakes were profound, but he

243

did not repeat them; in his West Virginian Campaign *Lee's* mistakes were equally profound, yet he learned nothing from them. Grant at Vicksburg is a totally different general from Grant at Belmont; but *Lee* at Gettysburg is the same man as *Lee* at Cheat mountain: there is the same lack of order, of combination, of central control and of authority. Whilst Grant learned how to stamp his mind on his operations, turning intellectual conceptions into co-ordinated actions, *Lee* merely continued to stamp his spirit on the hearts of his men. His outlook is complex, it is divided between his sense of duty and his sense of generalship, Providence and himself, the Government and himself, and himself and his subordinate commanders. Grant's outlook is simpler and, consequently, more all-embracing. He sees the war as a whole far more completely so than *Lee* ever saw it. His conceptions are simpler and less rigid; he is pre-eminently the grand-strategist, whilst *Lee* is pre-eminently the field strategian. His orders are simple, direct and unmistakable, *Lee's* more often than not are vague and frequently verbal. In the Official Records of the war it is conspicuous that no sooner is battle engaged than *Lee's* written orders cease.

In the realm of popular opinion, and historical opinion also, *Lee* was an imaginative genius, endowed with that supreme gift of generalship, namely, of being able to creep into his adversary's shoes and read his adversary's mind. Yet I believe that Grant was right when he said: *Lee* was not a highly imaginative man. It is true he read McClellan like a book, and rightly gauged during the first two years of the war the nervousness of Washington. Yet when McClellan had gone, who in his opinion was the ablest Federal general who ever confronted him and "by all odds,"[1] this magic began to wane; had he read Burnside aright he would have counter-attacked him at Fredericksburg, and had he read Hooker aright, on May 1, 1863, his army would have been far more effectively distributed than it was to attack him. Then, in the last year of the war, Grant was largely an enigma to him, and his misreading of the spirit of the North is proved by the fact that he once again attempted his now rusty sword-thrust of a raid down the Valley of Virginia.

In my own opinion *Lee* never fathomed Grant. It is true that after the war he is reported to have said: "I have carefully searched the military records of both ancient and modern history, and have never found Grant's superior as a general."[2] On the face of it such research work is so at variance with *Lee's* normal behaviour, that I am convinced this statement is a fabrication. The reason he never understood Grant is best given by Colonel Bruce:

"It has been said more than once that General Grant had not the gift of imagination. It is true that he had not that kind of imagination that sees an enemy where none exists; that multiplies by five the numbers of those who happen to be in his front; that discovers obstacles impossible to overcome whenever there is a necessity to act; that sees the road open and the way clear to victory when the foe is far away and not threatening; that conjures up, on his near approach, a multitude of impossible movements being made on the flanks and on the rear; that sets the brain of a commander into a whirl of doubt and uncertainty which generally ends in a hasty retreat or ignominious defeat. . . ."

This type of emotional imagination *Lee* could grasp, but Grant was not of this type.

"It was not through knowledge gained from books but through the gift of an historic imagination in part that he was enabled to see the true character of the great conflict in which he was engaged, its relation to the past and its bearing on the future; that enabled him to take in at a glance the whole field of the war, to form a correct opinion of every suggested and possible strategic

245

campaign, their logical order and sequence, their relative value and the interdependence of the one upon another; and finally at Appomattox, the moment *Lee* let drop his flag, to see that the end had come and the whole Southland was once more a part of a common country and her conquered soldiers were again his ountrymen." [3]

This type of imagination *Lee* could not understand, because he was not a highly imaginative man, and I think that far too much has been made of his powers of intuition. Of Grant, Badeau says: "He often said of those opposed to him: 'I know exactly what that general will do'; 'I am glad such an one is in my front'; 'I would rather fight this one than another.' " [4] His insight of *Floyd, Pillow, Buckner, Pemberton* and *Bragg* is quite as remarkable as *Lee's* of McClellan, Pope, Burnside and Hooker; but the difference was this, that whilst Grant used his imagination as a plummet line *Lee* used his as a trowel; *Lee* built his plans out of his intuitions, and time after time he failed because his intuition was at fault. Contempt for his enemy was the fruit of his imagination and not of his reason; and this contempt led him into the follies of Antietam and Gettysburg. Grant used his imagination not to build his plans upon it, but to rectify them by it. All said and done, before the outbreak of the war, the army being common to North and South, there is nothing remarkable in the fact that *Lee* understood McClellan, and Grant *Pemberton*. But whilst, in the Antietam campaign, *Lee* trusted this understanding so implicitly that he did not hesitate to scatter his army, at Vicksburg, as we have seen, Grant through an elaborate series of bluffs so played upon his adversary's weaknesses, that he was eventually able to carry out a hazardous campaign in complete safety. When, having started for Gettysburg, *Lee* suddenly asked Davis to mobilize a new army under

Beauregard to relieve the pressure on his own army by threatening Washington; Grant, before he advanced into the Wilderness, foresaw a possible move south of the river James and also the siege of Richmond. *Lee* lacked prevision, not only because he held his enemy in contempt, but because he had a horror of detail; Grant, from 1863 onwards, never failed to exercise it. He was a man of thought, *Lee* was a man of impulse; yet his impulses were always rigid—the relief of Virginia.

The Old and the New Tactics

Before I outline in greater detail the generalship of these two men, I must hark back to the question of tactics which I examined in Chapter I; for it is through a failure to appreciate the changes in the art of war which took place during the middle of the last century that most historians of the Civil War have gone astray. Unless these changes are fully realized, the stupendous task which confronted the North in its conquest of the South will be entirely overlooked and Grant's generalship obscured, as it has been in most histories.

This war opened with a clash between half-armed farmers and half-trained soldiers. From the first material resources preponderated in the North, and throughout the war were lacking in the South; consequently, had the rifle, the supreme weapon in this war, been more powerful in the attack than in the defence, there can be no question that the Confederacy would have been sooner crushed. This was, however, not so, for always and ever has the missile weapon excelled the shock weapon in the defence, and in this war it utterly outclassed it. Consequently, minor tactics were definitely against the Northern soldier, because his major tactics demanded the offensive; for without the offensive the South could not be brought to heel. It was the problem which had faced the French in La Vendée and in the peninsula of Spain, which had faced Napoleon in Russia, and the British in South Africa during the Boer War of 1899-1902. Not only was the Northern soldier, through force of circumstances, compelled to fight in his enemy's country, but he was compelled to devastate it as well as conquer it, in order to protect himself against the bands of irregular troops which were met with here, there and everywhere. The importance of this problem and the difficulties it entailed can be best appreciated by the fact that all of *Lee's* victories were gained in his own country, and that no single excursion into his enemy's territories proved successful.

I have examined this question fairly fully in my book *The Generalship of Ulysses S. Grant,* in which I wrote:

"In my opinion, few periods in military history have been so misunderstood as the one under review; and, consequently, few generals-in-chief have suffered greater injustice than Grant. The reason for this misunderstanding is obvious, directly it is appreciated that the Civil War was the first of its kind; by which I do not mean that it was the first of all such wars, but the first of all modern wars; and though strategically it can be compared to wars which preceded it, tactically it can only be judged correctly by those which followed it. In fact a writer who possessed no knowledge of the tactics of previous wars, and some knowledge of tactics since 1865, could not possibly have displayed so intense an ignorance of the nature of the tactics of this war as has been done by so many of the learned yet purblind historians who have obscured the very nature of the war through excess of strategical knowledge and paucity of tactical understanding.

"For instance, Ropes, and no man can doubt his knowledge or interest in the war, has but a faint idea of its tactical nature. To him there is no trace of Marlborough, Wellington or Napoleon in Grant's last campaign—'its terrible, bloody battles, its encounters of every day . . . the noble trees cut down by musket bullets . . . the thousands of thousands of brave men slain and maimed, and, above all, the indecisive results, amaze, terrify, repel, dishearten us.' And again: 'The experience of the Army of the Potomac in the campaign was in fact a new experience for soldiers. Sacrifices were demanded every day of the rank and file of the army which had hitherto been required only occasionally, and then only from those selected for some special post of honour or danger.' These things he cannot understand: 'To lie in a new-dug rifle-pit a hundred yards from the enemy for several days under constant fire is much like the experience of the engineer troops in a siege. To rush from this rifle-pit upon the enemy's works is the act of a forlorn hope, whose gallant performance is the admiration of a storming column, itself selected for a special and dangerous service. But it is not every day that the sap is pushed forward or the breach assaulted.'[5]

"Why cannot he understand them; why does he talk of Marlborough and Wellington, of new experiences, of rifle-pits, prolonged battles, siege-works and indecisive results? Because he does not understand that the rifle bullet has completely revolutionized tactics. His knowledge enables him to place his finger on the pulse of war, yet he cannot count its heart throbs, nor can he diagnose its fever. He is blind to the reality of rifle warfare; yet, though he wrote the above extracts in 1884, he was no blinder than the majority of generals of thirty years later, or many of to-day. The rifle bullet utterly changed tactics, and unless this is understood all knowledge is a blank, worse—a danger.

"The 1864-1865 campaign in Virginia was the first of the modern campaigns; it initiated a tactical epoch, and did not even resemble the wars of ten years before its date. It was not a campaign of bayonets but of bullets. . . . On the battlefields of the Wilderness and of Spottsylvania the Confederate ordnance officers collected for recasting more than 120,000 pounds of lead,[6] and even if this amount represents a twentieth part of the bullets fired, then, at two ounces apiece the number expended was 19,000,000. When did Marlborough, or Wellington, or Napoleon face such a hail of projectiles?

"It was the bullet which created the trench and the rifle-pit; which killed the bayonet; which rendered useless the sword; which chased away guns and horsemen; which, from May 5, 1864, to April 9, 1865, held the contending forces in 'constant close contact, with rare intervals of brief comparative repose,'[7] and which prevented the rapid decisions of the battles of preceding centuries. In 1861-1865 the rifle bullet was the lord of the battlefield as was the machine gun bullet in 1914-1918."[8]

249

This must be remembered, for otherwise it is futile to attempt to assess the generalship of Grant or *Lee*. Neither of them understood the tactics of the bullet, or its influences upon former tactical conceptions, morale and tactical organization. Both were like children playing with a new and complicated toy, and seeing that, in 1914-1918, Marshal Foch[9] understood the bullet no better, it is a remarkable fact that Grant and *Lee* understood it as well as they did. This lack in the appreciation of the power of the rifle bullet has constituted the supreme tragedy of modern warfare, a drama of insanity in which millions have perished for a dream—the bayonet clinch, the flash of steel, the stab and the yell of victory.[10]

Generalship and Grand Strategy

The correlation of all the forces of war and the resources of peace in accordance with the political object of the war is the main duty in grand strategy, a duty which in a democratic country must be divided between the head of the Government and the General-in-Chief. Without this correlation there can be no stable fulcrum whereon to move the lever of operations. The General-in-Chief must not only be acquainted with the national policy, but what is still more important he must be in a position to suggest modifications which are bound to arise during the war. His plans are based on this policy, and as they succeed, or fail, so must policy be modified.

When the Civil War was declared, grand strategy was conspicuous through its absence. There was no co-ordination of policy and plan in the North or in the South; all that existed was potential force on the one side and active idealism on the other, the one directed towards conquest and the other towards resistance. The impulse of the North soon, however, began to centralize into a vague ill-constructed grand strategical base; because the ideal of union, the necessity of conquest and command of the sea compelled co-ordination. In the South, from the beginning to the end of the war, no such manifestation took place; for State rights were antagonistic to unity; fractionizing ideas, they led to a dispersion of force, the adoption of an all-round defence, and reliance upon European intervention... Whilst the North was compelled through force of circumstances to develop its resources, the South, relying on Europe for its munitions of war, failed to do so; with the result, that more and more did Southern policy develop into a political game of chance, and this may clearly be seen from Jefferson Davis's communications to Congress, which are devoted more largely to the subject of foreign recognition than to the war itself.

As I have stated in the first chapter of this book, there were three sub-theatres of war, the economic, the political and the strategical. The importance of the first was at once recognized, but the North did not possess a sufficiency in naval power to carry out a complete blockade of the Southern ports; had it been able to do so, resistance would have rapidly collapsed, in fact without European assistance it would have been scarcely possible for the Confederacy to have maintained an organized army in the field. The importance of the second assumed an exaggerated form, overshadowing the first and the third, for the war rapidly developed into a contest between the two capital cities. This undoubtedly took place because both Lincoln and Davis were all but totally ignorant of strategy. The result of this misdirection of force was that the blockade was not pushed to the full, and that for nearly three years a series of disastrous battles was waged in the political theatre with little or no reference to the strategical theatre. Under Halleck's guidance, Lincoln was completely at sea; whilst Jefferson Davis was guided solely by his own military conceit, *Lee* exerting practically no influence whatsoever on his strategy. Davis, as I have already shown,[11] did not even understand what modern war entailed; he had no conception of the changes which industrial civilization had created in war and the methods of waging it. His military outlook was eighteenth century and not nineteenth century; it was in fact completely out of focus with reality.

Lee, as I have shown, was no grand strategist, and, consequently, a most indifferent General-in-Chief, or Chief of Staff, or adviser to his Government. His sole grand strategical work of importance was when he asked Colonel *Marshall* to prepare the draft of a bill "for raising an army by the direct agency of the Confederate Government," in other words, conscription; which measure "completely reversed the previous military legislation of the South." *Lee* rightly considered that European intervention was more likely if the South were strong. "He thought," writes *Marshall*, "that every other consideration should be regarded as subordinate to the great end of the public safety, and that since the whole duty of the nation would be war until independence should be secured, the whole nation should for the time be converted into an army, the producers to feed and the soldiers to fight."[12] Conscription was adopted, but with so many restrictions as to be largely vitiated in value, and though *Lee* realized this, he never once *demanded* an amendment to the Act.

That *Lee* could not see the grand strategical aspect would appear to be untrue, but that he could not bring himself to insist upon its importance, I think, I have proved beyond a doubt. *Marshall* tells us that his object was to draw the war out to indefinite length. "The means to accomplish this end were to frustrate the enemy's designs; to break up campaigns undertaken with vast expense and with confident assurance of success; to impress upon the minds of the Northern people the conviction that they must prepare for a protracted struggle, great sacrifice of life and treasure, with the possibility that all might at last be of no avail; and to accomplish this at the smallest cost to the Confederacy."[13] If this is so, then *Lee's* campaigns into Maryland show his lack in realizing how this Fabian strategy should be accomplished; why did he undertake them?

This question I have already answered: He was obsessed by Virginia and the moral aspect of war, the importance of the Federal capital casting a spell upon him. His one and only grand strategical principle was to terrify Washington. This would have been a perfectly sound object had his army been well administered and provided with a siege train, but without these two essentials it was really futile, and grew more and more so as the war was prolonged.

According to *Marshall*, *Lee* favoured Virginia because of the importance of Washington[14]; according to E. Townsend, because Virginia was his native State[15]; Grant, according to Sherman,[16] held a similar view. Pollard hints at the same thing when he writes: "The fact was that, although many of General *Lee's* views were sound, yet, outside of the Army of Northern Virginia, and with reference to the general affairs of the Confederacy, his influence was negative and accomplished absolutely nothing." Again: "His most notable defect was that he never had or conveyed any inspiration in the war." Also quoting from a Richmond paper, after the battle of the Wilderness: " 'When will he [*Lee*] speak? Has he nothing to say? What does he think of our affairs? Should he speak, how the country would hang upon every word that fell from him!' "[17]

That *Lee*, though loyal to Virginia, was at heart disloyal to the Confederacy, is absurd. But that *Lee* was so obsessed by Virginia that he considered it the most important area of the Confederacy to me is undoubted. To him the Confederacy was but the base of Virginia, not only because he was a Virginian, but because the only form of attack he really understood was the moral offensive, and Virginia enabled him to carry this out. Had the capital of the Union been situated in Kentucky, the Virginian within him would not have prevented him carrying out a war of nerves in that State.

At the beginning of the war he said to General *Imboden*:

"Our people are brave and enthusiastic and are united in defense of a just cause. I believe we can succeed in establishing our independence, if the people can be made to comprehend at the outset that they must endure a longer war and far greater privations than our forefathers in the Revolution of 1776. We will not succeed until the financial power of the North is broken. . . . The conflict will be mainly in Virginia. She will be the Flanders of America before this war is over and her people must be prepared for this. If they resolve at once to dedicate their lives and all they possess to the cause of constitutional government and Southern independence and to suffer without yielding as no other people have been called upon to suffer in modern times, we shall, with the blessing of God, succeed in the end; but when it will be no man can foretell. I wish I could talk to every man, woman and child in the South now and impress them with these views."[18]

The tragedy is not *Lee's* disloyalty, but his total inability to realize that the only way he could talk to the people of the Confederacy was through their

Government. This he could not do, because it would have been an infringement of the divine right of the Southern President to do as he pleased, and he believed in this right as fervently as a fanatical cavalier believed in the divine right of Charles I to rule, or misrule, England. "Of one thing I am certain," wrote Jones, the diarist, in January, 1865, "that the people are capable of achieving independence, if they only had capable men in all departments of the government."[19] *Lee* realized this as clearly as did Jones, but his sense of duty to God was such that he could not violate his trust in His divine power. It was not because *Lee* placed Virginia before the Confederacy that he failed to be a grand strategist, a true General-in-Chief, but because he placed his sense of duty to God before all things.

Nevertheless, *Lee* did not want to serve outside Virginia; consciously, or unconsciously, he seems to have realized that he lacked the personality of a General-in-Chief, or else entirely failed to realize what such a Commander should do. In May, 1863, we find Jefferson Davis writing: "I note your request to be relieved of the command of the troops between the James River and the Cape Fear. This is one of the few instances in which I have found my thoughts running in the opposite direction from your own. It has several times occurred to me that it would be better for you to control all the operations of the Atlantic slope, and I must ask you to reconsider the matter."[20] Davis was undoubtedly right, but *Lee* could not tolerate the complexities of so extensive a command; his thoughts were always concentrated on Virginia, consequently he never fully realized the importance of Tennessee, or the strategic power which resided in the size of the Confederacy. Not until Sherman was hammering at the back door of Richmond did he begin to see the importance of the Western areas, and then, as we have seen, during the first three months of 1865 he could not decide whether to strike south until it was too late to do so.

Taking no interest in politics, and holding the North in utter contempt, in place of assisting Southern policy he unbalanced it. After the battle of Manassas, in 1862, though it was strategically sound to move into Maryland, grand strategically it was fatal because policy was seeking peace with the North, and such a move could but rouse the North to increased effort. After Chancellorsville, the move into this same area was fatal, strategically because Grant's grip on Vicksburg demanded that every possible man should be sent to *Johnston's* assistance, and grand strategically because, once again as policy was seeking peace, the invasion of Maryland and beyond was the very worst means of gaining it.

Turning to Grant we find a totally different picture. Though he did not become General-in-Chief until March, 1864, the entire series of his Western campaign shows a deep-rooted appreciation of grand strategy. Unlike *Lee* he did not start out on his career as a close adviser to his Government, but as an orderly room clerk with none too good a reputation, because after the Mexican War drink had broken him. Having already dealt fairly fully with his grand strategical evolution, all I will here do is to recapitulate its salient points.

When at Cairo, in 1861, he at once saw the strategical importance of Paducah; after the capture of Donelson he saw the importance of the Mississippi, which led to his Vicksburg campaign, in which he gained control of this river. Immediately after the fall of Vicksburg he suggested[21] an expedition to capture Mobile, and why? So that from there operations might be directed *against the rear of Bragg's* army at Chattanooga. He saw quite clearly that, whilst Chattanooga was the back door to Virginia, Mobile was the side door to Georgia, and that once in Federal hands a Confederate force at Chattanooga was threatened in rear and a Federal force advancing from this town south would have its right flank and then its rear protected. I have already quoted the plan he suggested to Halleck on December 7, 1863, here I will quote from his *Memoirs*, he says: "I had great hopes of having a campaign made against Mobile from the Gulf. I expected after Atlanta fell to occupy that place permanently, and cut off *Lee's* army from the West by way of the road running through Augusta to Atlanta and thence south-west. I was preparing to hold Atlanta with a small garrison, and it was my expectation to push through to Mobile if that city was in our possession, if not, to Savannah; and in this manner to get possession of the only east and west railroad that would then be left to the enemy."[22] His whole idea was to operate against *Lee's* communications, and once he had cut them make use of them in order to operate against *Lee's* rear. This is shown quite clearly on the strategic map received by Sherman on April 2, and though the letter explaining it is lost, from Sherman's reply and from Grant's proposals to Halleck of December 7, it is clear that *Lee's* rear was his objective.

Thus we see that whilst Grant's outlook was general, embracing the whole theatre of war, his leading idea was single, namely, the destruction of the enemy's main army. In comparison *Lee's* outlook was local, he concentrated on a small corner of the entire theatre, his leading idea being to terrify the Northern Government by making the politicians so nervous as to the safety of Washington, which at no time in the

257

war he was capable of besieging, that they would leave Richmond alone. Though he took no interest whatever in politics, his object was a political one because his outlook was non-strategic. True, he understood the strategy of Virginia, that is how to make use of its communications, but the strategy of the entire theatre of war was all but a closed book to him. In spite of all his ability, his heroism and the heroic efforts of his army, because he would think and work in a corner, taking no notice of the whole, taking no interest in forming policy or in the economic side of the war, he was ultimately cornered and his cause lost.

Generalship and Grand Tactics

Whilst grand strategy is the correlation of the operations of war and the policy of the Government supported by the resources of the country, grand tactics may be defined as the organization and distribution of the fighting forces themselves in order to accomplish the grand strategical plan, or idea. The grand strategical object is the destruction of the enemy's policy, and whilst politically the decisive point is the will of the hostile nation, grand tactically it is the will of the enemy's commander.[23] According to Clausewitz, "There are three principal objects in carrying on war:

"(a) To conquer and destroy the enemy's armed forces;

"(b) To get possession of the material elements of aggression, and of the other sources of existence of the hostile army;

"(c) To gain public opinion."[24]

The first is gained by destroying the enemy's plan, the second by undermining his economic strength, and the third by winning victories which depress his national morale and by occupying his capital, which not only disorganizes his government but is a visible sign to all that its cause has failed.

From this it will be seen that grand tactics is concerned more with disorganization and demoralization than with actual destruction, which is the object of minor tactics. Whilst grand strategy embraces the resources of the entire nation, and grand tactics the plan, or plans, of all the fighting forces, field strategy and minor tactics bring these to fruition through manoeuvre and actual fighting. The terms "major tactics," which is sometimes made use of, is nothing more than the grand tactics of a single battle: the combination of arms, and not the immediate co-operation between weapons.

In Chapter I I pointed out that the causes of the war demanded that the grand strategy of the North should be offensive, and that of the South defensive. The one side had to press; the other—to resist. At the opening of the war both sides were totally unprepared to do so, and as is so often the case when preparation is lacking, both fell into the common error of attacking before they were morally and economically ready to attack.

Of Clausewitz's "three principal objects," the first and the third were aimed at, whilst at the outset of the war it was the second which was the all-important one. Before moving on Washington, as the South half-heartedly wanted to do after the first battle of Bull Run, and before moving on Richmond, as the North attempted to do the following year, the South should have made a far greater effort in the fortification of such of its sea-ports connected to the interior by railway, and the North should have made a far greater effort not merely in blockading them, but in

259

occupying them by concentrating its comparatively slender naval power against each one *in turn*, and against Wilmington first.

During 1861 *Lee* was directly concerned with their defence, and after he was summoned to Richmond in March, 1862, though he did not lose sight of their value, it is curious that he did not insist upon retaining them under his immediate command, for far more so than Richmond did they constitute his main base of operations.

With Grant it was otherwise, for though, until the spring of 1864, he was in no way directly concerned with the grand strategy, or grand tactics, of the war, from the occupation of Fort Donelson onwards his grand tactics were based on cutting off segment after segment of the Confederacy, and so restricting its resources, more so than in defeating his enemy's armies. He saw clearly the economic value of gaining the Mississippi, and once gained he realized the value of occupying Mobile. Yet, though Mobile still held his gaze after he had become General-in-Chief, it is extraordinary that he did not insist upon the occupation of Wilmington before the Wilderness campaign opened, or, if time were too short for this, as soon as possible after it had opened, for this seaport was *Lee's* supply base—it was the "rail-head" of the Confederacy.

Though Grant, as General-in-Chief, does not seem to have realized the intimate connection between sea-power and land-power, he did realize that the grand tactical problem was primarily one of reducing the size of the theatre of war, whilst *Lee* failed to see that the grand tactical problem of the South was diametrically the opposite, and that, consequently, his object should have been to draw out the war to an indefinite length. This was not to be gained by fighting aggressive battles *within* his enemy's country, but in place, to draw the enemy into his own country where a guerilla war could be waged against him, and then to manoeuvre him into a false position and compel him to assume the offensive at a disadvantage. For such grand tactics he required above all space to manoeuvre in, and though it was no fault of his that Richmond was so close to the enemy's frontier and the sea-coast, he failed to see that space could be gained in Tennessee.

From the major tactical point of view, both these generals excelled in the rear attack, which is the true decisive attack, and in this respect it is difficult who to admire most, whether Grant at Vicksburg and Appomattox, or *Lee's* move of *Jackson* during the Second Manassas campaign and at Chancellorsville. To the military student one point is of supreme interest, namely, that whilst approximately seven out of eight frontal attacks failed, seven out of eight outflanking, or rear, attacks succeeded. At Belmont a rear attack compelled Grant to fall back; at Donelson a flank thrust gained him this fortress; at Iuka and Corinth it was a rear attack which compelled the withdrawal of his enemy; at Vicksburg, the rear manoeuvre and the rear attack gained him this fortress; at Chattanooga it was Hooker's rear attack which clinched the battle; in 1864, it was Sherman's rear manoeuvre which brought the Confederacy to collapse, and in 1865 the war was brought to an end by an outflanking pursuit which ultimately blocked *Lee's* rear. With *Lee* it was the same: Whilst practically every one of his frontal attacks failed, his outflanking and rear attacks seldom were other than astonishingly successful. It was the rear attack which forced McClellan back from Richmond, and Pope back from the Rappahannock and over the Potomac, and an outflanking attack which ruined Hooker at Chancellorsville.

This does not mean that frontal attacks should be avoided, but that they should be mainly looked upon as holding attacks and not as decisive operations; as solid unshakable foundations, that is tactical bases of operation upon which to pivot outflanking movements. In fact the two are complementary, and whilst *Lee* seldom possessed a sufficiency of troops to combine them, and consequently was compelled to accept great risks, Grant never fully appreciated their interdependence, and this may clearly be seen in his overland campaign of 1864. It is true that time and again he succeeded in holding *Lee* and in turning his right flank; yet his idea was not so much to hold as to hit, manoeuvring being forced upon him after the hitting had failed. Whether *Lee* more fully appreciated this combination of "hinge and swing door" it is difficult to say; Gettysburg would seem to disprove it. One thing is, however, certain, namely, that whilst Grant fully recognised the importance of sieges, which are in fact nothing more than methodical holding operations, *Lee* never did. It is true that in resources the North was immeasurably superior to the South, but it is unbelievable that had *Lee* determined to equip his army with an efficient siege train he would have been unable to do so. In idea his attacks on the morale of Washington were sound enough, but not one of them could fully have succeeded without a siege train. Even had he won Antietam, or Gettysburg, he would have been no better off than Hannibal was after Cannae, or Gustavus after Breitenfeld. Hannibal could not besiege Rome, Gustavus could not besiege Vienna, nor could *Lee* after similar victories have taken and held Washington.

As regards the actual distribution of forces in battle,

neither Grant nor *Lee* showed exceptional ability, and this was probably due to the novelty of the weapons they used, namely, the rifled gun and the rifled musket. In this respect Chattanooga was undoubtedly Grant's masterpiece; for though he had intended to win this battle with his left, his distribution was so sound that, when Sherman was halted, Hooker succeeded in swinging round *Bragg's* left, which enabled Thomas to break his centre. Whilst *Lee's* offensive distributions were frequently faulty, seldom well organised and generally badly staffed, his defensive distributions, especially when fighting Grant in 1864, were admirable. Bearing in mind the range of the weapons of the day, his defensive order at Spottsylvania and on the North Anna was masterly; for it enabled him to put the whole of his numerically inferior army in line and yet maintain a reserve by refusing its wings, each wing of his inverted V formation being in fact a potential reserve for the other. As a defensive general *Lee* excelled, and had he realized this, and had he realized also the importance of organized guerillas in defensive warfare, and had he refused to be drawn away from the defensive policy which in the circumstances was the only sound policy the Confederacy could adopt, his grand tactics would have been of a vastly higher order.

Generalship and Field Strategy

Field strategy is grand tactics, or major tactics, set in motion, and as this motion is maintained by supply, supply is not only the foundation of strategy but its constant end, for to maintain supply and to threaten, or cut off, supply are in themselves the foundations of victory and defeat. Because of this, field strategy may be said to be woven on communications, not only roads, rivers and railways for troop movement but above all for supply movements; for without supplies an army is no more than an engine without fuel. For a time it may be kept working on rubbish, but only for a time.

The protection of communications and the threatening of them are the chief means of developing strategy, the object of which is not necessarily battle, but rather the disorganization of the enemy's plan, either by battle or by manoeuvre. Generally speaking, the weaker side is compelled to develop an offensive strategy and a defensive tactics, and the stronger side the reverse. In both cases, however, supply remains the foundation of strategy.

In this respect the first great difference between the strategy of Grant and *Lee* was, that whilst the former, after his victory at Donelson, never failed to base his strategy upon supply, more often than not the latter based his upon the search after supplies (notably during the Antietam and Gettysburg campaigns) and, consequently, suffered chronically from a shortage of supplies and a dispersion of forces. Adequate administration stabilized the strategy of the first, and inadequate administration unbalanced the strategy of the second of these generals.

From supply, as the base of strategical action, I will turn to movement; for field strategy, as I have said earlier in this book, is largely concerned with protected movement, which does not mean tactical protection, but security gained through correct distribution, such as the influence of *Jackson's* detachment in the Valley during McClellan's Peninsula campaign, and of Butler's army on Richmond during Grant's Wilderness campaign. In both these operations the detachment had a distracting influence on the main enemy forces, and though *Jackson's* succeeded and Butler's failed through his own incompetence, these and many other cases show that both Grant and *Lee* fully understood the strategical importance of distraction. And why? Because both realized, as I have shown, that *the true decisive point is the rear of the enemy's army.*

Protected movement and distraction seldom lead to decisive results unless the object is maintained; for, even if it be discovered that the object of a campaign is not the best one, any change in it will upset the plan. In the maintenance of the object there can be no doubt whatever that Grant eclipsed *Lee*, not only because his army was stronger, but because it was far better organized and supplied, and because by nature these two men were very different. Whilst Grant detested changing the central idea of a campaign, and frequently showed a pertinacity which bordered upon obstinacy, *Lee* was far more mercurial. By instinct a cautious soldier, as may be seen at Fredericksburg and after the battle of the Wilderness, when successful success frequently upset his equilibrium, leading him to substitute an offensive for a defensive tactics, and so violate the grand strategical object which was to weary the North out and gain European recognition. Not only were the Antietam and Gettysburg campaigns unsound grand strategically, but equally so from the point of view of field strategy, because they led to two wasteful battles. Except for the battle of Shiloh, which was not sought by Grant, though on account of his own lack of foresight it was thrust upon him, no single one of his battles was strategically wasteful, though at times his tactics were clumsy.

We see this again when we examine surprise, which is an important factor in strategy. Whilst Grant educated his enemy into a sense of security, as he did in his Vicksburg, in his Chattanooga and in his Overland Campaigns, *Lee* took advantage of his enemy's lack of security, as at Manassas Junction and Chancellorsville. The one was a strategical diplomatist, the other a strategical opportunist. Whilst Grant prepared his surprisals, such as turning Vicksburg from Grand Gulf and crossing the James River in June 1864, by months and weeks of careful preparation, *Lee* acted on the spur of the moment, and never once brought any one of his electrical manoeuvres to complete fruition, because he acted so impulsively as to be unprepared to take full advantage of them. The Seven Days' Campaign ended in the disaster of Malvern Hill, the Second Manassas campaign in that of Antietam, and the Chancellorsville campaign led to Gettysburg.

In the conception of a plan of campaign *Lee* was probably no whit inferior to Grant, but in execution there was a marked difference. For instance, compare the Seven Days' Campaign and the Vicksburg Campaign. In both, the conceptions are masterly, but the one was carried out in complete confusion whilst the other was pre-eminently methodical. Though both were of different calibre, it should not be overlooked that Grant was working without a base, was strange to the country and had to supply his army by foraging; whilst *Lee* struck from a fortified area, was operating in his own country and could supply himself from Richmond. The fact is that whilst Grant's strategy was progressive, *Lee's* was spasmodic. Grant's strategy at Vicksburg and after Cold Harbor was as brilliant as any strategical moves ever accomplished by *Lee*, and both culminated in decisive successes—the fall of the fortress and the ending of the war. *Lee's* strokes flashed like lightning, and resulted in much political thunder which has caused them even to-day to resound in the pages of history; but their effects however startling lacked purpose or permanence.

In audacity, which is the mainspring of strategy as it is of tactics, *Lee* has few equals. He once said to *D. H. Hill:* "If you can accomplish the object, any risk would be justifiable,"[25] and on another occasion: "There is always hazard in military movements, but we must decide between the possible loss of inaction and the risk of action,"[26] which is only too true. When he withdrew from Richmond and concentrated against Pope, when he moved *Jackson* on Manassas Junction, and when he divided his army at Chancellorsville and struck at Hooker's right, he took risks which were justified by his weakness only; but when he accepted battle at Manassas, at Antietam, and sought battle at Gettysburg, he took risks which were unnecessary, because whilst weakness demands strategical audacity, it equally demands tactical caution. Whilst Grant's determination, which is a form of audacity, was best when situations were tactically at their worst, *Lee's* audacity was worst when situations strategically were at their best, and though the reasons for these characteristics must be sought for in the personality of these two men, the fact remains that Grant's pugnacity fitted the general strategical situation—the conquest of the South, whilst *Lee's* audacity more than once accelerated rather than retarded this object.

Generalship and Minor Tactics

It is sometimes considered, and more so to-day than in former times, that tactics and more particularly the tactical use of weapons in contra-distinction to that of arms, is no part of a General-in-Chief's mental equipment. Such an assumption is untenable, and especially so during the warfare of the last eighty years in which one new weapon has succeeded another so rapidly that the tactical wood can barely be seen for its trees. If a General-in-Chief does not understand the limitations and powers of each weapon, it is totally impossible for him to combine them economically, that is to set them together in such an order that each will assist the other.

As the outbreak of the Civil War coincided with the change over from smooth-bore weapons to rifled ones, all generals of this period, and more especially those of professional armies, worked under quite exceptionally difficult circumstances; for the tactical knowledge they had absorbed before the war did not fit the majority of the weapons which were used during it. In this respect there is no difference between Grant and *Lee;* neither understood the full powers of the rifle or the rifled gun; neither introduced a single tactical innovation of importance, and though the rifle tactics of the South were superior to those of the North, whilst the artillery tactics of the North were superior to those of the South, these differences were due to circumstances outside generalship.

It is difficult to see how this could have been otherwise, for though the conflict had been boiling up for over a generation, its eruption came as a surprise to both sides, and so utterly unprepared were both, and so essential was it to raise and organize vast numbers of men that tactics went by the board, or rather the old tactics were at once foisted onto the new weapons.

Here we are confronted by a common and almost

universal error in the history of war, an error which has cost millions of lives and which has prolonged wars and rendered them unnecessarily brutal and destructive, for the longer they are waged the more animal do they become. This error is, that in war there is so little time wherein to elaborate tactics, that though strategy and administration may be of a high order, tactics are normally of a low. Yet of all the problems of war that of tactics is the simplest, consisting as it does of almost a mathematical equation between the elements of protection, mobility and offensive power on the one side, and supply, ground and human nature on the other. If the powers of the percussion-capped rifle and those of the flintlock musket had been carefully examined, and the characteristics of these two weapons carefully compared, certain tactical differences would have been discovered, which when applied to the normal operations of war—attacking, defending, pursuing, retiring, etc., would have produced a series of clear sketches of what the fighting would be like. This was, however, not done, with the result that not only were the powers of the new weapons wasted, but time and again human life was thrown away.

Tactics are the cutting edge of strategy, the edge which chisels out the plan into an action; consequently the sharper this edge is the clearer cut will be the result.

Not understanding the powers of the rifle, the tactics of this war were not discovered through reflection, but through trial and error. Thus, over a year of bitter fighting was necessary to open the eyes of both sides to the fact that the trench was a by-product of the rifle bullet, and like so many by-products, as valuable as the product itself. It is astonishing to find that *Lee*, an engineer officer, made no use of entrench-

269

ments at the battle of Antietam, and only less so Grant, who failed to construct them on the field of Shiloh. Later on we find every position entrenched, even if it is to be held only for a few hours, until Grant and *Lee* become past-masters in the art of manoeuvring entrenchments; yet though both grasped their protective properties, neither fully grasped their influence on the attack; this brings me to the much discussed problem of assaults.

In the day of sword, axe and lance the attack and the assault coincided, all fighting being hand-to-hand. In the day of the flintlock musket they were separated by so short a distance—30 to 100 paces—that the bullet was subordinated to the bayonet. Next we come to the day of the muzzle-loading rifle with an effective range of from 300 to 500 paces; obviously the whole tactical situation has changed, for the effective zone of fire has been extended over five-fold. Consequently the attack has become five times as dangerous, and a successful assault five times as unlikely. Add entrenchments to this picture, that is entrench one side, the defenders; then, whilst the attacker must expose the whole of his body, the defender exposes but a quarter of his, consequently the assault becomes more difficult still, so difficult as to become unprofitable.

What is the solution to this difficulty? It is to replace assaulting by holding, and to add manoeuvring to advancing. The attackers should advance close enough to the defenders to make it extremely dangerous for them to quit their trenches, whilst, under their fire, an outflanking manoeuvre is set in motion, which must now be carried out by infantry because cavalry are no longer sufficiently powerful to meet the rifle.

The defender may, and will whenever possible,

take up a position such as the summit of a ridge from which he can slip away, and behind which his reserves are immune from rifle and low angle artillery fire. Consequently, the attacker should be strongly supported by howitzers, not only because these can search the rear slope of the enemy's position and decimate his reserves, as well as make it difficult for him to retire from it, but because overhead fire can be maintained during the advance. Whilst the cannon using round-shot and ricochet fire was complementary to the musket, the howitzer using high-angle shell fire is complementary to the rifle. Had this been grasped, the assault would have gained considerably in strength. It was not—neither Grant nor *Lee* appreciated the influence of the rifle upon the gun, with the result that throughout the war few efforts were made to overcome the tactical difficulties of the assault. The common solution was to pile up numbers; the result was the high casualties in most of the battles fought.

Popularly, and what is far more reprehensible historically, *Lee* is supposed to have been an arch tactician whilst Grant was a tactical tiro; yet if we examine the attack tactics of these two generals, there is little to choose between them: *Lee's* assaults at Malvern Hill and Gettysburg are as hopeless as Grant's at Vicksburg and Cold Harbor, and far more costly. At Malvern Hill *Lee's* excuse was that his enemy was demoralized, which was Grant's excuse at Vicksburg. At Gettysburg and Cold Harbor ample time was given the defending side to entrench in, and in both cases artillery preparation heralded the assault, and most markedly so in the first of these battles. The results, however, were negligible, because low angle fire normally prohibits covering fire being maintained during the advance. When it was effective, notably in Upton's assault on the Salient at Spottsylvania, on May 10, 1864, the assault was successful. Other successful assaults, such as Smith's at Donelson, Thomas's at Missionary Ridge, and Hancock's, on May 12, 1864, at Spottsylvania, were due to special circumstances. In the first—the Confederates were exceptionally weak and surprised; in the second, Hooker's outflanking movement was felt before the assault took place, and in the third Hancock's assault, delivered in twilight, came as a surprise. On the whole, very few direct assaults proved successful; in fact, as I have already stated, less than one in eight. In my own opinion the only justification for those, which had they succeeded might have led to the shortening of the war—such as *Lee's* assault at Gettysburg and Grant's at Cold Harbor—was that two men died in the hospitals to every one killed in the field;[27] consequently, during the war sickness was twice as destructive of life as bullets and shells.

To turn from assaults to losses, there is nothing whatever to justify the common opinion that Grant wantonly sacrificed the lives of his men. It is true that during the last year of the war his losses were heavy, but it must be remembered that his efforts were continuous in order to prevent the Richmond Government from reinforcing *Johnston.* The following percentages[28] of losses are instructive, they speak for themselves:

GRANT, 1862-63

Battle	Date	Federal Losses per 100	Confederate Losses per 100
Fort Donelson	Feb. 12-16, 1862	9.6	9.5
Shiloh	April 6-7, 1862	16.2	24.1
Corinth	Oct. 3-4, 1862	10.4	11.2
Champion's Hill	May 16, 1863	7.6	10.9
Vicksburg	May 22, 1863	6.7	—
Chattanooga	Nov. 23-25, 1863	9.7	5.5

LEE, 1862-63

Battle	Date	Federal Losses per 100	Confederate Losses per 100
Mechanicsville	June 26, 1862	1.6	9.1
Gaines's Mill	June 27, 1862	11.7	15.3
Peach Orchard and Malvern Hill	June 29–July 1, 1862	6.0	9.9
Seven Days' Battle.. ..	June 25–July 1, 1862	10.7	20.7
Manassas and Chantilly ..	Aug. 27–Sept. 2, 1862	13.2	18.7
South Mountain	Sept. 14, 1862	6.8	10.5
Antietam	Sept. 16-17, 1862	15.5	22.6
Fredericksburg	Dec. 13, 1862	10.3	6.4
Chancellorsville	May 1–4, 1863	11.4	18.7
Gettysburg	July 1–3, 1863	20.0	30.1

From these two tables we learn the following: in Grant's six battles, the average percentage of men hit, that is killed and wounded, was 10.03 per cent., and in *Lee's* ten the average was 16.20 per cent.

I will now turn to the battles fought between Grant and *Lee* in 1864-65:

273

GRANT—LEE, 1864-65

Battle	Date	Grant	Lee
Wilderness and Spottsylvania ..	May 5–12, 1864	29.6	—
Cold Harbor	June 1–3, 1864	11.1	—
The Mine	July 30, 1864	13.8	—
Deep Bottom	Aug. 14–19, 1864	7.8	—
Weldon R.R.	Aug. 18–21, 1864	6.4	8.1
Boydton Plank Road	Oct. 27–28, 1864	2.8	—
Hatcher's Run	Feb. 5–7, 1865	3.9	—
Appomattox Campaign	March 29–April 5, 1865	8.0	—

As no accurate figures exist for *Lee's* losses they cannot be given, which in itself shows the indifferent staff work in his army, but as regards Grant's, his average loss in these eight battles was 10.42 per cent., which compares closely with his average during 1862-63, and is still considerably lower than *Lee's* during the same period. Of forty-six battles, great and small, tabulated by Livermore in *Numbers and Losses*, in which casualties for both sides are given, the Federal losses work out at 11.07 per cent., and the Confederate at 12.25 per cent.; both of which figures are higher than Grant's total average of 10.225 per cent., and decidedly below *Lee's* average of 16.20 per cent., for the years 1862-63, in spite of the fact that they include his losses. That Grant's casualties were abnormally high is thus proved a myth, and one of the most persistent in the history of this war. It may, however, be said that as the Federals were generally numerically superior to the Confederates these percentages are misleading. As to this I do not agree, because the Federals were normally the attackers, and it is a well known fact that the attacker loses much more heavily than the defender, and out of all proportion when the defender is entrenched. This can be seen quite clearly in the above tables.

I have already mentioned that lack in the appreciation of the powers of the rifle threw out of focus the true use of artillery, the object of which was either to assist or resist the infantry attack far more so than the assault, as the assault was becoming increasingly less profitable. With cavalry it was the same; in the assault they had no place, and on account of the increased range of the rifle their employment in the attack became more and more difficult. At the opening of the war the higher efficiency of the Confederate cavalry, especially in reconnoitring, was one of the main factors in the Southern successes. Yet neither Grant nor *Lee* seems to have realized that, on account of the rifle, reconnaissance was now their main rôle. In the Wilderness campaign, as we have seen, with some justification Grant detached nearly the whole of his cavalry under Sheridan to strike at *Lee's* communications. Again at the very end, when about to move on Five Forks, his first idea was for Sheridan to "cut loose and push for the Danville Road,"[29] attack *Lee's* communications and then join up with Sherman. Had he done so, it is not unlikely that *Lee* with part of his army would have escaped.

Lee's error in the use of cavalry was more accentuated. Before the opening of the Seven Days' Battle his instructions to *Stuart* were admirable; but when, on June 28, he sent this general with the whole of his cavalry to break up the York River railroad he unintentionally blinded himself, and he committed the same error, as we have seen, during the Gettysburg campaign.

The reason for these constant detachments of large forces of cavalry was the inability of cavalry to take part in battles pivoted upon assaults; this led to a doubt as how to use this arm. For so long in the past had cavalry been employed offensively that generals overlooked the fact that in a rifle war they had lost most of their offensive power, and realizing that they could no longer order them to strike the enemy in position, they ordered them to strike at his communications. To strike at communications is a sound operation of war, but for it to become fully effective it is first necessary *to pin down* the enemy who is making use of these communications, and before this can be done the enemy's position must be uncovered. Therefore, the first duty of cavalry is to assist the other arms in finding the enemy, that is reconnaissance, and when found, the second is to strike his communications *at a point sufficiently near to his front* as to cause him immediate and not "distant" anxiety; for such operations should aim at disorganizing as well as demoralizing the enemy. If close, they distract his attention, for they induce the enemy to weaken his front in order to protect his rear. And though always perturbing, the more distant they are the less distracting are they likely to be, and the less can they be supported by the other arms. The rear attack is an essential operation of war, but most of the cavalry operations in this war were not true rear attacks, in place—rear raids.

On this subject General Wilson's views are well worth quoting, for he was one of Sheridan's ablest subordinates, he says:

"To make a proper use of cavalry, you must get it into such a position that it can assail the flank or rear of an enemy, or operate upon his communications with effect. If I were called upon to command a force of 60,000 men, with authority to organize it as I pleased, I would have at least 20,000 on horseback. By using the mounted force to assail the flank and rear of the enemy, I should expect to conduct a more successful campaign than could be done by any other possible means in these days. The scattering of cavalry promiscuously along the front of an army is no longer necessary. Of course you must use cavalry to find out where the enemy is, and to gain early information of his movements, but a few squadrons can do it as well as a whole division. . . . With good cavalry, acting in conjunction with good infantry, you can accomplish almost anything in modern warfare. It is simply marvellous what can be done with men who are properly mounted. You can get them onto the flank and rear of the enemy every time."[30]

Throughout this war combined tactics were at a discount, because the full powers of the rifle were not fully appreciated; consequently, the inter-relationship of the three arms, infantry, artillery and cavalry, was not understood. Each weapon influences the use of all other weapons, and no improved weapon can be introduced without changing not only its old tactics but the tactics of all the other arms. This is a lesson little appreciated by both Grant and *Lee*.

Generalship

"War," writes Clausewitz, "is the province of chance";[31] it would have been more accurate, I think, had he written of "probabilities", for war is but an extended form of peace, and even in an anarchical society peace is more than a haphazard way of living. As in peace time probabilities are controlled for better or worse by statesmanship, so in war time are they controlled by generalship, which is nothing more than statesmanship under increased difficulties. As in peace time the abutments of statesmanship are authority and liberty, so likewise in war time are they of generalship; for an army, like a nation, must know how to obey and yet be able to adapt itself to its environment, therefore obedience must not cramp its initiative. As in civil wars the cause of the conflict is the desire to overthrow, or modify, authority, the generalship of the rebellious side is generally the more difficult though frequently the more brilliant. It is not bound by authority, yet unless it can establish authority, its cause is generally doomed.

In this American civil war, Grant stood for authority and *Lee* for liberty, neither were autocrats, but the servants of democratic governments. And of the two *Lee's* problem was the more difficult, for in order to win the war it was essential that he should exert his authority if only to establish a workable policy, and this he never did. Grant, on the other hand, had to gain that freedom of control which would enable him to mould the policy of his Government into strategical form; this, thanks to the good will of Lincoln, he was able to do. In both cases the deciding factor was personality. *Lee* could not impose his will upon Davis, and though Grant never attempted to impose his on Lincoln, his quiet unostentatious self-reliance and common sense imposed it for him. In *Lee's* place it is unlikely that he would have done much better than *Lee;* for neither he nor *Lee* was a true revolutionary general. Yet I much doubt whether in Grant's place *Lee* would have done half as well as Grant, for his outlook on war was narrow and restricted, and he possessed neither the character nor the personality of a General-in-Chief.

Of generalship in the field Napoleon once said:

"The first quality of a General-in-Chief is to have a cool head which receives exact impressions of things, which never gets heated, which never allows itself to be dazzled, or intoxicated, by good or bad news. The successive or simultaneous sensations which he receives in the course of a day must be classified, and must occupy the correct places they merit to fill, because common sense and reason are the results of the comparison of a number of sensations each equally well considered. There are certain men who, on account of their moral and physical constitution, paint mental pictures out of everything: however exalted be their reason, their will, their courage, and whatever good qualities they may possess, nature has not fitted them to command armies, nor to direct great operations of war." [32]

There can be no doubt whatsoever that both Grant and *Lee* did possess this first quality of generalship— self-command; but the remainder of Napoleon's description is far more applicable to the former than to the latter, because *Lee*, relying on intuition more than on reflection, was frequently misled by his assumptions, and particularly so as regards the morale of his enemy and the patriotism of the North.

"In war," writes Clausewitz, "it is only by means of a great directing spirit that we can expect the full power latent in the troops to be developed." [33] Intellectually Grant possessed such a spirit, in *Lee* this spirit was moral; the one relied upon strategy, the other upon sublimity; the one was the brain of his army, the other its soul. The one calculated and directed, the other impressed and compelled. Robert Jackson, one of the profoundest of military writers, once said: "Fear and love are coverings, behind them must lurk the spirit of genius which cannot be fathomed, for whether a commander be kind or severe, he cannot be great and prominent in the eye of the army unless he be admired for something unknown. It is thus that troops can only be properly animated by the superior and impenetrable genius of a commander, whose character stands before the army as a mirror, fixing the regards while it is bright and impenetrable, losing its virtue when the surface is soiled and softened so as to receive an impression. That a commander be a mirror, capable of animating an army, he must be impenetrable, but he cannot be impenetrable without possessing original genius. An original genius does not know his own powers. It thus commands attention, and it gives a covering of protection, in reality or idea, which proves a security against the impressions of fear."[34]

That Grant and *Lee* did possess such genius in totally different forms is beyond question, and that neither was aware of it, and hence its mysterious driving force, I think is also beyond doubt. One thing is, however, certain, few generals in history and none so submissive as *Lee*, have been able to animate an army as his self-sacrificing idealism animated the Army of Northern Virginia. To find a comparison we must go back to the days of the saints.

Of the general, Clausewitz says: "Ordinary men who follow the suggestion of others become . . . generally undecided on the spot; they think that they have found circumstances different from what they had expected, and this view gains strength by their again yielding to the suggestions of others. But even the man who has made his own plans, when he comes to see things with his own eyes, will often think he has done wrong . . . his first conviction will in the end prove true, when the foreground scenery, which fate has pushed on to the stage of war, with its accompaniments of terrific objects is drawn aside and the horizon extended. This is one of the great chasms which separate *conception* from execution."[35]

Clausewitz is undoubtedly right, for probably the commonest error in generalship is indecision, that is lack of faith in one's plan. Here Grant and *Lee* stand out as examples of extraordinary men. Grant's resolution knew no limit; *Lee's* faith in God knew no bounds. Both were men of first convictions, that is to say, once they had made up their minds there was no havering; consequently there was no chasm between conception and execution. The one followed naturally in the footsteps of the other, however faulty either might prove itself to be. Different though these two men were, Grant when he stepped ashore at Shiloh and *Lee* when he rallied his men after the fatal assault at Gettysburg, were men of a similar calibre, men who refused to succumb to "terrific objects"; men not only of cool heads but of firm hearts. To both may be applied the spirit of the following words of this great writer on war:

"As soon as difficulties arise—and that must always happen when great results are at stake—then things no longer move on of themselves like a well-oiled machine; the machine itself then begins to offer resistance, and to overcome this the commander must have a great force of will. . . . As the forces in one individual after another become prostrated, and can no longer be excited and supported by an effort of his own will, the whole inertia of the war gradually rests its weight on the will of the commander: by the spark in his breast, by the light of his spirit, the spark of purpose, the light of hope, must be kindled afresh in others: in so far only as he is equal to this he stands above the masses and continues to be their master; whenever that influence ceases, and his own spirit is no longer strong enough to revive the spirit of all others, the masses, drawing him down with them, sink into the lower region of animal nature, which shrinks from danger and knows not shame."[36]

Courage, moral and physical, self-reliance, resolution and self-command. . . . "Courage above all things is the first quality of a warrior,"[37] whether a simple soldier in the ranks or a General-in-Chief; for courage is of both and it unites both. "A man of courage," a man who fears not to die, a man who is possessed of something superior to mere living, this is the type of man who has always ennobled war. To the masses personal daring is like the lightning to the storm. "Ulysses don't scare worth a d——n!" . . . "General *Lee* to the rear, General *Lee* to the rear!"

. . . such was the lightning which fired the Army of the Potomac and the Army of Northern Virginia. Only in recent years, and I think quite unnecessarily so, have Generals-in-Chief, forgetting the virtue of courage, hidden themselves away in back areas to plot and to plan, and by not risking their lives, however precious they may be, have foresworn the valour of dying and so broken that magic link which connects the heart of the general to the hearts of his men.

Without personal leadership there can be no full manifestation of personality. Napoleon realized this when he said: "The personality of the general is indispensable, he is the head, he is the all of an army. The Gauls were not conquered by the Roman legions, but by Cæsar. It was not before the Carthaginian soldiers that Rome was made to tremble, but before Hannibal. It was not the Macedonian phalanx which penetrated to India, but Alexander. It was not the French Army which reached the Weser and the Inn, it was Turenne. Prussia was not defended for seven years against the three most formidable European Powers by the Prussian soldiers, but by Frederick the Great."[38] In a similar strain Robert Jackson writes: "Of the conquerors and eminent military characters who have at different times astonished the world, Alexander the Great and Charles the Twelfth of Sweden are two of the most singular; the latter of whom was the most heroic and the most extraordinary man of whom history has left any record. An army which had Alexander or Charles in its eye was different from itself in its simple nature, it imbibed a share of their spirit, became insensible of danger, and heroic in the extreme."[39]

Whether he be a subordinate general or the General-in-Chief, without the personal contact of the commander with his men such enthusiasm cannot be fired and such heroism created; for as Thomas Carlyle says, heroism is "the divine relation . . . which in all times unites a Great Man to other men."

This heroism, whether in peace or war, is the sheet-anchor of a people. Grant and *Lee* possessed it, as Washington possessed it, not only upon the summits of battle but in the vales of peaceful life. Hence, it seems to me, that I can find no better words wherewith to conclude this study of generalship than those of General *Gordon* when he wrote:[40]

"The strong and salutary characteristics of both *Lee* and
Grant should live in history as an inspiration to
coming generations. Posterity will find nobler
and more wholesome incentives in their
high attributes as men than in
their brilliant careers
as warriors."

FINIS

APPENDIX

BATTLES, NUMBERS AND LOSSES

Battles marked with an asterisk refer to Colonel Livermore's *Numbers and Losses in the Civil War in America, 1861-65.* Losses, etc., in other battles are taken from various sources and in some cases are estimated. Few things are more difficult in this war than to arrive at correct figures, and more especially so in the Confederate Army. Certain discrepancies will be noticed between strengths given in this table and in the text; these are due to differences in reckoning: in some cases "present for duty" is taken and in other cases "effectives" only. In actual fact it is impossible to disentangle these figures.

BATTLES, NUMBERS AND LOSSES

Battle	Date	Federal Casualties				Confederate Casualties			
		Strength	Killed	Wounded	Missing	Strength	Killed	Wounded	Missing
1st Bull Run or Manassas*	July 21, 1861	28,452	481	1,011	1,216	32,232	387	1,582	12
Belmont	Nov. 7, 1861	3,114	79	289	117	2,500	105	419	117
Fort Donelson*	Feb. 12–16, 1862	27,000	500	2,108	224	21,000		2,000	14,623
Shiloh*	April 6–7, 1862	62,682	1,754	8,408	2,885	40,335	1,723	8,012	959
Seven Pines or Fair Oaks*	May 31–June 1, 1862	44,944	790	3,594	647	41,816	980	4,749	405
Cross Keys	June 8, 1862		125	500				287	
Port Republic	June 9, 1862		67	361	574			657	
Mechanicsville*	June 26, 1862	15,631	49	207	105	16,356		1,484	
Gaines's Mill*	June 27, 1862	34,214	894	3,107	2,836	57,018		8,751	
Seven Days*	June 25–July 1, 1862	91,169	1,734	8,062	6,053	95,481	3,478	16,261	875
Cedar Mountain*	Aug. 9, 1862	8,030	314	1,445	594	16,868	231	1,107	89
2nd Bull Run or Manassas, and Chantilly*	Aug. 27–Sept. 2, 1862	75,696	1,724	8,372	5,958	48,527	1,481	7,627	800
South Mountain*	Sept. 14, 1862	28,480	325	1,403	85	17,852	325	1,560	
Harper's Ferry	Sept. 15, 1862		80	120	11,583			500	
Antietam or Sharpsburg*	Sept. 16–17, 1862	75,316	2,108	9,549	753	51,844	2,700	9,024	2,000
Iuka	Sept. 19, 1862		144	598	40			782	
Corinth*	Oct. 3–4, 1862	21,147	355	1,841	324	22,000	473	1,997	1,763
Fredericksburg*	Dec. 12, 1862	106,007	1,284	9,600	1,769	72,497	595	4,061	653
Chickasaw Bluff*	Dec. 27–29, 1862	30,720	208	1,005	563	13,792	63	134	10
Murfreesboro or Stone River*	Dec. 31, 1862	41,400	1,677	7,543	3,686	34,732	1,294	7,945	2,500
Chancellorsville*	May 1–4, 1863	97,362	1,575	9,594	5,676	57,352	1,665	9,681	2,018
Port Gibson	May 1, 1863		130	718	5			1,650	
Champion's Hill*	May 16, 1863	29,373	410	1,844	187	20,000	381	1,800	1,670
Vicksburg Assault*	May 22, 1863	45,556	502	2,550	147	22,301			
Vicksburg Campaign	May–July, 1863		1,243	7,095	535		10,000		37,000
Gettysburg*	July 1–3, 1863	88,289	3,155	14,529	5,365	75,000	3,903	18,735	5,425

Battle	Date	Strength	Killed	Wounded	Missing	Strength	Killed	Wounded	Missing
Chickamauga*	Sept. 19-20, 1863	58,222	1,657	9,756*	4,757	66,326	2,312	14,674	1,468
Chattanooga*	Nov. 23-25, 1863	56,359	753	4,722	349	46,165	361	2,160	4,146
Mine Run*	Nov. 27-Dec. 1, 1863	69,643	173	1,099	381	44,426	110	570	65
Pleasant Hill*	April 8-9, 1864	12,647	150	844	375	14,300	1,000	—	500
Wilderness*	May 5-7, 1864	101,895	2,246	12,037	3,383	61,025	7,750?	—	—
Spottsylvania Assault*	May 10, 1864	37,822	753	3,347	—	—	—	—	—
Spottsylvania Assault*	May 12, 1864	65,785	6,020		800	18,025	5,500?	1,941	4,000
Drury's Bluff*	May 12-16, 1864	15,800	390	2,380	1,390	66,089	355	9,187	210
Atlanta Campaign*	May, 1864	110,123	10,528		1,240	—	—	—	—
North Anna	May 23-27, 1864	—	223	1,460	290	—	2,000?	—	—
Cold Harbor	June 1-12, 1864	60,000	1,905	10,570	2,546	—	1,700?	—	—
Cold Harbor	June 3, 1864	—	1,100	4,517	1,400?	—	—	—	—
Petersburg Assaults*	June 15-18, 1864	63,797	8,150		—	41,499	—	—	—
Kenesaw Mountain*	June 21, 1864	16,225	1,999		52	17,733	270	—	172
Peach Tree Creek*	July 20, 1864	20,139	1,600?		—	18,832	2,500?	—	—
Atlanta*	July 22, 1864	30,477	430	1,559	1,783	36,934	7,000?	—	1,000
Atlanta*	July 28, 1864	13,226	559		73	18,450	4,100?	—	200
Petersburg Mine*	July 30, 1864	20,708	2,864		929	11,466	—	—	—
Weldon R.R.*	Aug. 18-21, 1864	20,289	198	1,105	3,152	14,787	1,200?	—	419
Opequon Creek or Winchester	Sept. 19, 1864	37,711	697	3,983	338	16,377	276	1,827	1,818
New Market Heights Va.	Sept. 28-30, 1864	—	400	2,029	—	—	—	—	—
Chaffins Farm*	Sept. 29-30, 1864	19,639	383	2,299	645	10,836	—	—	—
Cedar Creek*	Oct. 19, 1864	30,829	644	3,430	1,591	18,410	320	1,540	1,050
Boydton Plank Road*	Oct. 27-28, 1864	42,823	166	1,028	564	20,324	—	—	—
Franklin*	Nov. 30, 1864	27,939	189	1,033	1,104	26,897	1,750	3,800	702
Nashville*	Dec. 15-16, 1864	49,773	387	2,562	112	23,207	—	—	4,462
Fort Fisher	Jan. 13-15, 1865	—	184	749	22	—	—	—	—
Fort Steadman	March 24, 1865	45,247	2,080		583	20,030	2,483?	—	—
Dinwiddie Court House*	March 29-31, 1865	63,299	2,198		326	18,576	4,000?	—	—
Petersburg Assault*	April 2, 1865	112,892	625	3,189	1,714	54,000	1,050?	—	—
Appomattox Campaign*	March 29-April 5, 1865	—	1,316	7,750	—	22,349	—	—	—
Surrender of General Lee	April 9, 1865	—	—	—	—	—	—	—	—

REFERENCES

a—Denotes a Staff Officer to Grant or *Lee*
b—A person well acquainted with either Grant or *Lee*
c—A contemporary American witness, and
d—A contemporary foreign witness.

CHAPTER I

1 *John Brown's Body*, Stephen Vincent Benét, p. 375.
2 *The Rise and Fall of the Confederate Government*, Jefferson Davis,[b] vol. i, p. 154.
3 *ibid.*, vol. i, p. 155.
4 *Three Months in the Southern States, April-June, 1863*, Lieut-Colonel Fremantle,[d] p. 31.
5 *A Belle of the Fifties*, Mrs. Clay,[c] p. 167.
6 *The American Commonwealth*, James Bryce, vol. i, p. 329.
7 *The Rise and Fall of the Confederate Government*, Jefferson Davis,[b] vol. i, p. 32.
8 *Life in the Confederate Army*, William Watson,[c] p. 87.
9 *The Life and Campaigns of General Lee*, Edward Lee Childe,[b] p. 5.
10 *Madison Papers*, p. 1066.
11 *The American Commonwealth*, James Bryce, vol. i, p. 99.
12 *Robert E. Lee and the Southern Confederacy*, Henry Alexander White,[b] p. 68.
13 *The American Commonwealth*, James Bryce, vol. i, p. 423.
14 *Destruction and Reconstruction*, Richard Taylor,[b] p. 100.
15 *John Brown's Body*, Stephen Vincent Benét, pp. 25-26.
16 *ibid.*, p. 163.
17 *Recollections and Letters of General Robert E. Lee*, Captain Robert E. Lee,[b] p. 113.
18 *Three Months in the Southern States, April-June, 1863*, Lieut-Colonel Fremantle,[d] p. 58.
19 *The Life and Campaigns of General Lee*, Edward Lee Childe,[b] p. 11.
20 *The War of the Rebellion*, vol. xxviii, p. 644.
21 *Jefferson Davis, ex-President of the Confederate States*, Mrs. Davis,[b] vol. i, p. 191.

22 *Essays on American Government*, A. B. Hart, p. 283.

23 *A Diary from Dixie*, Mrs. Chesnut,[b] vol. i, p. 108.

24 *General Lee of the Confederate Army*, Fitzhugh Lee,[b] p. 382.

25 *An Aide-de-Camp of Lee*, Papers of Colonel Charles Marshall,[a] edited by Major-General Sir Frederick Maurice, pp. 10, 19.

26 *The Rise and Fall of the Confederate Government*, Jefferson Davis,[b] vol. ii, pp. 158-159.

27 *The War of the Rebellion*, vol. xliii, p. 31.

28 *History of the Civil War in America*, Comte de Paris,[d] vol. i, p. 613.

29 *Leading American Soldiers*, R. M. Johnston, p. 130.

30 *Memoirs of the Confederate War for Independance*, Heros von Borcke,[d] vol. i, p. 14.

31 *Battles and Leaders of the Civil War*, vol. i, p. 107.

32 *An Aide-de-Camp of Lee*, Papers of Colonel Charles Marshall,[a] p. 13.

33 *Memoirs of the Confederate War of Independence*, Heros von Borcke,[d] vol. ii, p. 7.

34 *A Belle of the Fifties*, Mrs. Clay,[c] pp. 186, 194-195.

35 *Four Years Under Marse Robert*, Robert Stiles,[b] p. 37.

36 *Battles and Leaders of the Civil War*, vol. i, p. 160.

37 *An Aide-de-Camp of Lee*, Papers of Colonel Charles Marshall,[a] p. 12.

38 *ibid.*, pp. 24-25.

39 *The Rise and Fall of the Confederate Government*, Jefferson Davis,[b] vol. i, p. 87.

40 *ibid.*, p. 149.

41 *ibid.*, p. 170.

42 *A Constitutional View of the Late War Between the States*, Alexander H. Stephens,[b] pp. 31, 34 and 35. See also *Rawle on the Constitution*, p. 85.

43 *The Life and Campaigns of General Lee*, Edward Lee Childe,[b] p. 62.

44 *Stonewall Jackson and the American Civil War*, Colonel G. F. R. Henderson, C.B., vol. i, p. 173. "A defensive war is apt to betray us into too frequent detachments. Those generals who have had but little experience attempt to protect every point, while whose who are better acquainted with their profession, having only the capital object in view, guard against a decisive blow, and acquiesce in smaller misfortunes to avoid greater." Frederick the Great's *Instructions to his Generals*.

45 *An Aide-de-Camp of Lee*, Papers of Col. Charles Marshall,[a] pp. 34-35. This Conscription Act completely reversed the previous military legislation of the South. Election of officers continued until just before the opening of the 1865

campaign, and was one of the root causes of ill-discipline. Owners of fifteen slaves were exempted from the Conscription law.

46 *Stonewall Jackson and the American Civil War*, Colonel G. F. R. Henderson, C.B., vol. i, p. 234.

47 *Reminiscences of the Civil War*, General John B. Gordon,[b] p. 315.

48 Another reason apparently was the "scourge of flies and bad food" at the Exchange Hotel, Montgomery, Jefferson Davis's headquarters.—*Jefferson Davis, Political Soldier*, Elisabeth Cutting, p. 154.

49 *Instructions to his Generals*, Frederick the Great.

50 *Stonewall Jackson and the American Civil War*, Colonel G. F. R. Henderson, C.B., vol. i, pp. 109-110.

51 *MacMillan's Magazine*, March, 1887, p. 328.

52 Introduction to Henderson's *Stonewall Jackson*, p. x.

53 *Leading American Soldiers*, R. M. Johnston, pp. 93-94. This battle was fought on January 8, 1815, sixteen days after peace was signed at Ghent between the United States and Great Britain. News travelled slowly then.

54 *Stonewall Jackson and the American Civil War*, Colonel G. F. R. Henderson, C.B., vol. ii, p. 341.

55 *ibid.*, vol. i, p. 170.

56 *Meade's Headquarters, 1863-1865*, Colonel Theodore Lyman,[b] p. 224.

57 *The Soldier in Battle, or Life in the Ranks of the Army of the Potomac*, Frank Wilkeson,[c] p. 99.

58 *Meade's Headquarters, 1863-1865*, Colonel Theodore Lyman,[b] p. 101.

59 *Southern Generals: Who They Are and What They Have Done*, W. Parker Snow,[c] p. 104.

60 *General Lee, His Campaigns in Virginia, 1861-1865*, Walter H. Taylor,[a] pp. 33-34.

61 *Life in the Confederate Army*, William Watson,[c] p. 217.

62 *Reminiscences of the Civil War*, General John B. Gordon,[b] pp. 5-6.

63 *Memoirs of the Confederate War for Independence*, Heros von Borcke,[d] vol. i, p. 63, and vol. ii, p. 50.

64 *Papers of the Military Historical Society of Massachusetts*, vol. xiii, p. 265.

65 *Battles and Leaders of the Civil War*, vol. iv, p. 212.

66 *Encyclopaedia Britannica*, Eleventh Edition, vol. xvii, p. 239.

67 *The Times*, Special Correspondent, January 1, 1863.

68 *Battles and Leaders of the Civil War*, vol ii, p. 513.

69 *Campaigns and Battles of the Army of Northern Virginia*, George Wise,[b] p. 160.

70 *The War of the Rebellion,* vol. lxix, pp. 888-889.
71 *Battles and Leaders of the Civil War,* vol. iv, p. 636.
72 *Papers of the Military Historical Society of Massachusetts,* vol. xiv, pp. 450-453.
73 *Meade's Headquarters, 1863-1865,* Colonel Theodore Lyman,[b] p. 284.
74 *Southern Generals: Who They Are and What They Have Done,* W. Parker Snow,[c] p. 105.
75 *The Soldier in Battle, or Life in the Ranks of the Army of the Potomac,* Frank Wilkeson,[d] p. 80.
76 *ibid.,* p. 72.
77 *Battles and Leaders of the Civil War,* vol. i, p. 169.
78 *The Soldier in Battle, or Life in the Ranks of the Army of the Potomac,* Frank Wilkeson,[d] p. 11.
79 *Life in the Confederate Army,* William Watson,[c] p. 171.
80 *Southern Historical Society Papers,* vol. xiii, p. 261.
81 *Meade's Headquarters, 1863-1865,* Colonel Theodore Lyman,[b] p. 100.
82 *Three Months in the Southern States, April-June, 1863,* Lieut-Colonel Fremantle,[d] pp. 121-123.
83 *Life in the Confederate Army,* William Watson,[c] p. 184.
84 *The Campaign of Chancellorsville,* Major John Bigelow, p. 175; *Campaigns of the Army of the Potomac,* William Swinton,[c] p. 272; *The War of the Rebellion,* vol. xl, pp. 554-555.
85 *General Lee, His Campaigns in Virginia, 1861-1865,* Walter H. Taylor,[a] pp. 176-177.
86 *Life in the Confederate Army,* William Watson,[c] p. 388.
87 *ibid.,* pp. 230, 294.
88 *Four Years Under Marse Robert,* Robert Stiles,[b] p. 200.

CHAPTER II

1 *A Personal History of Ulysses S. Grant,* Albert D. Richardson,[b] p. 122.
2 *Meet General Grant,* W. E. Woodward, p. 125.
3 *A Personal History of Ulysses S. Grant,* Albert D. Richardson,[b] p. 176. After Grant had become famous Yates prided himself on his selection and said: "God gave him to the country, and I signed his first commission."—*General Grant,* James Grant Wilson,[c] p. 85.
4 *A Personal History of Ulysses S. Grant,* Albert D. Richardson,[b] p. 186.

5   *General Grant*, James Grant Wilson,[c] p. 212.
6   *Campaigning with Grant*, General Horace Porter,[a] LL.D., pp. 96-97.
7   *A Personal History of Ulysses S. Grant*, Albert D. Richardson,[b] p. 492.
8   *Battles and Leaders of the Civil War*, vol. iv, p. 744.
9   *Campaigning with Grant*, General Horace Porter,[a] LL.D., p. 515.
10 *Personal Memoirs*, Ulysses S. Grant, vol. ii, p. 489.
11 *Meet General Grant*, W. E. Woodward, p. 117.
12 *Personal Memoirs*, Ulysses S. Grant.
13 *Campaigning with Grant*, General Horace Porter,[a] LL.D., p. 81.
14 *ibid.*, p. 56.
15 *Ulysses S. Grant*, William Conant Church,[b] p. 364.
16 *Meet General Grant*, W. E. Woodward, pp. 288-289.
17 *A Personal History of Ulysses S. Grant*, Albert D. Richardson,[b] p. 155.
18 *ibid.*, p. 132.
19 *Campaigning with Grant*, General Horace Porter,[a] LL.D., p. 25.
20 *Ulysses S. Grant*, William Conant Church,[b] pp. 227-228.
21 *A Personal History of Ulysses S. Grant*, Albert Richardson,[b] p. 176.
22 *Ulysses S. Grant*, William Conant Church,[b] p. 64.
23 *A Personal History of Ulysses S. Grant*, Albert Richardson,[b] pp. 176-177.
24 *ibid.*, p. 177.
25 *Campaigning with Grant*, General Horace Porter,[a] LL.D., p. 67.
26 *ibid.*, pp. 164-165.
27 *ibid.*, p. 244.
28 *Battles and Leaders of the Civil War*, vol. i, p. 422.
29 *Personal Memoirs*, Ulysses S. Grant, vol. i, pp. 307-308.
30 *Meade's Headquarters, 1863-1865*, Colonel Theodore Lyman,[b] p. 359.
31 *Campaigning with Grant*, General Horace Porter,[a] p. 31.
32 *ibid.*, p. 4.
33 *ibid.*, p. 241.
34 *A Personal History of Ulysses S. Grant*, Albert Richardson,[b] p. 186.
35 *Campaigning with Grant*, General Horace Porter,[a] p. 250.
36 *A Personal History of Ulysses S. Grant*, Albert Richardson,[b] p. 293.
37 *Battles and Leaders of the Civil War*, vol. iii, p. 678.
38 *Campaigning with Grant*, General Horace Porter,[a] p. 74.
    During this battle Shakespeare's words in his *Henry the Fifth* may aptly be applied to him:
        "The royal captain of this ruin'd band
        Walking from watch to watch, from tent to tent,

*   *   *   *   *   *

Upon his royal face there is no note
How dread an army hath enrounded him;

*   *   *   *   *   *

That every wretch, pining and pale before,
Beholding him, plucks comfort from his looks,
A largess universal like the sun
His liberal eye doth give to every one
Thawing cold fear. . . ."

39 *The War of the Rebellion*, vol. l, p. 219.
40 *Battles and Leaders of the Civil War*, vol. iii, p. 678.
41 *Campaigning with Grant*, General Horace Porter,[a] p. 59.
42 *ibid.*, pp. 63-70.
43 *Personal Memoirs*, Ulysses S. Grant, vol. i, pp. 29-30.
44 *A Personal History of Ulysses S. Grant*, Albert Richardson,[b] p. 480.
45 *A Personal History of Ulysses S. Grant*, Albert D. Richardson, p. 396.
46 *ibid.*, p. 396.
47 *Leading American Soldiers*, R. M. Johnston, p. 137.
48 *The Mississippi*, F. V. Greene,[c] p. 108.
49 *A Personal History of Ulysses S. Grant*, Albert Richardson,[b] p. 393.
50 *Military Miscellanies*, J. B. Fry,[b] pp. 295, 296, 301.
51 *Ulysses S. Grant*, William Conant Church,[b] pp. 188-189.
52 *Meade's Headquarters, 1863-1865*, Colonel Theodore Lyman,[b] p. 80. Of his personal appearance Horace Porter[b] says: "Slim figure, slight stoop, five feet eight inches high, and weight about 135 lbs. His manner gentle and modest, and his eyes—dark grey. A good listener, but his face gave little indication of his thoughts. Often laughed heartily at witty remarks. Square jawed, hair and beard a chestnut brown and closely and neatly trimmed. Brow high, broad and rather square; voice 'exceedingly musical,' his gait in walking unmilitary, no ear for music, never could keep step."—*Campaigning with Grant*, p. 14.
53 *Meade's Headquarters, 1863-1865*, Colonel Theodore Lyman,[b] p. 81.
54 *ibid.*, p. 83.
55 *ibid.*, p. 156.
56 *Personal Memoirs*, Ulysses S. Grant, vol. i, p. 116.
57 *ibid.*, vol. i, p. 279.
58 *Campaigning with General Grant*, General Horace Porter,[a] p. 302.
59 *ibid.*, p. 2.
60 *Personal Memoirs*, Ulysses S. Grant, vol. i, p. 250.
61 *The War of the Rebellion*, vol. xxxviii, p. 285.

62 *Military History of Ulysses S. Grant*, A. Badeau,[a] vol. i, p. 222.
63 *Personal Memoirs of P. H. Sheridan*,[b] vol. ii, p. 204.
64 *Ulysses S. Grant*, William Conant Church,[b] pp. 231-232.
65 *Campaigning with General Grant*, General Horace Porter,[a] p. 314.
66 *Ulysses S. Grant*, William Conant Church,[b] p. 3.
67 *Military Miscellanies*, J. B. Fry,[b] p. 297.
68 *Military History of Ulysses S. Grant*, A. Badeau,[a] vol. i, p. 616.
69 *ibid.*, vol. iii, p. 28.
70 *Grant's Campaigns of 1864 and 1865*, C. F. Atkinson. p. 287.
71 *Battles and Leaders of the Civil War*, vol. iv, p. 738.
72 *ibid*, vol. iv, p. 248.
73 *The Soldier in Battle, or Life in the Ranks of the Army of the Potomac*, Frank Wilkeson,[d] p. 66.
74 *The War of the Rebellion*, vol. lxviii, p. 627.
75 *Battles and Leaders of the Civil War*, vol. iv, p. 709.
76 *Lincoln and Men of War Times*, McClure, p. 179.

CHAPTER III

1 *Life and Letters of R. E. Lee, Soldier and Man*, J. W. Jones,[b] p. 118.
2 *Memoirs of Robert E. Lee*, A. L. Long,[a] pp. 88-89.
3 *Robert E. Lee and the Southern Confederacy, 1807-1870*, Henry Alexander White,[b] p. 50.
4 *Recollections and Letters of General Robert E. Lee*, Captain Robert E. Lee,[b] p. 168.
5 *General Lee of the Confederate Army*, Fitzhugh Lee,[b] p. 64.
6 *Memoirs of Robert E. Lee*, A. L. Long,[a] p. 417.
7 *Anecdotes of the Civil War*, E. Townsend, p. 29.
8 *Southern Historical Society Papers*, vol. xi, p. 360.
9 *Memoirs of the War in the Southern Department of the United States*, Henry Lee, and a Biography of the Author by Robert E. Lee, p. 25.
10 *The War of the Rebellion*, vol. xcvi, p. 1230.
11 *Stonewall Jackson and the American Civil War*, Colonel G. F. R. Henderson, vol. ii, pp. 262-263.
12 *The Life and Campaigns of General Lee*, Edward Lee Childe,[b] p. 22.
13 *General Lee, Man and Soldier*, Thomas Nelson Page, p. 38.
14 *General Lee, His Campaigns in Virginia, 1861-1865*, Walter H. Taylor,[a] p. 180. "His design was to free the State of Virginia for a time at least, from the presence of the enemy."
15 *The Life and Campaigns of General Lee*, Edward Lee Childe,[b] p. 331.

16 *Recollections and Letters of General Robert E. Lee*, Captain Robert
    E. Lee,[b] p. 133.
17 *Southern Historical Society Papers*, vol. xxvii, p. 317; and *The
    War of the Rebellion*, vol. xci, pp. 920, 922.
18 *Memoirs of Robert E. Lee*, A. L. Long,[a] p. 301.
19 *ibid.*, pp. 309-310.
20 *ibid.*, p. 302.
21 *Memoirs of the War in the Southern Department of the United
    States*, Henry Lee, and a Biography of the Author by
    Robert E. Lee, p. 75. In the Biography, p. 45, *Lee* writes:
    "Although his correspondence at this time [1792], as well
    as the course of his life, proves his devotion to the Federal
    Government, yet he recognized a distinction between his
    'native country' and that which he had laboured to associate
    with it in the strictest bonds of union." This is rather
    stretching the point, for on January 29, 1792, Henry Lee
    wrote to Madison: "No consideration on earth would
    induce me to act a part, however gratifying to me, which
    could be construed into disregard or forgetfulness of this
    Commonwealth. . . ."
22 *Robert E. Lee and the Southern Confederacy*, Henry Alexander
    White,[b] p. 124.
23 *Recollections and Letters of General Robert E. Lee*, Captain Robert
    E. Lee,[b] p. 89.
24 *A Diary from Dixie*, Mrs. Chesnut,[b] p. 94.
25 *Lippincott's Magazine*, vol. lxxix, p. 55.
26 *Recollections and Letters of General Robert E. Lee*, Captain Robert
    E. Lee,[b] pp. 304-305.
27 *General Lee of the Confederate Army*, Fitzhugh Lee,[b] p. 23.
28 *Memoirs of Robert E. Lee*, A. L. Long,[a] p. 65.
29 *General Lee of the Confederate Army*, Fitzhugh Lee,[b] p. 37.
30 *Memoirs of Robert E. Lee*, A. L. Long,[a] pp. 57-58.
31 *John Brown's Body*, Stephen Vincent Benét, p. 189.
32 *ibid.*, p. 374.
33 *General Lee, His Campaigns in Virginia, 1861-1865*, Walter H.
    Taylor,[a] p. 32.
34 *Memoirs of Robert E. Lee*, A. L. Long,[a] p. 435.
35 *Recollections and Letters of General Robert E. Lee*, Captain Robert
    E. Lee,[b] p. 138.
36 *Memoirs of Robert E. Lee*, A. L. Long,[a] p. 341.
37 *Reminiscences of the Civil War*, General John B. Gordon,[b] p. 279.
38 *Three Months in the Southern States, April-June, 1863*, Lieut-
    Colonel Fremantle,[d] p. 274.
39 *General Lee of the Confederate Army*, Fitzhugh Lee,[b] p. 209.

40 *ibid*, p. 152.
41 *ibid*., p. 42.
42 *ibid*., p. 91.
43 *Recollections and Letters of General Robert E. Lee*, Captain Robert E. Lee,[b] p. 271.
44 *Memoirs of Robert E. Lee*, A. L. Long,[a] pp. 259-260.
45 *Personal Reminiscences, Anecdotes and Letters of General Robert E. Lee*, J. W. Jones,[b] p. 50.
46 *General Lee of the Confederate Army*, Fitzhugh Lee,[b] p. 418.
47 *The Science of War*, Colonel G. F. R. Henderson, p. 314.
48 *Around the World with General Grant*, J. R. Young,[b] vol. ii, p. 459.
49 *Memoirs of Robert E. Lee*, A. L. Long,[a] p. 643.
50 *Recollections and Letters of General Robert E. Lee*, Captain Robert E. Lee,[b] p. 45.
51 *ibid*., pp. 105-106.
52 *Life and Letters of R. E. Lee, Soldier and Man*, J. W. Jones,[b] p. 438.
53 *General Lee of the Confederate Army*, Fitzhugh Lee,[b] p. 68.
54 *ibid*., p. 365.
55 *Memoirs of Robert E. Lee*, A. L. Long,[a] pp. 489-490.
56 *Lee, the American*, Gamaliel Bradford, pp. 244, 246.
57 *Memoirs of Robert E. Lee*, A. L. Long,[a] p. 465.
58 *Southern Historical Society Papers*, vol. xi, p. 360.
59 *Memoirs of Robert E. Lee*, A. L. Long,[a] p. 223.
60 *ibid*., p. 486.
61 *The Life and Campaigns of General Lee*, Edward Lee Childe,[b] p. 58. Also, *Recollections and Letters of General Robert E. Lee*, Captain Robert E. Lee,[b] p. 53.
62 *Life and Letters of R. E. Lee, Soldier and Man*, J. W. Jones,[b] p. 84.
63 *Der Bürgerkrieg in dem nordamerikanischen Staaten*, J. Scheibert,[d] p. 39.
64 *Recollections and Letters of General Robert E. Lee*, Captain Robert E. Lee,[b] p. 103. White says: "Nominally as military adviser to President Davis, *Lee* remained in official connection with the Confederate Cabinet."—*Robert E. Lee and the Southern Confederacy*, Henry Alexander White,[b] p. 108. Long says: "His advice in relation to the movements of other armies was constantly asked by the Government."—*Memoirs of Robert E. Lee*, A. L. Long,[a] p. 392. On January 17, 1865, the legislature of Virginia appealed to Davis to make *Lee* Commander-in-Chief of all the Confederate armies. On the 18th Davis offered the command to *Lee*. The intention of the legislature was that the entire military control should pass out of Davis's hands. *Lee*, however, accepted the office only "as the subordinate of the Presi-

dent," and refused to act as a true Commander-in-Chief.—
Lee's Confidential Dispatches to Davis, p. 322.

65 *Personal Reminiscences, Anecdotes and Letters of General E. Lee*, J. W. Jones,[b] p. 274.
66 *Memoirs of Robert E. Lee*, A L. Long,[a] p. 370.
67 *ibid.*, p. 454.
68 *Recollections and Letters of General Robert E. Lee*, Captain Robert E. Lee,[b] p. 287.
69 *Davis Memorial Volume*, p. 41.
70 *Battles and Leaders of the Civil War*, vol. ii, pp. 447-448.
71 *Memoirs of Robert E. Lee*, A. L. Long,[a] p. 478.
72 *The War of the Rebellion*, vol. xl, p. 726.
73 *ibid.*, vol. xxviii, p. 600.
74 *ibid.*, vol. xxxi, p. 1029.
75 *Memoirs of Robert E. Lee*, A. L. Long,[a] p. 587.
76 *An Aide-de-Camp of Lee*, Papers of Colonel Charles Marshall,[a] p. 275.
77 *ibid.*, p. 275.
78 *Lee, the American*, Gamaliel Bradford, p. 75.
79 *Reminiscences of War and Peace*, Mrs. Roger A. Pryor,[c] p. 358; and *Reminiscences of the Civil War*, General John B. Gordon,[b] p. 390.
80 *The War of the Rebellion*, vol. cxxix, p. 1012.
81 *Richmond Examiner*, February 16, 1865.
82 *The Lost Cause*, E. A. Pollard,[c] p. 655.
83 *John Brown's Body*, Stephen Vincent Benét, p. 188.
84 *The Life and Campaigns of General Lee*, Edward Lee Childe,[b] pp. 164-165.
85 *ibid.*, p. 190.
86 *Southern Historical Society Papers*, vol. xxviii, p. 295.
87 *General Lee, His Campaigns in Virginia, 1861-1865*, Walter H. Taylor,[a] p. 185.
88 *Memoirs of Robert E. Lee*, A. L. Long,[a] p. 295. Also *General Lee, His Campaigns in Virginia, 1861-1865*, Walter H. Taylor,[a] p. 215.
89 *The War of the Rebellion*, vol. cviii, p. 994.
90 *Life and Letters of R. E. Lee, Soldier and Man*, J. W. Jones,[b] p. 36.
91 *Lee, the American*, Gamaliel Bradford, p. 107.
92 *Three Months in the Southern States, April-June, 1863*, Lieut-Colonel Fremantle,[d] p. 255.
93 *MacMillan's Magazine*, March, 1887.
94 *Southern Historical Society Papers*, vol. ii, p. 65.
95 *Four Years with General Lee*, Walter H. Taylor,[a] p. 146.
96 *Southern Historical Society Papers*, vol. xvii, p. 37.

97 *Robert E. Lee and the Southern Confederacy*, Henry Alexander White,[b] p. 116.
98 *General Lee of the Confederate Army*, Fitzhugh Lee,[b] p. 280.
99 *Robert E. Lee and the Southern Confederacy*, Henry Alexander White,[b] p. 333.
100 *Destruction and Reconstruction*, Richard Taylor,[b] p. 70.
101 *Memoirs of Robert E. Lee*, A. L. Long,[a] p. 540.
102 *ibid.*, p. 537.
103 *Three Months in the Southern States, April-June, 1863*, Lieut-Colonel Fremantle,[d] p. 113.
104 *ibid.*, p. 160.
105 *Memoirs of Robert E. Lee*, A. L. Long,[a] p. 619.
106 *Four Years with General Lee*, Walter H. Taylor,[a] p. 148.
107 *MacMillan's Magazine*, March, 1887.
108 *Memoirs of Robert E. Lee*, A. L. Long,[a] p. 454.
109 *Lee's Confidential Dispatches*, p. 322.
110 *The War of the Rebellion*, vol. cxxi, p. 536.
111 *ibid.*, vol. xlviii, p. 405.
112 *Memoirs of Robert E. Lee*, A. L. Long,[a] p. 247.
113 *The War of the Rebellion*, vol. xcvi, p. 1210.
114 *ibid.*, vol. xl, p. 687.
115 *ibid.*, vol. xl, p. 1065.
116 *General Lee, His Campaigns in Virginia, 1861-1865*, Walter H. Taylor,[a] p. 25.
117 *ibid.*, p. 56.
118 *Memoirs of Robert E. Lee*, A. L. Long,[a] p. 223.
119 *Stonewall Jackson and the American Civil War*, Colonel G. F. R. Henderson, vol. i, p. 306.
120 *ibid.*, p. 411. See also vol. ii, p. 3.
121 *The War of the Rebellion*, vol. lxxi, p. 173.
122 *General Lee of the Confederate Army*, Fitzhugh Lee,[b] p. 420.
123 *Four Years with General Lee*, Walter H. Taylor,[a] p. 85.
124 *Campaigns in Virginia and Maryland*, Captain C. C. Chesney,[d] vol. i, p. 198.
125 *The Campaign of Fredericksburg*, Lieut-Colonel G. F. R. Henderson, p. 113.
126 *Four Years with General Lee*, Walter H. Taylor,[a] p. 99.
127 *General Lee, His Campaigns in Virginia, 1861-1865*, Walter H. Taylor,[a] p. 74.
128 *Three Months in the Southern States, April-June, 1863*, Lieut-Colonel Fremantle,[d] pp. 171 and 246. See also, *Campaigns in Virginia and Maryland*, Captain C. C. Chesney,[d] vol. i, p. 50.
129 *The Battle of Chancellorsville*, Augustus Choate Hamlin, p. 50.
130 *General Lee, His Campaigns in Virginia*, Walter H. Taylor,[a] p. 46.

131 *Memoirs of Stonewall Jackson*, Mary Anne Jackson, p. 43.
132 *ibid.*, p. 310.
133 *Life and Campaigns of Lieut.-Gen. Thomas J. Jackson*, Prof. R. L. Dabney,[b] vol. ii, p. 130.
134 *Recollections and Letters of General Robert E. Lee*, Captain Robert E. Lee,[b] p. 95.
135 *ibid.*, p. 153.
136 *ibid.*, pp. 223-224.
137 *ibid.*, p. 224.
138 *Memoirs of Robert E. Lee*, A. L. Long,[a] p. 456.
139 *ibid.*, p. 253.
140 *ibid.*, p. 457.
141 *ibid.*, p. 452.

CHAPTER IV

1 *Robert E. Lee and the Southern Confederacy*, Henry Alexander White,[b] p. 101.
2 *ibid.*, p. 103; and *The War of the Rebellion*, vol. ii, pp. 775-776.
3 *The War of the Rebellion*, vol. ii, p. 784; also pp. 777, 778, 788.
4 *ibid.*, vol. ii, p. 814.
5 *ibid.*, vol. ii, p. 505.
6 *Robert E. Lee and the Southern Confederacy*, Henry Alexander White,[b] p. 114.
7 *The War of the Rebellion*, vol. v, p. 1, footnote, and p. 757.
8 *ibid.*, vol. v, p. 773.
9 *ibid.*, vol. v, p. 774.
10 *ibid.*, vol. v, pp. 784-786, 792-794, 800, 804-805, 810, 868-869, 879.
11 *ibid.*, vol. v, p. 149.
12 *ibid.*, vol. v, p. 1099.
13 *ibid.*, vol. iv, p. 196.
14 *Meet General Grant*, W. E. Woodward, p. 212.
15 *The War of the Rebellion*, vol. vii, p. 529 and p. 533.
16 *ibid.*, vol. vii, p. 534.
17 *ibid.*, vol. viii, p. 509.
18 *ibid.*, vol. vii, p. 121.
19 *The Story of the Civil War*, J. C. Ropes, Pt. II, p. 18.
20 *The War of the Rebellion*, vol. vii, pp. 179-180.
21 *ibid.*, pp. 944 and 159. Badeau in *Military History of Ulysses S. Grant*, vol. i, p. 50, says: "65 guns and nearly 15,000 men."
22 *The War of the Rebellion*, vol. vii, p. 169.
23 *Battles and Leaders of the Civil War*, vol. i, p. 547.

REFERENCES

24 *Papers of the Military Historical Society of Massachusetts*, vol. viii, p. 142.
25 *ibid.*, vol. vii, p. 26.
26 *Personal Memoirs*, Ulysses S. Grant, vol. i, p. 317; and *The War of the Rebellion*, vol. vii, p. 648.
27 *The War of the Rebellion*, vol. vii, p. 616.
28 *Personal Memoirs*, U. S. Grant, vol. i, p. 326; *Military History of Ulysses S. Grant*, A. Badeau,[a] vol. i, p. 60-65; *Papers of the Military Historical Society of Massachusetts*, vol. vii, p. 37, and p. 108; and *The War of the Rebellion*, vol. vii, pp. 679, 680, 682, 683.
29 *Personal Memoirs*, U. S. Grant, vol. i, p. 327; *Papers of the Historical Society of Massachusetts*, vol. vii, p. 108.
30 *The War of the Rebellion*, vol. xi, p. 51.
31 *ibid.*, vol. xi, p. 91.
32 *Personal Memoirs*, U. S. Grant, vol. i, p. 333.
33 *ibid.*, vol. i, p. 357. *Lee* made the same mistake at Antietam.
34 *The Generalship of Ulysses S. Grant*, J. F. C. Fuller, Appendix I, pp. 423-429.
35 *The War of the Rebellion*, vol. xi, pp. 93-94.
36 *ibid.*, vol. x, p. 112; and *Papers of the Historical Society of Massachusetts*, vol. vii, p. 141.
37 *The Generalship of Ulysses S. Grant*, J. F. C. Fuller, pp. 108-110.
38 *Personal Memoirs*, U. S. Grant, vol. i, pp. 354-355.
39 *The Mississippi Valley in the Civil War*, J. Fiske,[c] p. 99.
40 *The War of the Rebellion*, vol. xi, pp. 146, 148 and 151.
41 *Narrative of Military Operations*, Joseph E. Johnston,[b] pp. 113-116.
42 *The War of the Rebellion*, vol. xviii, p. 844.
43 *ibid.*, vol. xviii, p. 859.
44 *ibid.*, vol. xiv, p. 568.
45 *ibid.*, vol. xviii, p. 893.
46 *ibid.*, vol. xiv, p. 557.
47 *ibid.*, vol. xiv, p. 590.
48 *The Life and Campaigns of Major-General J. E. B. Stuart*, H. B. McClellan,[b] p. 53.
49 *The War of the Rebellion*, vol. xviii, p. 810.
50 *An Aide-de-Camp of Lee*, Papers of Colonel Charles Marshall,[a] p. 82.
51 *The War of the Rebellion*, vol. xiv, p. 602, and vol. xviii, p. 913.
52 *An Aide-de-Camp of Lee*, Papers of Colonel Charles Marshall,[a] p. 85, and *The War of the Rebellion*, vol. xiii, p. 490.
53 *An Aide-de-Camp of Lee*, Papers of Colonel Charles Marshall,[a] p. 89.

54 *The War of the Rebellion*, vol. xiii, p. 490.
55 *ibid.*, vol. xiv, p. 620.
56 *ibid.*, vol. xiv, p. 620.
57 *General Lee, Man and Soldier*, Thomas Nelson Page, p. 304.
    Ropes, in *The Story of the Civil War*, Part II, p. 172, says
    that *Jackson* was "delayed by the fallen trees with which the
    Federal troops had obstructed the roads, and by the great
    fatigue of his men."
58 *Battles and Leaders of the Civil War*, vol. ii, pp. 352, 328-331, and
    The War of the Rebellion, vol. xiii, p. 623.
59 *The War of the Rebellion*, vol. xiv, p. 617. *Magruder*, in his
    report, says: "Had McClellan massed his whole force in
    column and advanced it against any point of our line of
    battle . . . though the head of his column would have
    suffered greatly, its momentum would have insured him
    success, and the occupation of our works about Richmond,
    and consequently of the city, might have been his reward."
    —*The War of the Rebellion*, vol. xiii, p. 686.
60 *ibid.*, vol. xii, p. 269.
61 *ibid.*, vol. xii, p. 60.
62 *ibid.*, vol. xiii, p. 492.
63 *ibid.*, vol. xiii, p. 686.
64 *ibid.*, vol. xiii, p. 494.
65 *From Manassas to Appomattox*, James Longstreet,[b] p. 130.
66 *The War of the Rebellion*, vol. xiii, p. 497.
67 *ibid.*, vol. xiii, p. 494.
68 *Life and Campaigns of Lieut.-Gen. Thomas J. Jackson*, Prof. R. T.
    Dabney,[b] p. 467.
69 *The Life and Campaigns of Major General J. E. B. Stuart*, H. B.
    McClellan,[b] p. 80. Henderson's account of *Jackson's* delay
    (*Stonewall Jackson and the American Civil War*, vol. ii, pp. 56-
    58) is so misleading as to be almost fictitious. For other
    accounts see Longstreet[b] in *From Manassas to Appomattox*,
    p. 150; articles in *Battles and Leaders of the Civil War*, vol. ii,
    pp. 402-403, 389 and 381, by Longstreet,[b] D. H. Hill[b] and
    Franklin[b] respectively; *Papers of the Southern Historical
    Society*, vol. xxv, p. 211; *The Army of Northern Virginia in
    1862*, William Allan,[c] p. 121; *Destruction and Reconstruction*,
    Richard Taylor,[b] p. 113; and very full and important
    accounts in *Military Memoirs of a Confederate*, E. P.
    Alexander,[b] pp. 146-153, and in *The Life and Campaigns of
    Major-General J. E. B. Stuart*, H. B. McClellan,[b] pp. 80-81.
    General *Hampton*, who was in command of two of *Jackson's*
    Brigades, says: As the Federal artillery commanded the

bridge *Jackson* discontinued building it. There were several other places where the stream could be crossed, *Hampton* selected one and was authorized by *Jackson* to build a bridge, then *Hampton* writes: "As soon as the bridge was constructed I made another reconnaissance of the enemy, whom I found in the same position and totally unsuspicious of our presence, though I approached their line to within 100 or 150 yards. Returning I reported to General *Jackson*, stated to him the admirable position we should secure for an attack, and urged that an attack should be made. He sat in silence for some time, then rose and walked off in silence. We remained in position all night and in the morning the enemy had withdrawn. We encountered him next at Malvern Hill, and I believe that battle would never have been fought had we struck them on the flank and in rear in White Oak Swamp."—See *An Aide-de-Camp of Lee*, Papers of Colonel Charles Marshall,[a] pp. 110-112.

70 *The War of the Rebellion*, vol. xiii, p. 628; see also *Battles and Leaders of the Civil War*, vol. ii, p. 391.

71 *Battles and Leaders of the Civil War*, vol. ii, p. 391.

72 *The War of the Rebellion*, vol. xiii, p. 495.

73 *The Army of Northern Virginia in 1862*, William Allan,[c] p. 135.

74 *Numbers and Losses in the Civil War in America, 1861-65*, Thomas L. Livermore,[c] p. 86. McClellan lost 1,734 killed, 8,062 wounded and 6,053 missing, and *Lee*—3,478 killed, 16,261 wounded and 875 missing.

75 *Destruction and Reconstruction*, Richard Taylor,[b] pp. 107-108; see also *Lee's* report—*The War of the Rebellion*, vol. xiii, pp. 811-812.

76 *The War of the Rebellion*, vol. xviii, pp. 435-436.

77 *ibid.*, vol. xvi, p. 21.

78 *ibid.*, vol. xiv, p. 371.

79 *ibid.*, vol. xviii, pp. 458, 467.

80 *ibid.*, vol. xii, p. 81.

81 *ibid.*, vol. xii, p. 51.

82 *ibid.*, vol. xiv, pp. 674-675 and vol. xviii, pp. 928-932.

83 *ibid.*, vol. xvi, pp. 29, 58, 726.

84 *ibid.*, vol. xviii, pp. 591, 603.

85 *An Aide-de-Camp of Lee*, Papers of Colonel Charles Marsall,[a] p. 130.

86 *The War of the Rebellion*, vol. xvi, p. 643.

87 *ibid.*, vol. xviii, pp. 653, 665.

88 *ibid.*, vol. xvi, pp. 70-72; and vol. xviii, p. 704.

89 *Numbers and Losses in the Civil War in America, 1861-1865,*
   Thomas L. Livermore,[c] p. 89.

90 *The War of the Rebellion,* vol. xvi, pp. 714, 566, 647.

91 In a conversation with Mr. Cassius Lee, *Lee* replied, when
   asked "why he did not come to Washington after second
   Manassas"—" 'Because my men had nothing to eat,' and
   pointing to Fort Wade, in the rear of our house, he said, 'I
   could not tell my men to take that fort when they had had
   nothing to eat for three days. I went to Maryland to feed
   my army.' "—*Recollections and Letters of General Robert E. Lee,*
   Captain Robert E. Lee,[b] p. 416.

92 *An Aide-de-Camp of Lee,* Papers of Colonel Charles Marshall,[a]
   p. 146; and *The War of the Rebellion,* vol. xxviii, pp. 590-591.

93 *The War of the Rebellion,* vol. xxviii, pp. 590-591.

94 *ibid.,* vol. xxviii, p. 592.

95 *ibid.,* vol. xxviii, pp. 593-594.

96 *ibid.,* vol. xxvii, p. 145; and vol. xxviii, pp. 604-605.

97 *ibid.,* vol. xxviii, p. 597.

98 *ibid.,* vol. xxviii, p. 600.

99 *ibid.,* vol. xxviii, pp. 604-605.

100 *ibid.,* vol. xxviii, p. 603.

101 *Battles and Leaders of the Civil War,* vol. ii, p. 673.

102 Marshall[a] (*An Aide-de-Camp of Lee,* p. 160) says *Lee* knew
    nothing about the lost order having been found. Allan[c]
    (*The Army of Northern Virginia in 1862,* p. 345), Alexander[b]
    (*Military Memoirs of a Confederate,* p. 230) say he did.

103 *The War of the Rebellion,* vol. cviii, p. 618, and *Battles and
    Leaders of the Civil War,* vol. ii, p. 627.

104 *The War of the Rebellion,* vol. xxviii, pp. 608-609.

105 *An Aide-de-Camp of Lee,* Papers of Colonel Charles Marshall,[a]
    p. 162. *Heros von Borcke*[d] gives an equally doubtful excuse:
    he says that *Lee* fought Sharpsburg to save the booty taken
    at Harper's Ferry (*Memoirs of the Confederate War of Indepen-
    dence,* vol. i, p. 240)—but why fight on the northern bank of
    the Potomac?

106 *Numbers and Losses in the Civil War in America, 1861-65,* Thomas
    L. Livermore,[c] p. 92.

107 *Robert E. Lee and the Southern Confederacy,* Henry Alexander
    White,[b] pp. 224-225.

108 *The War of the Rebellion,* vol. xxviii, pp. 626-627.

109 *Heros von Borcke*[d] writes: "This passage of the Potomac by
    night was one of those magnificent spectacles which are
    seen only in war. The whole landscape was lighted up with
    a lurid glare from the burning houses of Williamsport,

which had been ignited by the enemy's shells. High over
the heads of the crossing column and the dark waters of the
river, the blazing bombs passed each other in parabolas of
flame through the air, and the spectral trees showed their
every limb and leaf against the red sky."—*Memoirs of the
Confederate War of Independence*, vol. i, p. 255.

110 *The War of the Rebellion*, vol. xxvii, p. 71.
111 *ibid.*, vol. xxvii, pp. 152, 156.
112 *ibid.*, vol. xxviii, p. 711.
113 *ibid.*, vol. xxxi, p. 1041.
114 *ibid.*, vol. xxviii, pp. 549, 1021.
115 *ibid.*, vol. xxxi, pp. 1033, 1035.
116 *Report of the Joint Committee on the Conduct of the War*, vol. i, p. 683.
117 *The War of the Rebellion*, vol. xxxi, pp. 1121,1057.
118 *Memoirs of the Confederate War of Independence*, Heros von
     Borcke,[d] vol. ii, p. 114.
119 *ibid.*, vol. ii, p. 116.
120 *ibid.*, vol. ii, p. 117.
121 *Numbers and Losses in the Civil War of America, 1861-65*, Thomas
     L. Livermore,[c] p. 96.
122 *Campaigns in Virginia and Maryland*, Captain C. C. Chesney,[d]
     p. 185.
123 *Four Years with General Lee*, Walter H. Taylor,[a] p. 81.
124 *Four Years under Marse Robert*, Robert Stiles,[b] p. 137.
125 *Campaigns in Virginia and Maryland*, Captain C. C. Chesney,[d]
     p. 198.
126 *Memoirs of the Confederate War of Independence*, Heros von
     Borcke,[d] vol. ii, p. 129.
127 *ibid.*, vol. ii, p. 131.
128 *Three Months in the Southern States, April-June, 1863*, Lieut-
     Colonel Fremantle,[d] p. 132. Also, see Heros von Borcke,[d]
     vol. ii, p. 139.
129 *Memoirs of the Confederate War of Independence*, Heros von
     Borcke,[d] vol. ii, p. 147.
130 *Personal Memoirs*, U. S. Grant, vol. i, p. 420.
131 *The War of the Rebellion*, vol. xxv, p. 296.
132 *ibid.*, vol. xxiv, p. 467.
133 *The Mississippi*, F. V. Greene,[c] p. 58.
134 *The War of the Rebellion*, vol. xxiv, p. 468.
135 *ibid.*, vol. xxiv, p. 470.
136 *ibid.*, vol. xxiv, p. 470.
137 *ibid.*, vol. xxiv, p. 472.
138 *ibid.*, vol. xxv, p. 757.
139 *ibid.*, vol. xxv, p. 781.

140   *ibid.*, vol. xxiv, p. 477.

141   *Military History of Ulysses S. Grant*, A. Badeau,[a] vol. i, p. 140; and *Personal Memoirs*, U. S. Grant, vol. i, pp. 434-435.

CHAPTER V

1   *The War of the Rebellion*, vol. xxxvi, p. 44.
2   *Military History of Ulysses S. Grant*, A. Badeau,[a] vol. i, p. 180.
3   *Personal Memoirs*, U. S. Grant, vol. i, pp. 480-481.
4   *The Story of the Civil War*, William Roscoe Livermore,[c] Pt. III, Bk. II, p. 271.
5   *Personal Memoirs*, U. S. Grant, vol. i, pp. 491-492.
6   *ibid.*, vol. i, pp. 518-520.
7   *Military History of Ulysses S. Grant*, A Badeau,[a] vol. i, p. 281.
8   *The War of the Rebellion*, vol. xxxvi, p. 54.
9   *Military History of Ulysses S. Grant*, A. Badeau,[a] vol. i, p. 399; *The War of the Rebellion*, vol. xxxvii, p. 167 gives—9,362.
10   *The War of the Rebellion*, vol. xxxvi, p. 58.
11   *The Mississippi*, F. V. Greene,[c] pp. 170-171.
12   *The War of the Rebellion*, vol. xxxviii, pp. 529-530.
13   *The Battle of Chancellorsville*, Augustus Choate Hamlin, p. 5.
14   *History of the United States from the Compromise of 1850*, James Ford Rhodes, vol. xiv, p. 337.
15   *Report of the Joint Committee on the Conduct of the War*, vol. i, pp. 111-112.
16   *General Lee of the Confederate Army*, Fitzhugh Lee,[b] p. 238.
17   *The War of the Rebellion*, vol. xxxix, p. 1057.
18   *ibid.*, vol. xxxix, p. 171.
19   *ibid.*, vol. xxxix, p. 796.
20   *ibid.*, vol. xxxix, p. 797. See also: *Lee's Confidential Dispatches to Davis*, p. 86.
21   *Memoirs of Robert E. Lee*, A. L. Long,[a] pp. 254-255.
22   *The War of the Rebellion*, vol. xxxix, pp. 940, 966, 975.
23   *ibid.*, vol. xxxix, p. 386.
24   *Report of the Joint Committee on the Conduct of the War*, vol. i, p. 126.
25   *The War of the Rebellion*, vol. xxxix, p. 941.
26   *The Battle of Chancellorsville*, Augustus Choate Hamlin, p. 50.
27   *The Life and Campaigns of Major-General J. E. B. Stuart*, H. B. McClellan,[b] p. 235.
28   *The War of the Rebellion*, vol. xl, p. 769.
29   *Battles and Leaders of the Civil War*, vol. iii, p. 164.

30 *Numbers and Losses in the Civil War in America, 1861-65,* Thomas L. Livermore,[c] pp. 98-99.
31 *The War of the Rebellion,* vol. xl, p. 713.
32 *The Military Operations of General Beauregard,* Colonel Alfred Roman,[c] vol. ii, p. 84.
33 *The War of the Rebellion,* vol. xlv, p. 868.
34 *ibid.,* vol. xlv, pp. 880-882.
35 *ibid.,* vol. xlv, p. 882.
36 *A Constitutional View of the late War Between the States,* Alexander H. Stephens,[b] vol. ii, p. 563.
37 *ibid.,* vol. ii, p. 567.
38 *General Lee, His Campaigns in Virginia,* Walter H. Taylor,[a] p. 180.
39 *Memoirs of Robert E. Lee,* A. L. Long,[a] p. 269.
40 *The War of the Rebellion,* vol. xlv, p. 925.
41 *ibid.,* vol. xlv, p. 931.
42 *ibid.,* vol. xlv, p. 923; also see *Longstreet's* order to *Stuart,* vol. xlv, p. 915, and *Lee's* report, vol. xliv, pp. 313-325. Further important information is given in *An Aide-de-Camp of Lee,* Papers of Colonel Charles Marshall,[a] pp. 200-224 and *The Life and Campaigns of Major-General J. E. B. Stuart,* H. B. McClellan,[b] pp. 316-336.
43 *The War of the Rebellion,* vol. xliii, p. 61.
44 *Report of the Joint Committee on the Conduct of the War,* vol. i, pp. 329-330.
45 *The War of the Rebellion,* vol. xliv, p. 317; and *An Aide-de-Camp of Lee,* Papers of Colonel Charles Marshall,[a] p. 220.
46 *The War of the Rebellion,* vol. xliv, p. 308.
47 *From Manassas to Appomattox,* James Longstreet,[b] p. 361.
48 *General Lee of the Confederate Army,* Fitzhugh Lee,[b] pp. 276-277.
49 *Four Years with General Lee,* Walter H. Taylor,[a] p. 109.
50 *The Rise and Fall of the Confederate Government,* Jefferson Davis,[b] vol. ii, p. 441.
51 *Four Years with General Lee,* Walter H. Taylor,[a] p. 101.
52 *Three Months in the Southern States, April-June, 1863,* Lieut-Colonel Fremantle,[d] p. 262.
53 *An Aide-de-Camp of Lee,* Papers of Colonel Charles Marshall,[a] p. 233.
54 *Three Months in the Southern States, April-June, 1863,* Lieut-Colonel Fremantle,[d] p. 264.
55 *The War of the Rebellion,* vol. xliv, p. 230.
56 *From Manassas to Appomattox,* James Longstreet,[b] pp. 385-387.
57 *Four Years with General Lee,* Walter H. Taylor,[a] p. 106.
58 *ibid.,* p. 107.
59 *From Manassas to Appomattox,* James Longstreet,[b] p. 386.

60 *Battles and Leaders of the Civil War*, vol. iii, p. 372.
61 *Military Memoirs of a Confederate*, E. P. Alexander,[b] p. 423.
62 *The War of the Rebellion*, vol. xliv, p. 385.
63 *Battles and Leaders of the Civil War*, vol. iii, p. 365.
64 *Numbers and Losses in the Civil War in America, 1861-65*, Thomas L. Livermore,[c] pp. 102-103.
65 *Three Months in the Southern States, April-June, 1863*, Lieut-Colonel Fremantle,[d] p. 276.
66 *The Crisis of the Confederacy*, Capt. Cecil Battine, p. 177.
67 *The War of the Rebellion*, vol. xlix, p. 649.
68 *Personal Memoirs*, U. S. Grant, vol. ii, p. 25; *The War of the Rebellion*, vol. lvi, p. 216; and *Battles and Leaders of the Civil War*, vol. iii, p. 719.
69 *The War of the Rebellion*, vol. lv, p. 29; and *Battles and Leaders of the Civil War*, vol. iii, p. 716.
70 *The War of the Rebellion*, vol. lv, p. 32.
71 *ibid.*, vol. lv, pp. 718, 745 and 746.

CHAPTER VI

1 *The War of the Rebellion*, vol. lvi, pp. 349-350.
2 *Military History of Ulysses S. Grant*, A. Badeau,[a] vol. ii, p. 9.
3 *The War of the Rebellion*, vol. lx, p. 827.
4 *ibid.*, vol. lix, p. 262.
5 *ibid.*, vol. lix, p. 312.
6 *Battles and Leaders of the Civil War*, vol. iv, p. 99.
7 *The War of the Rebellion*, vol. lxvii, p. 15.
8 *ibid.*, vol. lx, pp. 1017-1018.
9 *ibid.*, vol. lx, p. 827.
10 *ibid.*, vol. lxvii, pp. 15-16; and vol. lx, pp. 828, 885, 904.
11 *ibid.*, vol. lx, pp. 880, 881, 889; and vol. cvii, p. 1158.
12 *ibid.*, vol. xlix, pp. 693, 699.
13 *ibid.*, vol. xlix, pp. 701, 702.
14 *The Military Operations of General Beauregard*, Colonel Alfred Roman,[c] p. 177.
15 *The War of the Rebellion*, vol. lvi, p. 779.
16 *ibid.*, vol. lvi, p. 785.
17 *ibid.*, vol. lvi, p. 792.
18 *ibid.*, vol. lviii, p. 541.
19 *ibid.*, vol. lviii, p. 566.
20 *ibid.*, vol. lviii, p. 809.
21 *ibid.*, vol. lix, p. 582.
22 *ibid.*, vol. lix, p. 595.

23 Essays in Modern Military Biography, Charles Cornwallis Chesney,[d] p. 285.
24 The War of the Rebellion, vol. ix, p. 1260.
25 ibid., vol. lx, p. 1262.
26 ibid., vol. lx, p. 1267.
27 ibid., vol. lx, p. 1272.
28 ibid., vol. lxviii, p. 948.
29 Military History of Ulysses S. Grant, A. Badeau,[a] vol. ii, p. 113.
30 Army of the Potomac, William Swinton,[c] p. 427.
31 Numbers and Losses in the Civil War in America, 1861-1865, Thomas L. Livermore,[c] pp. 110-111.
32 The War of the Rebellion, vol. lxvii, pp. 1028, 1029, 1030, 1032.
33 Meade's Headquarters, 1863-1865, Letters of Colonel Theodore Lyman,[b] pp. 99-100.
34 The War of the Rebellion, vol. lxviii, p. 967.
35 ibid., vol. lxviii, p. 974.
36 ibid., vol. lxviii, p. 968.
37 ibid., vol. lxviii, p. 970.
38 Reminiscences of the Civil War, General John B. Gordon,[b] p. 268.
39 The War of the Rebellion, vol. xlviii, p. 967.
40 Papers of the Military Historical Society of Massachusetts, vol. iv, p. 212.
41 The War of the Rebellion, vol. lxviii, p. 552.
42 An interesting account of this attack and its eventual repulse is given by General Gordon,[b] in his book—Reminiscences of the Civil War, p. 275 ff.
43 Papers of the Military Historical Society of Massachusetts, vol. iv, pp. 252-256.
44 Numbers and Losses in the Civil War in America, 1861-1865, Thomas L. Livermore,[c] pp. 112-113.
45 The War of the Rebellion, vol. xlviii, pp. 956, 957, 965, 967, 968, 974, 979, 986, 989, 992, 999, 1004, 1005, 1006, 1007.
46 The Military Operations of General Beauregard, Colonel Alfred Roman,[c] vol. ii, pp. 200-209. Also: The War of the Rebellion, vol. xlviii, p. 1024.
47 The War of the Rebellion, vol. lxviii, pp. 1021-1022.
48 Lee's Confidential Dispatches to Davis, Nos. 102, 104.
49 The War of the Rebellion, vol. lxix, p. 183.
50 The Virginia Campaign of '64 and '65, A. A. Humphreys,[b] p. 191. Livermore,[c] in Numbers and Losses, states, "Not over 7,000," p. 115.
51 Battles and Leaders of the Civil War, vol. iv, pp. 217-218.
52 The Virginia Campaign of '64 and '65, A. A. Humphreys,[b] p. 182.
53 Battles and Leaders of the Civil War, vol. iv, p. 217.

54 *Army of the Potomac*, William Swinton,[c] p. 485.

55 *The War of the Rebellion*, vol. lxix, p. 206.

56 *Military History of Ulysses S. Grant*, A Badeau,[a] vol. i, p. 85.

57 *The War of the Rebellion*, vol. lxvii, p. 22; and vol. lxix, pp. 598-599.

58 *Papers of the Military Historical Society of Massachusetts*, vol. i, p. 280.

59 *The War of the Rebellion*, vol. xlix, p. 879.

60 *ibid.*, vol. lxix, pp. 879, 884, 885.

61 *ibid.*, vol. lxix, p. 886. See also *Hill to Beauregard*, p. 896.

62 *ibid.*, vol. lxix, p. 755.

63 *Papers of the Military Historical Society of Massachusetts*, vol. v, p. 84.

64 *ibid.*, vol. v, p. 120.

65 *The War of the Rebellion*, vol. lxxxi, p. 36.

66 *ibid.*, vol. xcv, p. 24.

67 *ibid.*, vol. lxxxi, p. 645.

68 *Memoirs of Robert E. Lee*, A. L. Long,[a] p. 358.

69 *Lee's Confidential Dispatches to Davis*, No. 125.

70 *ibid.*, No. 131.

71 *Papers of the Military Historical Society of Massachusetts*, vol. v, p. 121.

72 *The War of the Rebellion*, vol. lxxxi, pp. 655, 657. See also: *The Military Operations of General Beauregard*, Colonel Alfred Roman,[c] vol. ii, pp. 227-246, and *Campaigns and Battles of the Army of Northern Virginia*, George Wise,[c] pp. 368-374.

73 *The War of the Rebellion*, vol. lxxxi, p. 659.

74 *ibid.*, vol. lxxxi, pp. 662, 663; see also, pp. 663 *Lee to Wade Hampton*, *Lee to W. H. F. Lee* and *Lee to Beauregard*, pp. 664, 665.

75 *ibid.*, vol. lxxxi, p. 667.

76 *Military Memoirs of a Confederate*, E. P. Alexander,[b] p. 547.

77 *The Military Operations of General Beauregard*, Colonel Alfred Roman,[c] vol. ii, p. 247.

78 *Lee's Confidential Dispatches to Davis*, No. 139.

79 *The War of the Rebellion*, vol. lxxxviii, p. 1229.

80 *ibid.*, vol. lxx, p. 769.

81 *ibid.*, vol. lxxi, p. 595.

82 *ibid.*, vol. lxxxii, pp. 44-45.

83 *Atlanta*, J. D. Cox,[c] pp. 25, 28.

84 *ibid.*, p. 127.

85 *The War of the Rebellion*, vol. lxxviii, p. 355.

86 *ibid.*, vol. lxxviii, p. 412.

87 *ibid.*, vol. lxxix, p. 202.

88 *ibid.*, vol. lxxix, p. 378.
89 *ibid.*, vol. lxxix, p. 576.
90 *ibid.*, vol. lxxix, p. 594.
91 *Atlanta,* J. D. Cox,[c] pp. 96-97.
92 *The War of the Rebellion,* vol. xcvi, p. 1035.
93 *ibid.*, vol. xcvi, p. 1099.
94 *ibid.*, vol. xcvi, p. 1143.
95 *ibid.*, vol. xcvi, p. 1199.
96 *ibid.*, vol. xcvi, p. 1247.
97 *ibid.*, vol. xcvi, p. 1250.
98 *The Military Operations of General Beauregard,* Colonel Alfred Roman,[c] vol. ii, p. 359.
99 *ibid.*, pp. 341, 355.
100 *Reminiscences of the Civil War,* General John B. Gordon,[b] pp. 385-394. See also: *The Rise and Fall of the Confederate Government,* Jefferson Davis,[b] vol. ii, pp. 648-649.
101 *Papers of the Military Historical Society of Massachusetts,* vol. xiii, p. 406.
102 *The War of the Rebellion,* vol. xcii, pp. 797, 820.
103 *ibid.*, vol. xcix, p. 190.
104 *ibid.*, vol. xcviii, p. 1044.
105 *ibid.*, vol. xcix, pp. 1453-1454; and vol. c, p. 682.
106 *Reminiscences of the Civil War,* General John B. Gordon,[b] pp. 397-408.
107 On the 28th Sheridan's instructions were, after passing through Dinwiddie, to "cut loose and push for the Danville road," then he was to destroy the South Side railroad between Petersburg and Burksville, after which he was to return or join Sherman. (See: *The War of the Rebellion,* vol. xcvii, p. 234.) On the night of the 29th, Grant modified this order saying: "I now feel like ending the matter. . . . I do not want you, therefore, to cut loose at once and go after the enemy's roads at present. In the morning push around the enemy if you can and get onto his right rear." (See: *The War of the Rebellion,* vol. xcvii, p. 266.) According to Grant (see: *Personal Memoirs,* vol. ii, p. 437), Sheridan was disappointed with the first of these instructions, consequently, Grant said to him: " 'General, this portion of your instructions I have put in merely as a blind. . . .' I told him that . . . I intended to close the war right here, with this movement, and that he should go no farther."
108 *The War of the Rebellion,* vol. xcv, pp. 603, 1017.
109 *Personal Memoirs,* U. S. Grant, vol. ii, p. 456.
110 *The War of the Rebellion,* vol. xcvii, p. 528.

111 *The Rise and Fall of the Confederate Government*, Jefferson Davis,[b] vol. ii, pp. 669-675.
112 Ord's Corps was formed out of the divisions of Butler's Army of the James. Butler had been relieved by Ord in December, 1864.
113 *The War of the Rebellion*, vol. xcvii, pp. 621, 633.
114 *ibid.*, vol. xcv, pp. 1109-1110.

CHAPTER VII

1 *Recollections and Letters of General Robert E. Lee*, Captain Robert E. Lee,[b] p. 416.
2 *General Grant*, J. G. Wilson, p. 367.
3 *Papers of the Military Historical Society of Massachusetts*, vol. vii, pp. 7-8.
4 *Military History of Ulysses S. Grant*, A. Badeau,[a] vol. iii, p. 141.
5 *Papers of the Military Historical Society of Massachusetts*, vol. iv, pp. 365, 405.
6 *Battles and Leaders of the Civil War*, vol. iv, p. 244.
7 *The Virginia Campaign of '64 and '65*, A. A. Humphreys,[b] p. 118.
8 *The Generalship of Ulysses S. Grant*, J. F. C. Fuller, pp. 359-361.
9 This is made very clear in *Foch, the Man of Orleans*, B. H. Liddell Hart, 1931.
10 Since 1917, that is for nearly half a generation, I have preached almost daily that the answer to half an ounce of lead is half an inch of steel; that is to say, the crucial tactical problem in modern warfare is the introduction of bullet-proof armour. This would seem so obvious a fact as to require no accentuation. All I can say is that my failure has been complete but not altogether wasted; for my efforts have led me to appreciate why for a hundred years the chivalry of France, in spite of dreadful losses, continued to charge the English archers.
11 *The Rise and Fall of the Confederate Government*, Jefferson Davis,[b] vol. ii, pp. 158-159.
12 *An Aide-de-Camp of Lee*, Papers of Colonel Charles Marshall,[a] pp. 30-32.
13 *ibid.*, p. 74.
14 *ibid.*, p. 75.
15 *Anecdotes of the Civil War*, E. Townsend,[c] p. 29.
16 *Memoirs of W. T. Sherman*, W. T. Sherman,[b] vol. iii, p. 224.
17 *The Lost Cause*, E. A. Pollard,[c] pp. 429, 655.
18 *Galaxy*, vol. xii, p. 628.

19 *A Rebel War Clerk's Diary*, J. B. Jones, January 1st, 1865.
20 *The War of the Rebellion*, vol. xxvi, p. 1084.
21 *ibid.*, vol. xxxviii, pp. 529-530.
22 *Personal Memoirs*, Ulysses S. Grant, vol. ii, pp. 100-101.
23 For a more detailed analysis of grand tactics see *The Foundations of the Science of War*, Colonel J. F. C. Fuller, Chapter VI.
24 *On War*, Clausewitz, vol. iii, pp. 209-210.
25 *The War of the Rebellion*, vol. xiv, p. 590.
26 *ibid.*, vol. xlv, p. 868.
27 *Statistical Records of the Armies of the United States*, F. Phisterer,[c] p. 70.
28 Extracted from *Numbers and Losses in the Civil War in America, 1861-65*, Thomas L. Livermore,[c] Table A.
29 *The War of the Rebellion*, vol. xcvii, p. 234. According to Grant (see: *Personal Memoirs*, vol. ii, p. 437) this order was meant as a blind. (See: footnote 107 to Chapter VI.)
30 *Papers of the Military Historical Society of Massachusetts*, vol. xiii, pp. 87-88.
31 *On War*, Clausewitz, vol. i, p. 49.
32 *Correspondance de Napoléon 1er*, vol. xxxii, pp. 182-183.
33 *On War*, Clausewitz, vol. i, p. 74.
34 *A Systematic View of the Formation, Discipline and Economy of Armies* (1804), Robert Jackson, pp. 228-229.
35 *On War*, Clausewitz, vol. i, p. 77
36 *ibid.*, vol. i, pp. 54, 55, 57.
37 *ibid.*, vol. i, p. 47.
38 *Mémoirs écrits a Sainte-Helène*, Montholon, vol. ii, p. 90.
39 *A Systematic View of the Formation, Discipline and Economy of Armies* (1804), Robert Jackson, pp. 218-219.
40 *Reminiscences of the Civil War*, General John B. Gordon,[b] p. 463.

INDEX

Adams, C. F., 22
Alabama, 175, 206
Aldie (Va.), 164
Alexander, Gen. *E. P., quoted* 200, 227
Alexandria (Va.), 170
Allatoona (Ga.), 231
Alleghany Mountains, 32, 38, 136, 139
Amelia Court House, 240
Amissville (Va.), 164
Anderson, Gen. R., 133
Anderson, Gen. *R. H.,* 189, 191, 217, 227
Aquia Creek (Va.), 170-1
Arkansas, 40
Armies, Federal—
 Cumberland, 177, 203, 230
 Mississippi, 174
 Ohio, 174, 231
 Potomac, 67, 83, 92, 145, 150, 185, 207, 213, 217, 230, 238, 282
 Tennessee, 174, 231
 Tennessee and Mississippi, 174
Armies, Confederate—
 East Virginia and North Carolina ,156
 Northern Virginia, 113, 117, 120, 123-24, 128, 164, 169, 200, 215, 240, 253, 280
Armistead, Gen., 200
Ashby's Gap (Va.), 165
Ashland (Va.), 157-58
Atlanta (Ga.), 32, 40, 42
Augusta (Ga.), 232, 257

Badeau, A. (biographer of U. S. Grant), *quoted,* 87, 90, 207, 214, 222, 224, 246
Baltimore, 167
Banks, Gen. N. P., 153-54, 156, 163, 184, 208
Bardstown (Ky.), 177
Barlow, Gen. F. C., *quoted,* 218
Baton Rouge (La.), 181
Battine, Capt. C., *quoted,* 200
Beaufort (N.C.), 33
Beauregard, Gen. *P. G. T.,* 57, 127, 175, 176, 193, 195, 201, 210, 247. At Shiloh, 75, 147-48; bombards Fort Sumter, 133-34; at First Bull Run, 135-36; at

Drury's Bluff, 219; at Petersburg, 222-27
Beaver Dam (Va.), 157-58
Benét, S. V. (Virginian poet), *quoted,* 18, 64, 103, 117
Bermuda Hundred (Va.), 219-20, 226. Neck, 223
Berryville (Va.), 165
Big Black River, 181-83
"Bloody Angle" (at Battle of Spottsylvania), 218
Blue Ridge, 167, 179
Boggs, Henry (partner of U. S. Grant), 59
Boonville (Mo.), 134
Bottom Bridge (Chickahominy river), 161
Bowling Green (Ky.), 141-42, 176-77
Bradford, G. (biographer of *Robert E. Lee*), *quoted,* 119
Bragg, Gen. *Braxton,* 54, 179, 184, 208, 219, 246, 257, 263. At Shiloh, 147; Commander-in-Chief in the West, 175; at Murfreesborough, 176-77; 201; at Chattamauga, 202; at Chattanooga, 203-204
Branch, Gen., 154-55
Branchville (S.C.), 32, 237
Brandy Station (Va.), 213
Breckinridge, Gen. *J. C.,* 222; Confederate Secretary of War, 235
Bridgeport (Tenn.), 176, 203
Bristoe Station, 164
Brown, John, 64
Bruce, Col., *quoted,* 144; on U. S. Grant, 245-46
Bruinsburg (Miss.), 181
Brunswick (Ga.), 33
Bryce, Lord, *quoted,* 19
Buckner, Gen. *S. B.,* 84, 97, 144, 246
Buell, Gen. D. C., 141-42. At Shiloh, 145-49; at Corinth and Iuka, 174-77; relieved of command, 177
Bull Run, 209
Burkesville (Ky.), 235, 239
Burnside, Gen. A. E., 91, 127, 176, 246. Defeated at Fredericksburg, 170-74; relieved of command,

318

INDEX

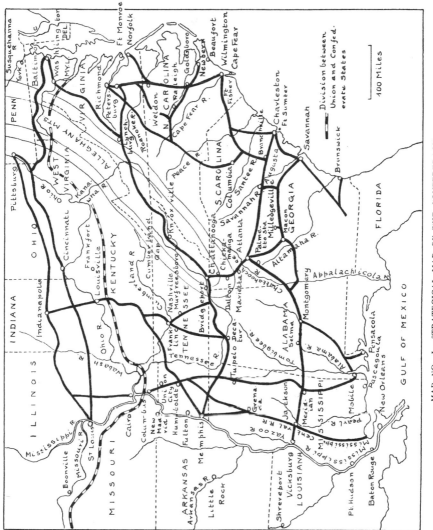

MAP NO. I—STRATEGICAL MAP OF THE CONFEDERACY

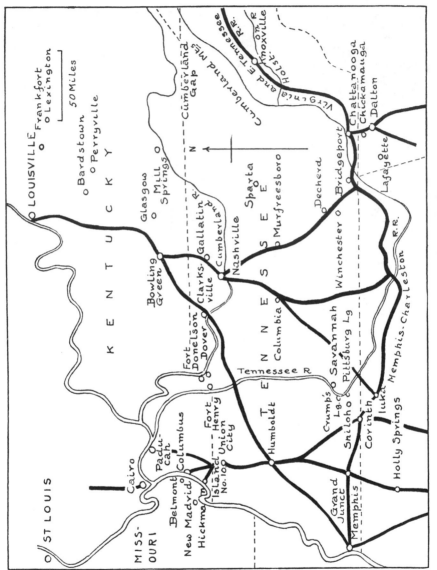

MAP NO. 2—TENNESSEE AND KENTUCKY

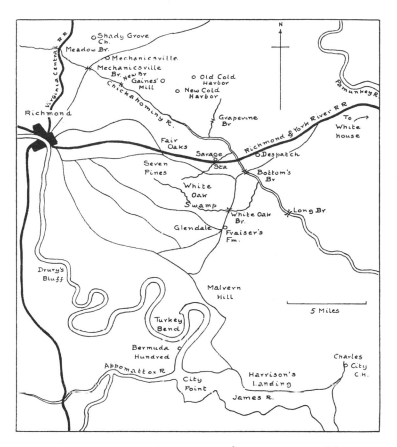

MAP NO. 3—THE SEVEN DAYS' CAMPAIGN, 1862

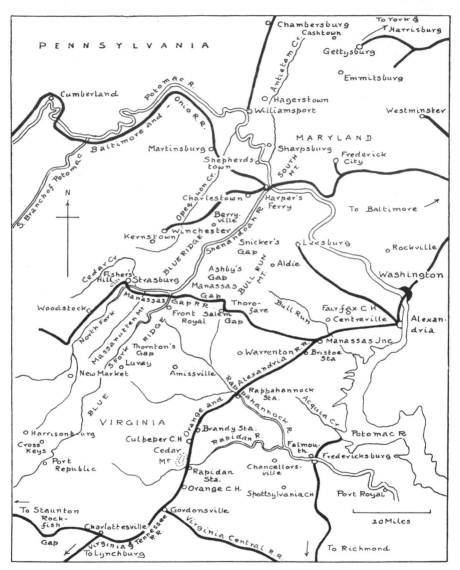

MAP NO. 4—NORTHERN VIRGINIA

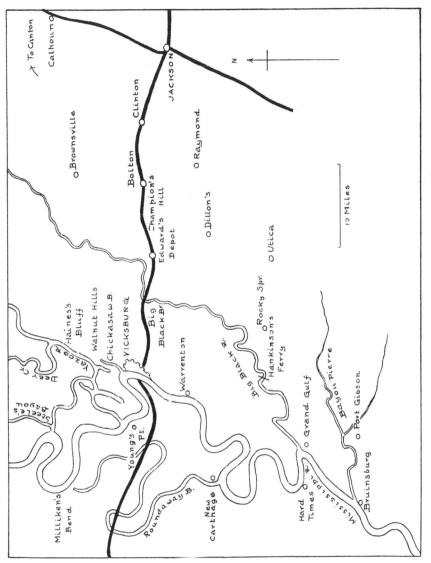

MAP NO. 5—VICKSBURG CAMPAIGN, 1863

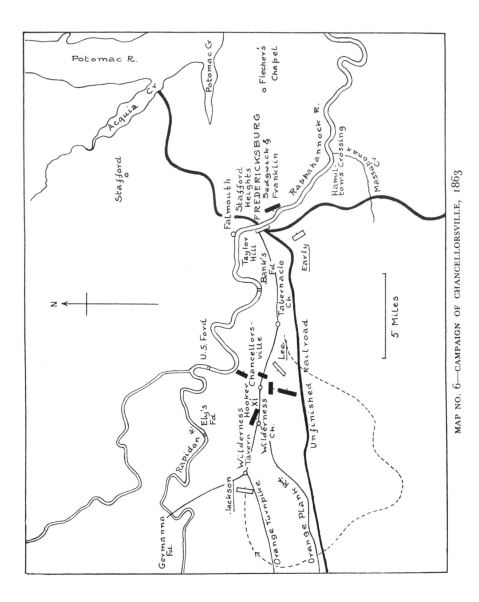

MAP NO. 6—CAMPAIGN OF CHANCELLORSVILLE, 1863

Potomac R.

Potomac Cr

o Flecher's
Chapel

Acquia Cr

Rappahannock R.

Stafford o

Falmouth
Stafford
Heights
FREDERICKSBURG
Sedgwick &
Franklin

Hamil-
ton's Crossing

Massaponax C.

Taylor
Hill

Bank's
Fd

Early

Tabernacle
Ch.

Z

U.S. Ford

5 Miles

Lee

Chancellors-
ville

Unfinished Railroad

Rapidan R.

Ely's
Fd

Wilderness
Tavern

Hooker

XI

Wilderness
Ch.

Jackson

Germanna
Fd.

Orange Turnpike

Orange Plank R.

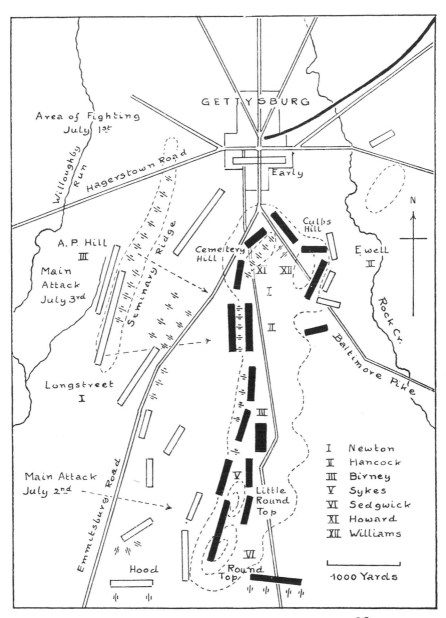

MAP NO. 7—THE BATTLE OF GETTYSBURG, 1863

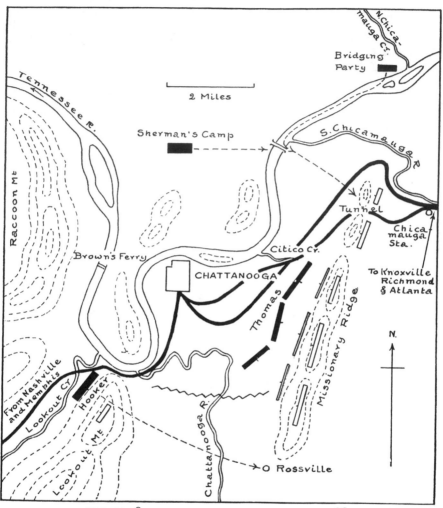

MAP NO. 8—THE BATTLE OF CHATTANOOGA, 1863

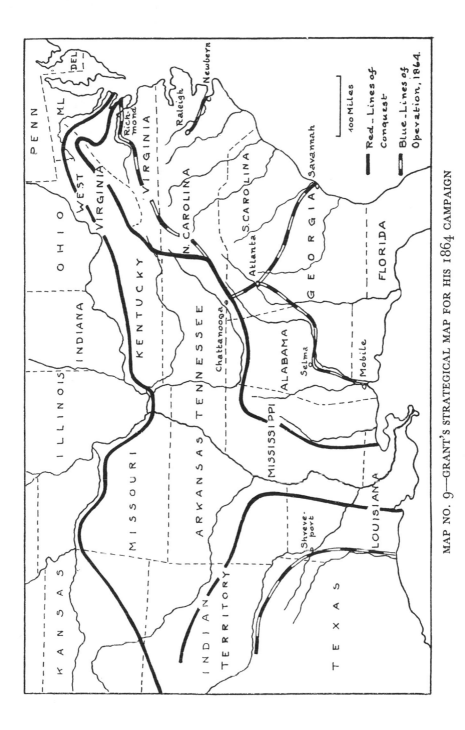

MAP NO. 9—GRANT'S STRATEGICAL MAP FOR HIS 1864 CAMPAIGN

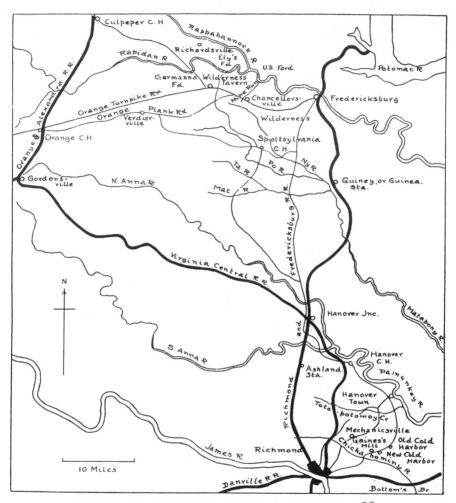

MAP NO. 10—OPERATIONS NORTH OF RICHMOND, 1864

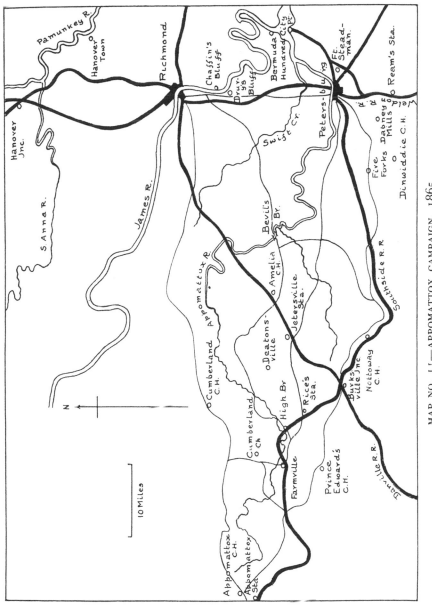

MAP NO. 11—APPOMATTOX CAMPAIGN, 1865